LAS

THE MINI ROUGH GUIDE

Bellagio's - very nice
good buffet - go for
lunch not
dinner!

There are more than one hundred and fifty
Rough Guide travel, phrasebook, and music titles,
covering destinations from Amsterdam to Zimbabwe,
languages from Czech to Vietnamese, and musics
from Jazz to Opera and World

Forthcoming titles include

Beijing • Cape Town • Croatia
Ecuador • Switzerland

Rough Guides on the Internet

www.roughguides.com

Rough Guide Credits

Text editor: Andrew Rosenberg
Series editor: Mark Ellingham
Typesetting: Helen Ostick
Cartography: Melissa Baker

Publishing Information

This first edition published March 2000 by
Rough Guides Ltd, 62–70 Shorts Gardens, London, WC2H 9AB

Distributed by the Penguin Group:

Penguin Books Ltd, 27 Wrights Lane, London W8 5TZ
Penguin Books USA Inc., 375 Hudson Street, New York 10014, USA
Penguin Books Australia Ltd, 487 Maroondah Highway,
PO Box 257, Ringwood, Victoria 3134, Australia
Penguin Books Canada Ltd, 10 Alcorn Avenue,
Toronto, Ontario, Canada M4V 1E4
Penguin Books (NZ) Ltd, 182–190 Wairau Road,
Auckland 10, New Zealand

Typeset in Bembo and Helvetica to an original design by Henry Iles.
Printed in Spain by Graphy Cems.

© Greg Ward, 304pp, includes index
A catalogue record for this book is available from the British Library.
ISBN 1-85828-463-5

The publishers and authors have done their best to
ensure the accuracy and currency of all the information
in *The Rough Guide to Las Vegas*; however, they can
accept no responsibility for any loss, injury or
inconvenience sustained by any traveller as a result of
information or advice contained in the guide.

LAS VEGAS

THE MINI ROUGH GUIDE

by Greg Ward

We set out to do something different when the first Rough Guide was published in 1982. Mark Ellingham, just out of university, was travelling in Greece. He brought along the popular guides of the day, but found they were all lacking in some way. They were either strong on ruins and museums but went on for pages without mentioning a beach or taverna. Or they were so conscious of the need to save money that they lost sight of Greece's cultural and historical significance. Also, none of the books told him anything about Greece's contemporary life – its politics, its culture, its people, and how they lived.

So with no job in prospect, Mark decided to write his own guidebook, one which aimed to provide practical information that was second to none, detailing the best beaches and the hottest clubs and restaurants, while also giving hard-hitting accounts of every sight, both famous and obscure, and providing up-to-the-minute information on contemporary culture. It was a guide that encouraged independent travellers to find the best of Greece, and was a great success, getting shortlisted for the Thomas Cook travel guide award, and encouraging Mark, along with three friends, to expand the series.

The Rough Guide list grew rapidly and the letters flooded in, indicating a much broader readership than had been anticipated, but one which uniformly appreciated the Rough Guide mix of practical detail and humour, irreverence and enthusiasm. Things haven't changed. The same four friends who began the series are still the caretakers of the Rough Guide mission today: to provide the most reliable, up-to-date and entertaining information to independent-minded travellers of all ages, on all budgets.

We now publish more than 150 titles and have offices in London and New York. The travel guides are written and researched by a dedicated team of more than 100 authors, based in Britain, Europe, the USA and Australia. We have also created a unique series of phrasebooks to accompany the travel series, along with an acclaimed series of music guides, and a best-selling pocket guide to the Internet and World Wide Web. We also publish comprehensive travel information on our Web site: **www.roughguides.com**

Help Us Update

We've gone to a lot of effort to ensure that this first edition of *The Rough Guide to Las Vegas* is as up to date and accurate as possible. However, if you feel there are places we've underrated or over-praised, or find we've missed something good or covered something which has now gone, then please write: suggestions, comments or corrections are much appreciated.

We'll credit all contributions, and send a copy of the next edition (or any other Rough Guide if you prefer) for the best letters. Please mark letters: "Rough Guide Las Vegas Update" and send to: Rough Guides, 62–70 Shorts Gardens, London, WC2H 9AB, or Rough Guides, 375 Hudson St, New York NY 10014. Or send email to: **mail@roughguides.co.uk**. Online updates about this book can be found on Rough Guides' Web site (see opposite).

The Author

Greg Ward has worked for Rough Guides since 1985, in which time he has also written *Rough Guides* to Southwest USA, Hawaii, Honolulu, Maui, the Big Island, Brittany and Normandy, and Essential Blues CDs, edited and co-written the *Rough Guide to the USA*, contributed to books on China, Mexico, California, France, Spain and Portugal, edited several more, and helped to set up the company's desk-top publishing system. He has also worked on travel guides for Fodors and Dorling Kindersley.

Acknowledgements

Thanks above all to Sam Cook, for her love, support and encouragement, and the many good times divided between London, Las Vegas, and New Orleans. Thanks too to Edie Jarolim for friendship and input, and Rob Faust for a virtuoso performance at *Bellagio*. Mark Baldwin, Wayne Bernath, Myram Borders, Deke Castleman, Bill Doak, Maria Gladowski, John Hessling, Jayne Innes, Shelley Mansholt, Pien Koopman, and Michelle Rikard all offered valuable assistance in Las Vegas, while back home, Jules Brown, Rob Humphreys, and Rob Jones gave me a healthy perspective on things.

At Rough Guides, it was a real pleasure to have Andrew Rosenberg as an editor; his committed editing and enthusiastic interest was much appreciated. Thanks too to Helen Ostick for typesetting, Melissa Flack for mapmaking, and Margaret Doyle for proofreading.

CONTENTS

Contexts

Introduction

Shimmering from the desert haze of Nevada like a latter-day El Dorado, **Las Vegas** is the most dynamic, spectacular city on earth. At the start of the twentieth century, it didn't even exist; at the start of the twenty-first, it's home to well over one million people, with enough newcomers arriving all the time to need a new school every month.

Las Vegas is not like other cities. No city in history has so explicitly valued the needs of visitors above those of its own population. All its growth has been fueled by tourism, but the tourists haven't spoiled the "real" city; there is no real city. Las Vegas doesn't have fascinating little-known neighborhoods, and it's not a place where visitors can go off the beaten track to have more authentic experiences. Instead, the whole thing is completely self-referential; the reason Las Vegas boasts nineteen of the world's twenty largest hotels is that more than thirty million tourists each year come to see the hotels themselves.

Each of these monsters is much more than a mere hotel, and more too than the casino that invariably lies at its core. They're extraordinary places, self-contained fantasylands of high camp and genuine excitement that can stretch as much as a mile from end to end. Each holds its own flamboyant permutation of showrooms and swimming pools, luxurious guest quarters and restaurants, high-tech rides and attractions.

The casinos want you to gamble, and they'll do almost anything to lure you in; thus the huge moving walkways that pluck you from the Strip sidewalk, almost against your will, and sweep you into places like *Caesars Palace*. Once you're inside, on the other hand, the last thing they want is for you to leave. Whatever you came in for, you won't be able to do it without criss-crossing the casino floor innumerable times; as for finding your way out, that can be virtually impossible. The action keeps going day and night, and in this windowless – and clock-free – environment you rapidly lose track of which is which.

> **"Little emphasis is placed on the gambling clubs . . .**
> **No cheap and easily parodied slogans have been**
> **adopted to publicize Las Vegas, no attempt has been**
> **made to introduce pseudo-romantic architectural**
> **themes or to give artificial glamour or gaiety."**
> *WPA Guidebook to Nevada*, 1940

Las Vegas never dares to rest on its laurels, so the basic concept of the Strip casino has been endlessly refined since the Western-themed resorts and ranches of the 1940s. In the 1950s and 1960s, when most visitors arrived by car, the casinos presented themselves as lush tropical oases at the end of the long desert drive. Once air travel took over, Las Vegas opted for Disney-esque fantasy, a process that started in the late 1960s with *Caesars Palace* and culminated with *Excalibur* and *Luxor* in the early 1990s.

These days, after six decades of capitalism run riot, the Strip is locked into a hyperactive craving for thrills and glamour, forever discarding its latest toy in its frenzy for the next jackpot. First-time visitors tend to expect Las Vegas to be a repository of kitsch, but the casino owners are far too canny to be sentimental about the old days. Yes, there are a few Elvis impersonators around, but what characterizes the city far more is its endless quest for novelty. Long before they lose their sparkle, yesterday's showpieces are blasted into rubble, to make way for ever more extravagant replacements. The Disney model has been discarded in favor of more adult themes, and Las Vegas demands nothing less than entire cities. Replicas of New York, Paris, Monte Carlo and Venice now jostle for space on the Strip.

The customer is king in Las Vegas. What the visitor wants, the city provides. If you come in search of the cheapest destination in America, you'll enjoy paying rock-bottom rates for accommodation and hunting out the best buffet bargains. If it's style and opulence you're after, by contrast, you can dine in the finest restaurants, shop in the most chic stores, and watch world-class entertainment; it'll cost you, but not as much as it would anywhere else. The same guidelines apply to gambling. The Strip giants cater to those who want sophisticated high-roller heavens, where tuxedoed James Bond lookalikes toss insouciant bankrolls onto the roulette tables. Others prefer their casinos to be sinful and seedy, inhabited by hard-bitten heavy-smoking low-lifes; there is no shortage of that type of joint either, especially downtown.

On the face of it, the city is supremely democratic. However you may be dressed, however affluent or otherwise you may appear, you'll be welcomed in its stores, restaurants, and above all its casinos. The one thing you almost certainly won't get, however, is the last laugh; all that seductive deference comes at a price. It would be nice to imagine that perhaps half of your fellow visitors are skillful gamblers, raking in the profits at the tables, while the other half are losing, but the bottom line is that almost nobody's winning. In the words of Steve Wynn, as the owner of *Bellagio* and the *Mirage*, currently Las Vegas's prime mover – "The only way to make money in a casino is to own one." What's so clever about Las Vegas is that it makes absolutely certain that you have such a good time that you don't mind losing a bit of money along the way; that's why they don't even call it "gambling" anymore, but "gaming."

Finally, while Las Vegas has certainly cleaned up its act since the early days of Mob domination, there's little truth in the notion that it's become a family destination. In fact, for kids, it's doesn't begin to compare to somewhere like Orlando. Several casinos have added theme parks or fun rides to fill those odd non-gambling moments, but only five percent of visitors bring children, and the crowds that cluster around the exploding volcanoes and pirate battles along the Strip remain almost exclusively adult.

Climate and when to go

Las Vegas is at the heart of the hottest, harshest **desert** in North America, and so receives less than four inches of rain (10cm) per year. Temperatures, however, vary enormously, with daytime maximums averaging over 100°F (38°C) in July and August, and night-time minimums dropping below freezing in December and January. The mid-summer heat on the Strip is unbearable, making it impossible to walk any distance during the day, so the ideal times to visit are between April and May and between September and October. Hotel swimming pools tend to be closed between October and March inclusive.

The city is at its quietest, and room rates are therefore lowest, during the first few weeks of December and the last few weeks of January, and also during June and July, while Christmas and New Year are the busiest periods of all.

Climate

	°F		°C	
	Average daily		Average daily	
	MAX	MIN	MAX	MIN
January	60	29	16	-2
February	67	34	20	1
March	72	39	22	4
April	81	45	27	8
May	89	52	32	12
June	99	61	37	17
July	103	68	40	20
August	102	66	39	19
September	95	57	35	14
October	84	47	29	9
November	71	36	22	2
December	61	30	17	-1

THE GUIDE

Introducing the city

I t doesn't take long to come to grips with Las Vegas. **Downtown**, slightly southeast of the intersection of I-15 and US-95, may stand at the center of an urban sprawl that stretches fifteen miles both east to west and north to south, but it's the legendary **Strip**, starting two miles south of downtown, where all the action takes place. In fact, by no coincidence at all, the Strip begins at the point where Las Vegas Boulevard leaves the city limits, and casino owners are therefore not liable to city taxes.

   The Strip itself consists of the four miles of Las Vegas Boulevard between the *Sahara* and *Mandalay Bay*, and thus now reaches as far south as McCarran Airport. Almost every building along the way is a casino, each frantically clamoring for the attention of the tourists who throng the road day and night. For the sake of convenience, it's often loosely divided into the **South Strip**, from *Mandalay Bay* up to the *MGM Grand* and *New York–New York*; the **Central Strip**, which includes *Bellagio*, *Caesars Palace* and the *Venetian*; and the **North Strip**, from the *Stardust* to the *Sahara*.

Whatever you might expect, **downtown Las Vegas** is not a bustling area of shops and offices where locals go about their business far from the mayhem of the Strip. Instead, it too is utterly dominated by casinos. Its center-piece, the **Fremont Street Experience**, is an extraordinary architectural conceit, in which four blocks of its main thoroughfare have been roofed over to give it the feel of a theme park rather than a real city. An unfortunate side effect has been to make the rest of downtown seem even more derelict and menacing than before; it is not an area any visitor should attempt to explore.

The telephone area code for all phone numbers in the text, unless otherwise indicated is ©702.

In between the Strip and downtown lie two somewhat seedy miles of gas stations, fast-food drive-ins, and wedding chapels, parts of which have been optimistically but point-lessly promoted as the **Gateway District**.

Being closely paralleled by both the I-15 interstate and the (currently inactive) railroad line, the Strip also serves as the dividing line between east and west Las Vegas, and marks the zero point for street addresses. The closest attempt to match the success of the Strip has been along **Paradise Road**, immediately to the **east**, which is home to the *Las Vegas Hilton*, the Convention Center, the *Hard Rock*, and several popular restaurants. A large campus to the east of Paradise Road, between Flamingo and Tropicana avenues, houses **UNLV** – the University of Nevada Las Vegas – whose students tend to hang out on **Maryland Parkway**, another block east.

Although the area to the **west** of the Strip is less suscepti-ble to generalization, the *Rio* has encouraged tourists to stray across to the far side of the interstate, and **Decatur Boulevard**, especially around Sahara Avenue, is a thriving shopping district.

City residents, of course, can distinguish between the demographic profiles of any number of Las Vegas **neighborhoods**, but tourists spend so little of their time anywhere other than the Strip or downtown that they can remain oblivious. Broadly speaking, the northeast and northwest quadrants of the city are its less affluent areas, while its most fashionable district is **Henderson** to the southwest – ranked in its own right as one of America's fastest-growing cities – with the new **Summerlin** development to the east tipped as a future rival.

ARRIVAL

By air

The runways of Las Vegas's busy **McCarran International Airport** (©261-5743) start barely a mile east of the southern end of the Strip, though the main terminal is a three-mile drive via Tropicana Avenue and Paradise Road.

Car rental is readily available at the airport (see p.8). There's no public bus service, but both Bell Trans (©739-7990) and Ray & Ross (©261-3230) run around-the-clock **minibuses** to the Strip ($3.50) and downtown ($5), leaving from immediately outside the terminal. In addition, certain hotels run free shuttle buses for their guests.

A line of **taxis** is always waiting outside the arrivals area. In theory, the ride should cost between $8.50 and $12 for hotels at the southern end of the Strip; from $10 to $14 for the Central Strip area; up to $15 for the North Strip; and between $15 and $19 for destinations both downtown and out on Boulder Highway. However, traffic delays can easily force those fares up by another $5 or so.

If you want to arrive in style, Bell Trans (see above) can also provide **limousine** service from around $30.

By car

Much the busiest **driving route** into Las Vegas is the **I-15** freeway from southern California. Traffic congestion, especially close to the state line, can mean that the 269-mile drive from LA takes as long as eight hours. Las Vegas Boulevard South, which becomes the Strip, parallels I-15 well before it reaches the city, but the quickest way to reach your final destination will almost certainly be to stay on the interstate as long as possible. I-15 also connects Las Vegas with Salt Lake City, 421 miles northeast.

From the major cities of Arizona, direct access is provided by **US-93**, which leaves I-40 at Kingman, a hundred miles southeast. It joins **US-95**, running north from Needles, California, outside Boulder City; together, the two become **I-515**, which crosses I-15 immediately northwest of downtown Las Vegas.

Four hundred miles northwest of Las Vegas, US-95 meets I-80 thirty miles east of Reno. Using that interstate is the fastest way to get between Las Vegas and San Francisco, but threading cross-country via Yosemite and Death Valley national parks is a much more scenic option.

By bus

Greyhound's long-distance **buses** to and from Los Angeles, Phoenix, Salt Lake City, Denver and other cities use a terminal alongside the *Plaza* hotel at 200 S Main St downtown. For schedules and fares, call ©1-800/231-2222, or access *www.greyhound.com*.

By rail

Amtrak stopped running passenger **trains** to Las Vegas in 1997, and its downtown terminal was demolished. As this book went to press, however, it seemed likely that a new high-speed Amtrak service between Los Angeles and Las Vegas would soon come into operation, with a projected journey time of 5hr 30min. Some level of subsidy from the casinos is anticipated; individual carriages may belong to specific casinos, and be equipped with slot machines to be switched on as soon the train crosses the Nevada state line. For Amtrak information, call ©1-800/USA-RAIL, or access *www.amtrak.com*.

GETTING AROUND

Driving and rental cars

If you're happy to see no more of Las Vegas than the Strip and perhaps downtown – and on a short visit, there's no great reason to venture any further – then you can survive without a **car**. However, the metropolitan area is very large, so driving is the only practical way to explore it in any detail, while all the excursions detailed in Chapter Five require the use of your own vehicle. Even the Strip is too long to explore comfortably on foot; walking more than a couple of blocks in summer is exhausting.

Las Vegas as a whole is plagued by severe **traffic** problems, and nowhere more so than the Strip. That said, so long as you're not in a hurry to get anywhere, driving along the Strip is an exhilarating sensory blast, and worth experiencing both by day and by night. For trips on which speed is your main priority, it's usually worth using **I-15** where possible, even for short hops. The fastest east–west route across town tends to be **Desert Inn Road**, which passes under the Strip and over I-15, with connections to neither.

All the Strip casinos offer free **parking** to guests and non-guests alike, usually in huge garages around the back of the entire complex. The snag is that the walk from your car to wherever you actually want to go – your hotel room, for example – can be as much as a mile in places like *Caesars Palace* or the *MGM Grand*. If you're spending a day touring the Strip, you may prefer to go through the rigmarole of parking once only, somewhere central like *Harrah's*. **Valet parking**, usually available at the main casino entrance, can save a lot of stress; it's nominally free, although a tip of around $2 is all but obligatory.

Typical **car rental** rates in Las Vegas are $30 per day, $150 per week. All the major chains have outlets at the airport, and nearly every sizable hotel is affiliated with at least one car rental outfit. Specifically, Dollar (✆1-800/421-6868) is also represented at ten Strip casinos, Avis (✆1-800/331-1212) at *Bally's*, *Caesars Palace* and the *Las Vegas Hilton*, and Hertz (✆1-800/654-3131) at the *Desert Inn*. Allstate (✆1-800/634-6186) is an inexpensive local alternative, with additional locations at the *Riviera*, *Sahara* and *Plaza* casinos. To rent a Harley Davidson **motorcycle**, contact Drive With Passion (✆736-2592 or 1-800/372-1981).

Taxis

Every casino has a line of **taxis** waiting at its front entrance. Standard fares are $2.20 for the first mile and $1.50 for each additional mile, but the meter continues to run when you're caught in traffic. A $1.20 surcharge is added for trips to the airport; sample fares for the airport run are listed on p.5. Tip the driver between fifteen and twenty percent.

If you need to call a cab, try ABC (✆736-8444); Ace (✆736-8383); or Checker, Star and Yellow (all ✆873-2000).

Buses

CAT **buses** (℡228-7433) serve the entire city from their hub at the **Downtown Transportation Center** (daily 6am–10pm), a couple of blocks north of Fremont Street at Stewart Avenue and Casino Center Boulevard.

Two routes, **#301** and **#302**, run the length of the Strip and continue to downtown, with services every ten minutes between 5.30am and midnight, and every fifteen minutes from midnight until 5.30am. The flat fare is $1.50. Services in the rest of town operate between 5.30am and 1.30am only, for a flat fare of $1. A monthly pass for all CAT buses costs $20.

Trolleys

The oak-veneered streetcars of the **Las Vegas Strip Trolley** (℡382-1404) ply the Strip daily between 9.30am and 1.45am, with a flat fare of $1.40 and departures every fifteen minutes. Their route extends from *Mandalay Bay* as far north as the *Stratosphere*, with stops at the front doors of the major casinos, plus the Fashion Show Mall and Wet'n'Wild, and a brief detour to the *Las Vegas Hilton*.

The similar **Downtown Trolley** (℡229-0624) circles between downtown and the *Stratosphere* at thirty-minute intervals between 7am and 11pm daily, for a flat fare of 50¢.

Monorails

Several Strip properties are connected by means of free **monorail** services. Such systems link *Excalibur* with *Mandalay Bay* via *Luxor*; the *MGM Grand* with *Bally's* (potentially via the *Aladdin*); *Bellagio* with the *Monte Carlo*; and the *Mirage* with *Treasure Island*.

There has long been talk of constructing a single light-rail system that would run the length of the Strip and perhaps even extend as far as downtown. Such plans have traditionally been stymied by the refusal of the *Desert Inn*'s management to allow it to pass over their property, so its recent change of ownership may finally signal progress.

For the moment, however, the four existing segments do not meet up. In any case, they hardly make for a model of public transit. Designed to serve the needs of the casinos rather than the visitors, most can only be reached by walking through the whole of the relevant casinos.

Casino shuttle services

Several casino operators run **free shuttle services** either to connect different properties in the same chain, or between outlying casinos and the Strip. These include services between the various members of the Stations chain; between the *Barbary Coast* on the Strip and *Orleans* and the *Gold Coast* (next to the *Rio*) to the west; between *Sam's Town* and both the *Stardust* on the Strip and the *California* and *Fremont* hotels downtown; and between the *Rio* and the northeast corner of Harmon Avenue on the Strip.

In addition, a $10 round-trip bus service connects the *MGM Grand* with the town of **Primm**, forty miles southwest on the California border, which is home to a couple of large casinos and the Fashion Outlet Las Vegas mall; call ℅874-1400 for details.

Cycling

Cycling in Las Vegas proper is not a good idea. Cops do it to beat the traffic on the Strip, but for visitors there's too much danger for too little reward. Red Rock Canyon (see p.112) is very popular with recreational cyclists, however. If you want to rent a bike to join them, go to *Cyclery'n'Cafe*, 7016 W Charleston Blvd (℅228-9460).

Sightseeing tours

Las Vegas is not a city that lends itself to organized **sightseeing tours**. On foot, you'd have to walk too far; on a bus, you couldn't visit the Strip casinos that are the main focus of interest. What bus tours there are head out from the city instead, mainly to the destinations described in Chapter Five – Hoover Dam, Lake Mead, Red Rock Canyon, and so on. Several companies also offer free trips to the state-line casinos at Primm and Laughlin, of appeal to die-hard gamblers only. Most of the operators listed below also run flights or tours from Las Vegas to the Grand Canyon; see p.122.

Gray Line ©384-1234. Red Rock Canyon and Mount Charleston ($30); Hoover Dam ($22, or $37 with Lake Mead cruise); Death Valley ($99); Bryce Canyon ($125).

Jeep Tours ©796-9355. Red Rock Canyon ($50); Mount Charleston ($50); Valley of Fire ($60).

Las Vegas Tour and Travel ©739-8975. Hoover Dam ($18); Hoover Dam plus Lake Mead cruise ($34); night helicopter flights over Las Vegas ($55).

Magic Tours ©380-1106. Hoover Dam ($20); Laughlin (free).

Maverick Helicopter Tours ©261-0007. Las Vegas by night ($69); helicopter flight with rafting trip ($369).

Teddy Bear Express ©737-6062. Laughlin (free); Primm (free).

Valen Transportation & Tours ©734-5110. Bryce Canyon ($129), Disneyland (one-way $49, round-trip $89).

INFORMATION AND MAPS

There are two official **visitor centers** in Las Vegas. One, run by the **Las Vegas Convention & Visitors Authority**, is just inside the vast Convention Center at 3150 Paradise Rd (Mon–Fri 8am–6pm, Sat & Sun

8am–5pm; ✆892-0711 or 1-800/332-5333), half a mile east of the Strip. The other, the headquarters of the **Las Vegas Chamber of Commerce**, is at 711 E Desert Inn Rd (Mon–Fri 8am–5pm; ✆735-1616).

To receive an information pack by mail before you visit, call the Las Vegas Convention & Visitors Authority (✆892-0711) or the Nevada Commission on Tourism (✆1-800/638-2328).

However, there's very little point in visiting either. Neither is easily accessible on foot, while parking at the Convention Center is a real pain. Both merely hold much the same array of glossy brochures and leaflets that you'll find displayed in the lobby of your hotel. All Las Vegas's major attractions are run for profit, and you'll be bombarded with all the information you need without having to go out in search of more.

Similarly, it should be easy to pick up a decent **map** of the city at the desk of your hotel or car rental agency. The streetscape changes so fast, especially along the Strip, that it's essential for that map to be as recent as possible. Surprisingly enough, free handouts tend to be more reliable than commercial publications that may have been on the shelves for years.

To see our detailed color maps of Las Vegas, turn to the section at the back of the book. A map of the area covered in Chapter Five appears on pp.110–11.

THE MEDIA

The two principal daily **newspapers** in Las Vegas are the *Las Vegas Review-Journal*, which is published each morning

Las Vegas on the Internet

The following is a selective list of useful Web sites to help you plan before and during your trip. Web sites run by individual casinos, and by hotel reservation services, are listed in the Accommodation chapter (p.130).

www.experiencelasvegas.com A copious city directory.

www.gayvegas.com The best source for information on the city's gay scene.

www.ilovevegas.com Extensive listings and reviews from *What's On* magazine, plus on-line reservation service.

www.lasvegas24hours.com Official site of the Las Vegas Convention & Visitors Authority; comprehensive but unexciting.

www.lasvegastaxi.com Entertaining but infrequently updated "inside scoop" from Las Vegas's taxi drivers.

www.lvol.com Information and reservations, plus personal reviews and rankings of restaurants and hotels.

www.lvrj.com *Las Vegas Review-Journal*, with the latest details from the paper's *Neon* supplement and a useful searchable archive.

www.thegamblersedge.com Not Vegas-specific, though it does have links to the casinos, but a primer of rules, strategy, and the like for all types of casino games.

www.vegasresorts.com/new All the latest photos and details of hotel construction in Las Vegas.

and features a useful listings supplement, *Neon*, on Fridays, and the *Las Vegas Sun*, which appears every afternoon. *City Life*, a free "alternative" weekly, is the best source of up-to-date listings, but can be hard to find on the Strip – try the *Virgin Megastore* in *Caesars Palace*.

In addition, any number of freesheets and magazines –

usually bursting with discount vouchers, plus details of accommodation, buffets and the latest shows – provide local information. The fortnightly magazine *What's On* carries the most extensive reviews, while the weekly *Today in Las Vegas* offers the most accurate entertainment schedules and prices.

Stores in all the casinos sell local newspapers plus *USA Today* and the major Californian dailies, but for most out-of-town papers you'll need to head either to the Las Vegas International Newsstand, 3900 Paradise Rd (✆796-9901), or one of the bookstores listed on p.236.

The Strip

For its razor-edge finesse in harnessing sheer, magnificent excess to the deadly serious business of making money, there's no place like the **Strip**. Little more than fifty years ago, as Hwy-51, **Las Vegas Boulevard** was just a dusty desert thoroughfare, scattered with the occasional edge-of-town motel as it set off south toward California. Now, as a four-mile showcase of the most extravagant architecture on earth, it's a tourist destination in its own right, surpassed only by Orlando as the most popular in the US.

Las Vegas was not the first city to acquire an ever-lengthening "strip" of new businesses, as it expanded along a single straight line. In fact Las Vegas Boulevard got its nickname because it reminded former LA police captain Guy McAfee of Sunset Strip back home. McAfee moved to Las Vegas in 1938, after being obliged to resign as commander of LA's vice squad merely because he controlled a string of illegal gambling joints. He took over the *Pair-O-Dice Club*, which had recently opened as Las Vegas Boulevard's first casino. During the next ten years, it was joined by *El Rancho*, the first real resort, in 1941; the *Last Frontier* in 1942, which in due course incorporated the *Pair-O-Dice*; Bugsy Siegel's legendary *Flamingo* in 1946; and the *Thunderbird* in 1948.

For casino owners, much of the appeal of the nascent Strip was that it lay outside the city limits of Las Vegas proper. Instead it was in Clark County, where they completely dominated what little political life there was, and were thus spared the legal and financial scrutiny suffered by their rivals downtown. Their control of the county machine enabled them to resist repeated attempts to bring the Strip under the jurisdiction of the city authorities, and they've been free to pursue untrammeled development ever since.

....

The Strip is shown in detail on the color maps at the back of this book: the South Strip on map 2 and the North Strip on map 3.

....

While the essential spur for every innovation on the Strip remains the desire of each casino to attract gamblers, seduction strategies have changed over the years. When most Las Vegas visitors drove up from California, the Strip was entirely geared toward motorists. Until the 1980s, roadside signs advertising lodging, dining and entertainment bargains were taller and more prominent than the casinos themselves. These days, the tourists fly in, with their accommodation pre-booked, and the Strip itself is too clogged with traffic for aimless cruising to be a pleasure. The twin aims of the latest generation of giant casinos have become to keep their own guests on the premises for as much time as possible, and to lure in the pedestrian sightseers who throng the sidewalks outside. Pure spectacle is the name of the game, be it the volcano at the *Mirage* or the Sphinx at *Luxor*. Time was when each casino was a stand-alone oasis; now they're crammed so tightly together that they feed off each other – the Eiffel Tower at *Paris*, for example, sells itself as the ideal place to watch the fountain ballet at *Bellagio* across the street.

The northern end of the Strip is traditionally regarded as being the intersection of Las Vegas Boulevard with Sahara Avenue, although since 1996 the *Stratosphere*, a few blocks north, has made a brave attempt to change public perceptions. Its southern end, by contrast, is constantly shifting. The empty spaces south of the most recent casino to appear – the latest, but almost certainly not the last, is *Mandalay Bay* – have always presented the double advantage of offering plenty of room to build, and also the closest location to both California and the airport. Broadly speaking, therefore, in following the Strip from south to north, this chapter also journeys back through the history of the city.

MANDALAY BAY

Map 2, B8. 3950 Las Vegas Blvd S. *Mandalay Bay* hotel accommodation is reviewed on p.138, and the *Four Seasons* on p.136; restaurants include the *Bayside Buffet* (p.153), *China Grill* (p.159), and *rumjungle* (p.169); the *House of Blues* is described on p.199.

Since March 1999, the forty-story sentinel of **Mandalay Bay** has marked the southern limits of the Strip, glowing like a beacon as its gilded windows commandeer the sunset. Built by Circus Circus Enterprises on the site of the former *Hacienda* – blown up at midnight on New Year's Eve 1996–97 – it's an explicit attempt to match the showpieces constructed by Steve Wynn's Mirage organization.

Traditionally regarded as a canny but resolutely downmarket operator, Circus Circus Enterprises has followed a steady upward progression since the mid-1960s, from *Circus Circus* itself via *Excalibur* and *Luxor*. It celebrated completion of *Mandalay Bay*, which shares its trefoil design with *Bellagio* and the *Mirage*, and its gold-plated exterior with the *Mirage* and the *Golden Nugget*, with the logical final step of renaming itself the Mandalay Resort Group.

MANDALAY BAY

For each new Circus Circus casino, the target clientele has been envisaged as more affluent and more inclined to prize style over novelty. Not that *Mandalay Bay* is intended for existing customers, grown older and richer – it's aimed squarely at the next generation, not yet tied down by kids and eager to party at the *House of Blues* and its other music venues. The problem is that in eschewing the eye-catching gimmickry of *Excalibur*, while not (yet) being able to equal the opulence of *Bellagio*, *Mandalay Bay* risks falling between two stools and satisfying no one.

Mandalay Bay was not helped by its poor advance publicity. Subsidence delayed construction by almost a year; before it could be stabilized, the tower sank sixteen inches into the sand. At that stage, it was known as "Project Paradise," with the overall theme variously reported as being South Seas, Tropical, or Southeast Asian. The casino's first general manager resigned before it even opened, allegedly because promised efforts to attract Asian high-rollers had not materialized.

The name "Mandalay Bay" is supposed to conjure up romantic images from Rudyard Kipling's poem *The Road to Mandalay*. Though Mandalay itself is a real city, in Myanmar (which Kipling knew as Burma), the theming of the property remains generic. Landscaped gardens and walkways at both front and back abound in Asiatic motifs like pagodas and winged dragons, but both the interior and the extensive pool area opt for a softer-focus tropical feel of palm trees combined with upscale resort trimmings.

When the *Hacienda* was first built, in 1955, it stood well over a mile south of the Strip. Though *Mandalay Bay* now counts as being on the Strip, it's still perceived as off the beaten track. For motorists, it's easy enough to reach, with its own dedicated freeway exit. Pedestrians, however, face a discouraging slog; that few bother in the heat may explain the rudimentary feel of the Strip-level entrance. The styrofoam "boulders" piled here are so flimsy that they're crumbling where sightseers have climbed on them, releasing tiny white pellets to drift across the sidewalk.

Most visitors instead approach *Mandalay Bay* by means of the **monorail** that leaves from outside *Excalibur* at the intersection of the Strip and Tropicana Avenue. By Las Vegas's usual standards, this is a convenient ride; at least it's out front rather than right at the back. However, just to make sure you don't give *Mandalay Bay* a miss, the trains don't stop at *Luxor* on the way south, while on the return trip they don't take you back to where you started, but force you to walk through *Excalibur*.

Entering *Mandalay Bay* from the monorail stop or the parking garage, you arrive at the edge of the central casino floor, close to the *House of Blues* or the main restaurant area respectively. The dominant feature when the casino first opened was a huge statue of Lenin outside the *Red Square* restaurant. Allowing such a communist icon to overlook this cathedral to capitalism was too much for many palates, however. To mimic the destruction of similar statues in eastern Europe, Lenin was splattered with paint and then beheaded, before in a last indignity his head was stolen by persons unknown.

The main lobby area centers on a mock temple encasing a tank of tropical fish. Presumably in an attempt to match *Bellagio*'s Gallery of Fine Art (see p.42), there's also a little museum. Known as the **Treasures of Mandalay Bay**, it holds an inconceivably awful collection of dull coins from early Nevada (daily 9.30am–11pm; $7).

Panoramic windows at the far end of the lobby look out on an attractive tiled fountain topped by a griffin, but oddly enough the pool beyond belongs to the **Four Seasons** hotel and not *Mandalay Bay*. The 424 guest rooms of the *Four Seasons* occupy floors 35 through 39 of the *Mandalay Bay* tower, but they're accessed not only via separate elevators but through an entirely different lobby building. If you're curious, you can stroll in using a discreet door alongside the *Sea Breeze* juice bar on the lower level of *Mandalay Bay*. As a gaming-free zone, the *Four Seasons* is eerily silent, the clamor of the slots being replaced by the clink of bone china teacups.

> **Afternoon tea and scones in the *Four Seasons'* elegant *Lobby Lounge* cost $10; $19 gets you a plate of neatly trimmed sandwiches as well.**

While *Mandalay Bay* makes little effort to entertain rubbernecking tourists based elsewhere in town, its real strength stems from providing a full-on resort experience for its own guests. Unless you're staying here, you won't get to enjoy its superb open-air pool complex, complete with a scallop-shaped wave pool fringed by a broad sandy beach, and the "Lazy River" tubing ride.

On top of that, the place really comes alive at night. Boasting over a dozen top-class restaurants certainly helps, but the cornerstone of its strategy to lure hip contemporary customers is the *House of Blues* (see p.199). Run independently as part of the national *HoB* chain, this attracts the kind of big-name rock, soul and rap artists previously to be seen only off-Strip, at the *Hard Rock*. The crowds that spill out after the show's over tend to stick around into the small hours, grazing in the late-night lounges or gambling in the massive, ultra-modern Race and Sports Book. For really major events *Mandalay Bay* also has its own 12,000-seat arena, while the musical *Chicago* plays six nights a week.

The Mandalay Resort Group currently owns twelve thousand hotel rooms in its three adjacent properties south of Tropicana Avenue. Depending on the success of *Mandalay Bay*, it may yet add a fourth consecutive casino on the plot it owns immediately to the south. It is in any case committed to the construction of a giant shopping mall between *Mandalay Bay* and *Luxor* to the north.

LUXOR

Map 2, B7. 3900 Las Vegas Blvd S. Hotel accommodation is reviewed on p.137; restaurants include *Hamada* (p.163) and *Isis* (p.163); the show *Imagine* is reviewed on p.194, and the *Ra* nightclub on p.187.

When it opened in October 1993, **Luxor** was heralded as the ultimate in-your-face Las Vegas casino. A stark, forbidding pyramid of black glass, it dominated the southern approach to the Strip, its colossal Sphinx standing guard over not merely this one casino but all the splendors of the city. These days, however, it's surprisingly easy to forget that *Luxor* is even there, not least because its owners, Mandalay Resort Group (formerly Circus Circus), have comprehensively overshadowed it by building the mighty tower of *Mandalay Bay* next door. Furthermore, once the initial novelty wears off, black glass is one of the least conspicuous construction materials imaginable – especially at night, when the rest of the Strip comes into its own – and the entire exterior of *Luxor* is so featureless that it's hard to get any sense of the sheer scale of the place. That said, *Luxor* has been a great success, and recent improvements to its originally weak Egyptian theming have made it a better place to visit, or stay, than ever before.

For the record, the pyramid itself is 350 feet high, and it has been flanked since 1997 by two huge yet equally inconspicuous step-pyramids, bringing the total number of hotel rooms to 4427. In theory, it's approached from the sidewalk via a palm-fringed avenue of ram-headed sphinxes, though the only pedestrians around are in fact *Luxor* guests briefly braving the sun for a photo opportunity. Semi-constant construction work in this area gives *Luxor* the feel of an

LUXOR

archeological site, as though it's being unearthed rather than erected. The transit system that connects *Excalibur* to the north with *Mandalay Bay* to the south drops its passengers in front of the main multistory Sphinx, which also doubles as a porte-cochère, sheltering the vehicles that drive between its front and rear paws.

The spectacle that greets you inside the portals is every bit as dramatic. To reach the casino proper, you pass through a reconstruction of the temple of Abu Simbel, guarded by two huge seated statues. *Luxor* employees in gold Egyptian costumes patrol the precincts, posing for souvenir photos. As the pyramid is hollow, you're now in the world's largest atrium, which takes up 29 million cubic feet. Unfortunately, none of the elevators – those that follow the 39° slope of the pyramid are known as inclinators – offers any views to speak of, so the only way to see *Luxor* is by wandering around the lower levels. The gaming area is no more exciting than any other Vegas casino, but around the periphery you'll find some great friezes, statues, hieroglyphic inscriptions and other Pharaonic paraphernalia – look out for the high-camp bare-breasted maidens outside the *Ra* nightclub.

There are in fact no pyramids in Luxor, Egypt.

Escalators climb from the casino floor to the **Attractions Level**, the one place where *Luxor*'s theming goes wrong. Supposedly this area represents "the future," but its half-hearted "skyscrapers" are more of a weird hybrid of modern New York and medieval Cairo. Amid the mess are a small food court, a couple of restaurants, and a Sega games arcade. A meticulous replica of the **Tomb of King Tutankhamen** attempts to strike a highbrow note, though most of the visitors who shuffle through it appear bemused by its ersatz treasures. After all, the original – which stands

Top Ten Strip attractions for kids

*Older children may prefer the attractions
listed in the Top Ten for Adults, on p.37.*

across the river Nile from the city of Luxor, Egypt – remained undiscovered for millennia precisely because it was so small and pokey. Nearby, **In Search of the Obelisk** is a two-part simulator ride that punctuates an incoherent saga of Indiana-Jones-style derring-do with nauseating mechanical bumps and lurches. Admission to both, plus the assorted non-related films shown in the two IMAX movie theaters (one of them 3-D), costs a pricey $21.

Luxor's 36 stories taper to a point overhead; all the guest rooms face outward, and with so much free space to play with they're abnormally large by Vegas standards. The most powerful artificial light beam ever created shines up into the sky from the very apex. Though it's said to be visible from planes circling over LA, 250 miles west, it's barely noticeable in the general neon glare of the Strip. Around the back of the pyramid, the large, attractively landscaped swimming pool – open to guests only, and very short on shade – is over-looked by more counterfeit colossi, as well of course as several thousand hotel rooms and a couple of huge parking lots.

EXCALIBUR

Map 2, B6. 3850 Las Vegas Blvd S. Hotel accommodation is
reviewed on p.134; restaurants include the *Roundtable Buffet*
(p.155); and *King Arthur's Tournament* is reviewed on p.194.

The oldest of the three casinos owned by Mandalay Resort
Group (formerly Circus Circus) at the southern end of the
Strip, the mocked-up medieval castle of **Excalibur** now
makes a crude and unsophisticated neighbor for *Luxor* and
Mandalay Bay. Hastily erected in 1990, in the hope of beat-
ing the recently opened *Mirage* at its own game, it only cost
half as much to build – and it shows. Circus Circus
Enterprises pioneered the concept of the child-oriented
casino with the original, cheerfully downmarket *Circus
Circus* itself (see p.70). *Excalibur* went a stage further by
appearing to be both designed and assembled by children,
with its oversized primary-colored turrets drawn straight
from a kindergarten art class, and its sharp angles and visible
seams giving it the air of a cheap Christmas construction
kit.

When Circus Circus was planning *Excalibur*, architect
Veldon Simpson – later also responsible for both the *MGM
Grand* and *Luxor* – was dispatched to Europe to check out
hundreds of genuine castles. The model he chose to follow
was itself a playful, romantic fantasy. Neuschwanstein in
Bavaria was built in the late nineteenth century by Mad
King Ludwig, a devoted Wagner fan, who stuck the fairy-
tale flourishes of a French château atop the redoubtable
walls of a German fortress. If that sounds familiar, it's probably because Neuschwanstein was also the blueprint for
Sleeping Beauty's Castle in Disney World.

The name "Excalibur" was the winning entry in a
public competition.

In truth, no one ever intended *Excalibur* to look like a real castle. Its colors are deliberately clashing, and its proportions distorted. Basically it's a gigantic billboard, designed to draw in tourists who see it from a distance. The castle itself is all but engulfed by the two huge hotel towers that hold its four thousand guest rooms, so you can only see it properly either from the Strip, diagonally opposite the main entrance, or from the air.

For its first three years, *Excalibur* was the world's largest hotel, and it prospered enough for Circus Circus to use its cash profits to build *Luxor* next door. At the root of that success was its appeal to low-budget tour groups – it was the first casino to have a separate driveway specifically for tour buses – and even now, as it starts to age, its popularity with family vacationers remains undimmed.

The pedestrian entrance to *Excalibur* has recently been revamped, to make room for the monorail system that ferries passengers to *Mandalay Bay*. The castle itself is set so far back from the Strip that you have to approach via a long system of moving walkways, on which almost no expense has been lavished. In theory there's a sort of moat down below a sort of drawbridge, but you get little impression of either. A purple-robed figure of Merlin, dwarfed by his surroundings, waves benignly from high on the central turret, while a booming, genial English voice welcomes all "loyal subjects" to King Arthur's domain of Camelot.

Once inside, you're plunged as ever into the maelstrom of the main casino floor, but it's easy to escape to the non-gaming areas both above and below. Upstairs you'll find most of *Excalibur*'s restaurants – quite what the TV-wrestling-themed *WCW Nitro Grill* is doing tucked between *Merlin's Ice Cream Shoppe* and the always packed *Roundtable Buffet* is anyone's guess – together with family-fun opportunities such as photo studios equipped with extensive wardrobes for dressing-up, plus the Canterbury

EXCALIBUR

Wedding Chapel for single travelers seized by the urge to settle down. Downstairs the atmosphere is more like a traditional fairground, filled with sideshows where kids can spend real money attempting to win plastic swords and other Arthurian memorabilia. A large indoor arena hosts *King Arthur's Tournament*, a twice-nightly mixture of jousting, joshing and noshing.

There are plenty more places in Vegas to tie the knot of course; see Chapter Thirteen, Getting Married p.252.

THE TROPICANA

Map 2, C6. 3801 Las Vegas Blvd S. Hotel accommodation is reviewed on p.142.

On its opening day in 1957, the **Tropicana** was not literally alone in the desert – the now-vanished *Hacienda* had gone up nearby the previous year – but it stood a mile removed from the body of the Strip, and considered itself as a class apart. Bankrolled by the New Orleans Mafia, the "Tiffany of the Strip" was aimed squarely at high-rollers, and its flamboyant paradise-island trimmings epitomized Las Vegas luxury. In the decade since *Excalibur* came along, however, the crossroads of Tropicana Avenue and Las Vegas Boulevard has become one of the Strip's two principal intersections, rivaled only by the spot where *Caesars Palace* and *Bellagio* face off across Flamingo Road. These days, and despite recent upgrading, the *Tropicana* palls in comparison to its three mighty neighbors. Even so, it continues to do well, thanks in large part to refugees from *Excalibur* and the *MGM Grand* who cross the pedestrian bridges over the Strip either to find a more traditional place to gamble, or simply to escape the kids.

Though the "tropical" theme of the "Island of Las Vegas"

is pretty vague, and not based on any specific location, that didn't stop the *Tropicana* from trying to sue Steve Wynn, when he was building the *Mirage*, for allegedly copying the idea. Appropriately enough, its new facade suspiciously resembles the Caribbean village at Wynn's *Treasure Island* (see p.56), minus the pirates but plus false storefronts in pastel colors. The corresponding shops can be found within, just not behind the relevant "doors."

The interior of the *Tropicana* is a muddled maze that offers scant reward to those who try to penetrate it. It owes the "Tiffany" nickname to the ornate **domed ceiling** of stained glass that hangs above its central gaming tables. The ceiling is modeled on a San Francisco bank destroyed in the 1906 earthquake; its impact, however, is diminished by the fact that it only covers a small proportion of the total room space, which is otherwise so low-ceilinged as to make it almost unnoticeable.

Devotees of Las Vegas history can spend a happy half-hour browsing through the **Casino Legends Hall of Fame**, on the first floor (daily 7am–9pm; $4). A bit too much space is given over to a collection of chips from every casino that's ever existed – many are for sale, priced from $4 to $600 – but when the focus shifts to the personalities of the past, things become more interesting. The entertainment section kicks off with Sophie Tucker, who starred at the *Last Frontier* in 1944, runs through Frank Sinatra and Liberace, and includes a bevy of showgirls from the *Tropicana*'s own long-running *Folies Bergeres*. So far Elvis doesn't seem to have been elected to the Hall of Fame, but at least he's represented in the movies section, where *Viva Las Vegas* is one of four classic flicks on display. Some spectacular footage of planned casino implosions also runs constantly, along with strangely tasteless film clips of the city's most disastrous fires. The "Bad Guys" section lingers lovingly on the skeletons in Las Vegas's closet, describing

Bugsy Siegel as more of a "colorful uncle" than a founding father. The *Tropicana*'s tribulations are not ignored – it's widely acknowledged as having remained under Mob domination until 1979, when it was taken over by Ramada – as it moves to the surprisingly downbeat conclusion that "today Las Vegas's casinos are relatively Mob-free."

Where the *Tropicana* really does come up trumps is with its **swimming pool**, which is among the best in Las Vegas. Covering five landscaped acres, it's more of a waterpark really, surrounded by lush gardens and complete with hot tubs, fish-filled lagoons, a swim-up bar, and an outdoor wedding chapel.

In terms of traffic volume, the intersection of Las Vegas Boulevard and Tropicana Avenue is said to be the busiest in America.

NEW YORK–NEW YORK

Map 2, B5. 3790 Las Vegas Blvd S. Hotel accommodation is reviewed on p.139; restaurants include *America* (p.158), *Il Fornaio* (p.163), and *Motown Cafe* (p.165).

Architects have played many strange and inventive games in Las Vegas during the last fifty years, but for sheer weirdness there's never been anything quite like **New York–New York**. On the one hand, it looks utterly unlike the conventional idea of a "building," and yet on the other it's immediately recognizable as being an entire city compressed into a single structure. The motives behind the creation of this miniature Manhattan were much the same as for the original; when space is at an absolute premium, the best way to build is upward. Thanks to its exuberant attention to detail, it's an absolute triumph. Owned by MGM Grand and Primadonna Resorts, and unveiled at the start of 1997, it's the most perfectly realized of all the Strip's themed casinos.

From street level, *New York–New York* looks stunning, its twelve pastel skyscrapers silhouetted with absolute clarity against the blue desert sky, and fronted by a proud, pristine **Statue of Liberty**. The various components range between a third and a half of the size of the originals, with the highest point of the whole ensemble, naturally enough, being the 510-foot, 47-story **Empire State Building**. This squashed-up cityscape is not simply a static tableau. Matching red and green fireboats jet arcs of water across New York Harbor, while a Coney Island roller coaster loops and swoops around the skyline in full view – and earshot – of the Strip.

For once, *New York–New York* is as much fun inside as out. Not that the distinction is all that clear; there's only a minimal correlation between the interior and the exterior, so you step through the doors to find yourself not safely inside Grand Central Station, but walking through Central Park at nightfall. Stuffed owls gaze down on the gaming tables from fake trees strung with fairy lights, and the carpeted walkways are disguised as footpaths strewn with fallen leaves. The one drawback is that by Las Vegas standards, *New York–New York* is a small joint, with a mere two thousand hotel rooms, and its narrow aisles can often feel overcrowded with sightseers.

As well as the obligatory casino, the ground floor holds several unexpected delights. The Greenwich Village section comes complete not only with fast-food outlets and a fake subway station, but even fire hydrants, trashcans and mailboxes sprayed with impressive (if firmly PG-rated) graffiti. Elevators up to the hotel rooms leave from lobbies styled to resemble specific buildings – one reproduces the Art Deco embellishments of the Chrysler Building – but unfortunately the towers above don't correspond to what's visible from outside. Among several scattered eateries are the excellent *Il Fornaio* deli, the *America* diner, with its massive relief map of the US suspended alarmingly from the ceiling, and the *Motown Cafe* (even Las Vegas will probably never build a *Detroit Detroit*, so this makes as good a place to put it as any).

Most of the upper floor is given over to traditional carnival sideshows and attractions intended for kids, though its corridors also accommodate the often lengthy lines waiting to climb aboard the little yellow taxicabs of the Manhattan Express **roller coaster** (Sun–Thurs 10.30am–10.30pm, Fri & Sat 10.30am–midnight; $8). This is by far the best such ride in Vegas, racing out into the open air at speeds of up to 65mph, and spiraling through some fearsomely tight rolls; not an experience theme-park neophytes should undertake lightly.

THE MGM GRAND

Map 2, C5. 3799 Las Vegas Blvd S. Hotel accommodation is reviewed on p.138; restaurants include *Coyote Cafe* (p.160), *Emeril's New Orleans Fish House* (p.162), *Rainforest Cafe* (p.169), and *Wolfgang Puck Cafe* (p.172); and the show *EFX* is reviewed on p.193.

A lot of careful thought and planning went into the construction of the world's largest hotel, the **MGM Grand**; most of it turned out to be hopelessly wrong. In the early Nineties, the concept of Las Vegas as the family destination of the future was in its heyday, and the prospects of this billion-dollar project were seen as resting on its own state-of-the-art **theme park**, MGM Grand Adventures. From the moment the hotel opened in 1993, however, the theme park was universally panned. For audiences reared on its rivals in LA and Orlando, it simply wasn't big enough or thrilling enough. Not only has the theme park now all but closed down, but the *Grand*'s original *Wizard of Oz* theme, which meant little or nothing to modern kids, has had to be abandoned. And yet the *MGM Grand* itself is going from strength to strength; if the theme park does disappear, which seems a real possibility, it's most likely to be replaced with yet more hotel space to complement the original world-record five thousand rooms.

Spreading over 114 acres of a site previously occupied by the *Tropicana*'s golf course and the *Marina* hotel complex, the *MGM Grand* is bigger than *Luxor* and *Excalibur* combined. Its owner, Armenian billionaire **Kirk Kerkorian** – who like Howard Hughes is a former aviator – has twice before erected the world's largest hotel. The first was what's now the *Las Vegas Hilton* (see p.95); the second, also called the *MGM Grand*, became *Bally's* in 1985, after being devastated by a horrific fire in which 84 people died (see p.39). Kerkorian sold everything but the name.

Until recently, visitors entered the complex through the gaping jaws of a lion that may have been a great copy of the one seen at the start of classic MGM movies, but to unsentimental eyes looked downright tacky. Asian customers also considered it unlucky to walk through the mouth of a lion – especially into a casino, of all places. It has been replaced by a more naturalistic stand-alone bronze lion, towering seventy feet above the intersection of Tropicana Avenue and Las Vegas Boulevard, and gleaming in front of a copper-colored wall of lights. Small pedestrian entrances are located on either side, but the main entrance for hotel guests and all other traffic is a hundred yards or so east along Tropicana Avenue.

Getting rid of the Emerald City attraction just inside the doors – it also said goodbye Yellow Brick Road to the walkway that led on from it, relegated Dorothy to an alcove near the monorail station at the back, and toned down the general greenness of the whole building – left the *MGM*

Grand with little for casual sightseers to look at. Shamelessly taking a leaf from the *Mirage* and its tigers, as well as stealing some thunder from the nearby *Rainforest Cafe*, it developed the **Lion Habitat**, a wooded zoo close to the front entrance where real lions lounge around a ruined temple beneath a naturally lit dome. You can either watch the lions from the casino floor or walk through the enclosure via a glass tunnel, quite possibly as they pad directly overhead (daily 11am–11pm; free). Paying $20 entitles you to partici-pate in the grotesque charade of having your photo taken with a cute little lion cub; oblivious to your presence, it's made to look wistful and winsome by having its milk bottle whisked away for a fraction of a second (daily except Tues 11am–5pm).

The child-friendly *Rainforest Cafe* and the all-too-adult *Studio 54* nightclub are also close to the Strip entrance, but most of the hotel's prestigious array of **restaurants** – big names include *Emeril's*, *Coyote Cafe*, and *Wolfgang Puck Cafe* – are way back, beyond the casino. Together with the pop-ular *MGM Buffet*, these ensure that the hotel is always crowded, but it steps up another gear whenever a big-name **boxing match** is being staged in its fifteen-thousand-seat arena.

As for the *MGM Grand*'s casino, it's so big that it's divided into four separate sections. Just to stock the slot machines in the first place required $3.25 million-worth of quarters – that's thirteen million of them. Turnover on its gaming tables (covered with blue rather than green felt, for no apparent reason) is so phenomenal that when the crowds after the Holyfield–Tyson ear-biting debacle in June 1997 mistook the popping of champagne corks for gunfire, and the resulting furor forced the casino to close down for two hours, the loss was estimated in millions of dollars. There's a chance to familiarize yourself with the sound of genuine gunfire downstairs, where the kids' play area includes a shooting range as well as arcade games, pinball machines, and virtual-reality rides.

What remains of the theme park is outside in the back lot, near the extensive swimming pools; the only noteworthy feature here is the **Sky Screamer**, a cross between a bungee-jump and a giant swing in which one victim at a time takes the plunge from twin 250-foot towers (summer daily 10am–10pm, winter Mon–Thurs 10am–6pm, Fri & Sun 10am–8pm; $22.50 for one ride, $35 for two, $37.50 for three).

A mile-long monorail connects the *MGM Grand* to *Bally's*, by way of the *Aladdin*. It's a long walk to reach it from the Strip, however, as it runs at the rear of those properties.

THE SHOWCASE MALL

Map 2, C5. 3769 Las Vegas Blvd S.

Immediately north of the *MGM Grand*, the **Showcase Mall** is a real rarity for the Strip – a gleaming new development that's not a casino. It is, however, every bit as thumpingly themed as any casino, with its most prominent feature being the multistory Coke-bottle-cum-elevator of the **World of Coca-Cola** (Sun–Thurs 10am–10pm, Fri & Sat 10am–11pm; $3.50). Set bang opposite *New York–New York* (which has an exclusive contract with Pepsi), this "museum" charges visitors for the privilege of watching "those memorable commercials" and admiring Hadden Sundblom's original oil paintings of "Visions of Santa." His early twentieth-century canvases are credited with giving the world the notion of Father Christmas as a white-bearded old man with a fur-trimmed red coat. Space-age soda fountains at the end of the self-guided tour jerk out a variety of sickly sodas, including a lychee-flavor Fanta that's said to go down a treat in Thailand.

If shopping for souvenirs is your main aim, you can get into the store area, on the lower levels, without paying, and put the money you saved on the admission fee toward buying a $950 crystal paperweight featuring the Coca-Cola polar bear. Watch out, too, for the endearing little robot who roams the Strip outside, singing the praises of Coca-Cola and cajoling passers-by into giving it a cuddle.

Elsewhere in the Showcase Mall, **Game Works** (daily 10am–4am) is a Spielberg-owned arcade of up-to-the-minute video games and virtual-reality machines that also holds a 75-foot rock-climbing wall ($10), while the **All-Star Cafe** nearby may serve unenthralling food, but it's bursting with sports memorabilia, including plenty from Las Vegas's favorite son, co-owner Andre Agassi. A twelve-screen movie theater rounds off the entertainment.

THE MONTE CARLO

Map 2, B5. 3770 Las Vegas Blvd S. Hotel accommodation is reviewed on p.139, and the *Lance Burton* show on p.195.

Many visitors to Las Vegas like to imagine the city as still being under the thumb of the Mob, with each casino fighting a quasi-legal cutthroat war against all the rest. The **Monte Carlo** conclusively puts the lie to that notion. Remarkably enough, it's a joint venture between Las Vegas's two major rivals: the Mandalay Resort Group (formerly Circus Circus), who put up the money to build it and are wholly responsible for running it, and Mirage Resorts, which owns the land on which it stands but, busy with *Bellagio*, did not at the time have the spare cash to create another casino. That potent combination meant that despite having over three thousand rooms, and therefore ranking among the world's ten largest hotels, the *Monte Carlo* took a mere fifteen months to go from the drawing board to its opening night in June 1996.

The *Monte Carlo* is by a long way the soberest new casino to appear in Las Vegas in the last ten years. The usual Circus Circus thrills and gimmickry are nowhere to be seen, and you can't help suspecting that Mirage made it a condition of its construction that it never tried to steal the thunder of *Bellagio* next door. Its nominal theme is that it's modeled on the Place du Casino in Monte Carlo, so there's plenty of sub-*Caesars* classical statuary around, and a certain Belle Epoque elegance about its plush Victorian trimmings. However, apart from its ornate 1200-seat theater, home to the show of the excellent illusionist Lance Burton, the theming does not extend to its restaurants and other facilities, and is probably of minimal significance to most guests. They tend to be an affluent and slightly older-than-average group, both because they see the *Monte Carlo* as being a quieter and classier place to both sleep and gamble than almost anywhere on the Strip, and because the hotel is shorter on crowds in general and kids in particular. The one place they can let their hair down is the *Monte Carlo Pub & Brewery*, a massive brewpub reviewed on p.184.

....

Another light monorail system links the *Monte Carlo* with *Bellagio* to the north; it can't continue to the *Mirage* and *Treasure Island* because *Caesars Palace* is in the way.

....

THE ALADDIN

This book went to press before the unveiling of the new **Aladdin**. The new hotel-casino is designed to expand upon the Arabian Nights theme of the original 1966 version, and is ambitiously scheduled to open on April 27, 2000, two years to the day after the first was imploded.

Topped by an extravaganza of Moorish domes, its facade centers on a "Lost City" perched atop an artificial cliff.

Its two major selling points are the **Desert Passage** – a shopping and entertainment mall intended to rival the Forum (see p.46) – and an as-yet-undefined "**Music Project**." Targeted at younger visitors, the latter hopes to lure contemporary music fans away from the *Hard Rock* and *Mandalay Bay*. It was initially envisaged as a joint venture with *Planet Hollywood*, but financial difficulties forced the chain to withdraw, and the search for a new partner may delay its opening by a year or more. In the interim, the *Aladdin's* renovated 7000-seat **Theatre of the Performing Arts** will doubtless play host to major musical events.

For updated details on the *Aladdin*, try their Web site at *www.aladdincasino.com* or call ©736-7114.

Among restaurants signed up for the property are outposts of New Orleans' legendary haute-Creole *Commanders Palace*, *Anasazi* from Santa Fe, *Lombardi's* from Dallas, and the *Macanudo Steakhouse* from Chicago.

PARIS

Map 2, C3. 3645 Las Vegas Blvd S. Hotel accommodation is reviewed on p.140; restaurants include *Le Village Buffet* (p.154); *La Rotisserie des Aristes* (p.164); and *Le Provencal* (p.165).

By opening in September 1999, **Paris**, immediately north of the *Aladdin*, became the last Strip casino of the twentieth century. It's the handiwork of the same team of designers as *New York–New York* (see p.28), who found themselves operating under similar spatial constraints. To make the most of its smallish site, they planted three legs of its centerpiece Eiffel Tower smack in the middle of the casino floor, and allowed it to straddle the Arc de Triomphe and the

Top Ten Strip attractions for adults

A Top Ten for Kids appears on p.23.

Opera. In this case, however, it's somewhat of a shame; feeling squashed up and claustrophobic is part of the fun of Manhattan, but Paris should surely be a bit more spacious and elegant.

It's slightly misleading to think of *Paris* as a separate casino at all. Technically it was built by Park Place, and licensed by the Nevada Gaming Commission, as a major extension to *Bally's* next door, to which it's linked by a broad corridor at the back. At $785 million, it cost around half of either *Bellagio* or the *Venetian*, and it shares much of its infrastructure and management with *Bally's*. Ultimately, perhaps, the tail may come to wag the dog, with *Bally's* being seen as a minor adjunct to *Paris*.

The Strip-front exterior of *Paris* is a well-realized miniature, incorporating a welcome strolling and picture-taking area focused around a sparkling fountain and a handful of trees; a colorful replica Montgolfier balloon; and a sidewalk brasserie, *A Mon Ami Gabi*, that's the only spot on the central Strip where you can sit down to eat or drink and watch

PARIS, TOP TEN STRIP ATTRACTIONS FOR ADULTS

the crowds go by. The Eiffel Tower itself – strictly speaking, the **Eiffel Tower Experience** – is also, of course, an extravagant sign in the finest Las Vegas tradition. Standing 540ft tall, it's half the size of the 1889 original, and made of welded steel rather than wrought iron, with "false rivets" added for cosmetic effect. Some components, most obviously the elevators, had to be built at full size so people could actually use them, thus it's not a perfect scale model. Taking the ninety-second ride straight through the roof and up to the summit – for which you might have to wait in line for up to thirty minutes – offers amazing views over the city, at their best after dark, and most specifically across to *Bellagio*'s water ballet (daily 10am–1am; $8). There's also a very expensive dinner-only restaurant, *La Tour Eiffel*, on its first level, seventeen stories high and reached by separate elevators.

The joyful wealth of detail inside *Paris* matches *New York–New York*, though in a slightly more twee and Disney-fied manner. Beret-wearing bicyclists whistle Gallic tunes as they pedal basket-loads of baguettes along its streets, dodging stripey-shirted accordionists and smart *gendarmes*. Every member of staff (or "citizen of Paris") has a twenty-word French vocabulary, which is splendidly inadequate to cope with any genuine situation. As well as a fine assortment of top-notch French restaurants, you'll find authentic bakeries, pastry shops, and even toy stores where the *Sesame Street* dolls talk in French. As any true Parisian could have warned you, the cobbled alleyways wreak havoc on high heels, strollers, and wheeled suitcases, but no one seems too concerned.

An air of French glamour wafts appealingly over the gaming tables, which are covered by metalwork canopies modeled on the metro stations of Paris, and the appeal of all that fabulous French food is unlikely to pall. Whether *Paris*'s intention of programming predominantly French entertainment will pay off, however, remains to be seen;

Marcel Marceau has reared his doleful features, while the showcase production at the 1200-seat theater is *Notre Dame du Paris*, a musical based on *The Hunchback of Notre Dame*.

BALLY'S

Map 2, C3. 3645 Las Vegas Blvd S. Hotel accommodation is reviewed on p.132; restaurants include *Bally's Big Kitchen Buffet* (p.152).

Though long since outclassed by its mighty neighbors, the casino now known as **Bally's** was twenty years ago the most famous, and infamous, hotel in the world. This is the original *MGM Grand*, which opened in 1973. Setting out to prove that there was far more money to be made in the casino business than in producing movies, entrepreneur Kirk Kerkorian had sold off almost the entire assets of MGM Studios in order to built the biggest hotel that had ever existed. Named after the 1932 movie *Grand Hotel*, the *MGM Grand* did indeed generate vast profits. However, it was devastated in November 1980 by the worst hotel fire in history, when faulty wiring in the deli caused a blaze that killed 84 people and injured over seven hundred more. The *MGM Grand* reopened in identical shape within eight months, but four years later Kerkorian sold it to Bally's, the pinball and slot-machine manufacturers, who had recently had a tremendous cash windfall from the worldwide success of their Pac-Man machines. That company later ran into difficulties, and sold the hotel to the Hilton corporation in 1996, which chose to keep on calling it *Bally's*. It's now run in conjunction with *Paris* next door by Park Place, who took over Hilton's casinos early in 1999 and also own *Caesars Palace*. Kerkorian, meanwhile, had retained the *MGM Grand* name for his own future use (see p.31).

The fact that *Bally's* is actually one of the Strip's dullest buildings, consisting of little more than two monolithic rectangular towers, has been disguised by turning the whole thing into a giant neon sign. Not only the towers, but also the tubular walkway that carries pedestrians into the casino, shift constantly through a spectrum of four garish colors. The walkway moves so slowly, however, above a shallow pool, that you'll probably have tired of the light show long before you reach the end.

There's little to detain you inside the hotel, which is used more by conventioneers and business people than vacationers. Non-guests tend to head straight for either the good-value *Big Kitchen Buffet*, up on the second floor of the South Tower; the large, high-tech Race & Sports Book, hidden away in the basement of the North Tower; or the monorail, right at the back of the property, which connects *Bally's* and the current version of the *MGM Grand*. At least the pedestrian walkway runs in both directions, so it's not too hard to find your way out again.

BELLAGIO

Map 2, B3. 3600 Las Vegas Blvd S. Hotel accommodation is reviewed on p.133; restaurants include *The Buffet* (p.153), *Aqua* (p.159), *Le Cirque* (p.164), *Olives* (p.167), and *Picasso* (p.168); the Via Bellagio shops are reviewed on p.229, and the Cirque du Soleil show *O* on p.196.

Steve Wynn, the presiding genius of Mirage Resorts, set himself a very tall order when he started to plan **Bellagio**. His goal was not to build merely the best hotel in Las Vegas – he felt he'd done that with the *Mirage* – or even the best hotel in the world. He wanted nothing short of the best hotel there has ever been, anywhere. Though Wynn's obsession has ensured that *Bellagio* is a breathtaking achievement – since it opened in October 1998, it has clearly been a quantum leap ahead of all its Vegas competitors – it has also demanded that it be judged according to standards that it could not conceivably meet. Seen as the latest in the long line of casinos that have set out to redefine Las Vegas, *Bellagio* is a triumph, but that's all it is: just another casino.

By all accounts, Wynn is not a modest man, and he can't help taking it personally that some people continue to look down their noses at Las Vegas. With *Bellagio*, he aimed "to impress everyone without being pretentious." Traditionally, the theming in Vegas casinos has always been playful – you're not supposed to think that being in *Luxor* is like being in ancient Egypt, just that it's fun to pretend. *Bellagio* takes itself much more seriously. No longer is it enough to create an illusion; *Bellagio*, rather pointlessly and self-defeatingly, wants to be real. Not only does it have to be an improvement on the Italian lakeside village for which it's named, it also has to outdo what's generally thought of as the greatest hotel in history, the nineteenth-century *Ritz* in Paris – hence the Belle Epoque late-Victorian flourishes tacked onto its understated Italian provincial elegance. And it even has to do so by somehow being more authentic than the original. The trouble is that *Bellagio* is not in Europe, it's in Las Vegas, and it's stuffed full of slot machines. Inlaid with jewel-like precision into marble counters, perhaps, but still slot machines.

The main hotel block, a stately curve of blue and cream pastels, stands aloof from the Strip behind an eight-acre artificial lake. The mere presence of so much water in the desert announces the wealth at *Bellagio*'s disposal, but the point is rubbed in every half-hour at night when hundreds of submerged fountains erupt in Busby-Berkeley water ballets, choreographed with booming music and colored lights. At the foot of the hotel, the lake is bordered by a reproduction of a small Italian village. Several of the structures here are restaurants, which offer lakeshore terrace dining.

Most pedestrians approach *Bellagio* from its northeast corner, crossing the bridges from *Caesars Palace* or *Bally's* where

BELLAGIO

Flamingo Road meets the Strip. Ponderous mosaic-floored revolving doors grant admittance not to the usual moving walkway but to the **Via Bellagio**, a covered mall of impossibly glamorous designer boutiques. At the far end of this plush paisley-carpeted corridor, the cacophony of the casino looms ever louder. Although only bona-fide guests are allowed to bring children aged under 18 inside the building, there's no dress code, and the staff are unfailingly polite to all comers.

Hotel guests, by contrast, sweep up to *Bellagio* along a grand waterfront drive, to enter a sumptuous lobby that's deliberately distinct from the casino. Mosaic butterflies and insects writhe across the floor, while the ceiling is filled by a brooding sort of semi-chandelier of glass flowers, made by sculptor Dale Chihuly. It's all said to be hand-blown, but "over-blown" would be closer to the mark. Even the area behind the check-in desks is themed; to reach the executive offices, disguised as a Venetian villa, the clerks have to make their way through a fully fledged Roman garden.

The lobby leads in turn to *Bellagio*'s real showpiece, the opulent **Conservatory**. Beneath a Belle Epoque canopy of copper-framed glass, a network of flowerbeds is replanted every six to eight weeks with ornate seasonal displays. Thus fall is heralded by resplendent gold and yellow blooms surrounding a colossal cornucopia of harvest fruits, December sees Martha Stewart decorate a glittering Christmas tree, and so on. Individual spotlights can be trained on each flower, so the place is at its most spectacular at night.

Bellagio's most overt bid for high-culture kudos is towards the rear of the property, across from the pool. Purists may profess to be appalled at the idea of displaying top-quality original art in a casino, but the **Bellagio Gallery of Fine Art** (daily 9am–11pm; $12) is nothing to sneer at. Yes, it only has a very small, "Greatest Hits"-

style collection – the product of a three-year, thirty-million-dollar shopping spree by Wynn himself – and yes, the admission fee is expensive by the standard of the world's major art galleries. However, the thirty or so pieces on display (the precise number varies) are uniformly excellent. Most artists are represented by a single canvas, but there are no lesser works or makeweights. The oldest is a Renoir from 1874, the newest a Lichtenstein from 1995; highlights include Edgar Degas' delicate, graceful *Dancer Taking A Bow* (1877), Monet's *Water-Lily Pond With Bridge* (1905), and a Warhol *Elvis* (1962–64). Paying $4 extra rents an audio "wand," featuring a Wynn-narrated tour that culminates in his revealingly Freudian interpretation of Picasso's 1942 *Portrait of Dora Maar*, though why he seems to imagine that this will be his guests' first exposure to high culture – he invites visitors to "join [him] in discovering the power of fine art" – is hard to fathom. Incidentally, all the art is for sale; a big enough win on the tables and you could walk out with a painting tucked under your arm.

To get the full benefit of *Bellagio's* facilities, which include a luxurious spa and beauty salon, and an array of six superb landscaped swimming pools, you need to stay at the hotel. For any visitor to Las Vegas, however, it has instantly become a must-see attraction in its own right, representing the best the city has to offer in almost any category you care to think of (with the obvious exception of parking spaces). Unless you're as hung up on authenticity as Steve Wynn, swooning at the cost of its construction materials swiftly ceases to be a thrill, but there's still plenty to enjoy. For sheer ambition and energy, its major production show, the Cirque du Soleil's *O*, offers by far the best theatrical experience in town, while around a dozen top-quality restaurants are arrayed along the lakefront, with the astonishing *Buffet* tucked away further back.

BELLAGIO

CAESARS PALACE

Map 2, B2. 3570 Las Vegas Blvd S. Hotel accommodation is reviewed on p.133; restaurants include *Chinois* (p.160), *The Palm* (p.168), and *Spago's* (p.170); the Forum Shops are described on p.227; and the *Magical Empire* dinner-cum-magic-show is reviewed on p.196.

Still going strong after more than thirty years in the business, **Caesars Palace** is a Las Vegas anomaly. In a city that's forever discarding the old in pursuit of the new, it remains the most famous name, the one casino all first-time visitors rush to see for themselves. Of course, much about *Caesars Palace* has changed since Vegas's definitive themed casino was unveiled in August 1966, but much has also stayed constant. The trademark Italianate fountains out front are still there, albeit joined by an ever-expanding array of pseudo-classical statuary and pavilions, while the half-naked Roman centurions and Cleopatra-cropped cocktail waitresses within now have a vast fake Forum through which to strut their stuff.

> **The one thing *Caesars Palace* will *never* have is an apostrophe – it does not belong to Caesar, it's filled by the thousands of Caesars who choose to visit it.**

To build *Caesars Palace* originally cost under $25 million – less than the volcano at the *Mirage*. The brainchild of entrepreneur Jay Sarno, who had owned progressively more elaborate motels in Atlanta, Dallas and (in partnership with Doris Day) Palo Alto, it was the first Vegas casino to be financed through loans from the pension fund of Jimmy Hoffa's Teamsters' Union. A powerful Mob presence was barely concealed from the word go, and became even more apparent after Sarno sold out in 1969 for $60 million. Under pressure from repeated Federal fraud investigations throughout the Seventies, *Caesars* passed into sanitized corporate control at the start of the Eighties. It was sold to ITT for $1.7 billion in 1995; taken over by Starwood Hotels & Resorts in 1998; and then passed into the hands of Park Place in 1999, at which time Steve Wynn of Mirage Resorts was among the unsuccessful bidders. Sarno himself, who went on to build the first, disastrous incarnation of *Circus Circus* (see p.70), died in a suite at *Caesars* in 1984. His crucial legacy lay in having set *Caesars* up on an expanse of land that has so far proved extensive enough to hold every enlargement architects have been able to imagine.

The exterior of *Caesars Palace* most matches its theme, the public spaces of ancient Rome, by being a haphazard accretion of disparate, often jarring, elements. Some are accurate depictions of classical Rome; some reproduce the architecture of much later periods; and others, like the geodesic dome of the Omnimax theater, the globe of *Planet Hollywood*, and the four-ton, four-faced bronze Brahma on the sidewalk, have absolutely nothing to do with it.

Caesars was originally designed to be approached by car; its distance from the highway was not a drawback, but instead made it seem even more majestic. When pedestrians started to cruise the Strip, *Caesars* was the first casino to respond by constructing moving walkways to haul them in – and it also established the tradition of making it as hard as possible for them to get away again. That first walkway, at the southern end, dates from 1972, and is marked by a simple circular "temple" across from *Bellagio*. A second was erected in the center in 1986, alongside the giant statue of Caesar that beckons in vehicles from the Strip. Marked "Enter Caesars World," it starts from a larger pavilion that holds a small diorama of ancient Rome. The third and most flamboyant walkway was added at the north end in 1989, to lure in guests from the new *Mirage*. Here the entrance pavilion is flanked by twin winged lions, and topped by a charioteer urging on his rampaging horses. One section of walk-way trundles into the Forum Shops, while the other leads to *Caesars'* huge, dimly lit Sports Book. Not only does the latter move in one direction only, but there isn't even a pedestrian exit here at all.

In terms of hotel space, *Caesars* is relatively "small"; ini-tially 1600 rooms, it has recently grown to around 2500. Nonetheless, its interior is a bewildering labyrinth, vast enough that it takes half an hour's brisk walk to get from one end to the other. And that's if you know the place well; with its low ceilings, low lights, and lack of signs, it's designed to be as disorienting as possible, and you're all too likely to be distracted by the appearance of an armor-clad Roman legionary atop a bank of slot machines.

One side passage from the casino proper – the hub around which everything else revolves – connects with the **Appian Way**, a shopping mall where the replica of Michaelangelo's David beneath the central dome is identical to the original in every respect except for remaining uncir-cumcised. Another obliges you to squeeze between the golden prow of *Cleopatra's Barge* (a floating nightclub and bar), and an exclusive sushi restaurant. Keep on heading back behind the scenes, and you'll find yourself in the actu-al hotel, which is every bit as huge again. Large plate-glass windows look out over the Garden of the Gods pool area, built using Carrara marble and modeled after the baths of Pompeii.

A high proportion of visitors to *Caesars* are here to explore the hugely successful **Forum** mall, where a com-plex play of lights transforms the blue-domed, cloud-strewn ceiling between dawn and dusk every hour. As well as a top-notch collection of stores and restaurants, this is home to the interactive **Race for Atlantis** attraction (Sun–Thurs 10am–11pm; Fri & Sat 10am–midnight; $9.50). Once you've been enticed in by the free extravaganza in the plaza outside, where a fountain of Neptune erupts amid a panoply of special effects, you're in for Las Vegas's only 3-D Imax simulator ride. What you pay is expensive for what you get – shaken to smithereens in front of a short sci-fi B-feature – but few kids seem to leave disappointed. A more conventional **Omnimax** big-screen movie theater, not far from the Forum entrance, puts on hourly wildlife-and-wonders shows (Sun–Thurs 2–10pm, Fri & Sat noon–10pm; $7).

Caesars has been renowned for big-name **entertainment** ever since it secured the services of Frank Sinatra in September 1967 at the rate of $100,000 a week. Its heyday as a Rat-Pack hangout came to an abrupt end when Sinatra and the hotel's executive vice president exchanged blows on the casino floor while discussing a baccarat debt, but Sinatra himself was persuaded to return in 1974 by a four-hundred percent payrise – an event promoted with the slogan "The Noblest Roman Has Returned."

More formal fisticuffs made *Caesars* for many years the city's premier **boxing** venue. During the early 1980s, it would erect a temporary arena capable of accommodating thirty thousand fight fans; however, that role has since been threatened in turn by the *Mirage*, the *MGM Grand*, and *Mandalay Bay*.

For more on boxing events in Las Vegas, see p.246.

THE BARBARY COAST

Map 2, C2. 3595 Las Vegas Blvd S. Hotel accommodation is reviewed on p.133.

Slotted in between several of the city's greatest names, the tiny, 200-room **Barbary Coast** feels like a throwback to a long-lost Las Vegas. Its main distinguishing feature is a classic piece of old Vegas neon, the hourglass-shaped sign above its front entrance. That entrance is always thrown open to the Strip, and with clattering tables and slots just inside the door the *Barbary Coast* is kept ticking nicely by walk-in gamblers weary of ogling its outsize neighbors.

Amenities on the *Barbary Coast*'s ground floor are minimal; apart from the chilled shrimp cocktails in the cabinets behind the main bar, there isn't even any food on sale. Inconspicuous elevators, however, lead to two expensive and highly rated restaurants: *Drai's*, down in the basement, and *Michael's* upstairs. The latter is named for proprietor Michael Gaughan, who also owns the newer *Orleans* out on Tropicana Avenue. Guest accommodation too is better than the rather faded elegance of the gaming area might lead you to expect.

THE FLAMINGO HILTON

Map 2, C2. 3555 Las Vegas Blvd S. Hotel accommodation is reviewed on p.136.

Though neither brick nor bloodstain remains of Bugsy Siegel's original resort, the very name of the **Flamingo** is dripping with Las Vegas legend. Popular myth regards it as having been, in 1946, the first of the great Strip casinos. In fact, *El Rancho Vegas* and the *Last Frontier* had already blazed the trail by then, and the *Flamingo* when it started out – with barely a hundred hotel rooms – was much more a consummately stylish Forties motel than a foretaste of the neon extravaganzas of the Fifties. What it did offer, however, was the ambition to look beyond its bleak desert setting in both theming and ambience, not to mention a glamorous hint of underworld menace.

Benjamin "don't call me Bugsy" Siegel's background was as a New York mobster, co-founder with Meyer Lansky of the infamous Murder, Inc syndicate. He headed west in the early 1940s in the hope of making it as a movie star; failing that, he settled for making it with movie stars. Though Las Vegas initially beckoned as a good base for running a horse-racing betting racket, the casino business swiftly caught his eye. Hearing about the cash-flow problems of LA restaurateur Billy Wilkerson, who was building a new casino a mile beyond the *Last Frontier*, he put together a million-dollar package that enabled him to squeeze Wilkerson out and take control.

Construction materials were expensive and in short supply after the war, and Siegel soon found himself in trouble. There are tales of contractors delivering supplies to the site by day, stealing them back at night, and then delivering them again the next day, not so much to defraud Bugsy as to avoid his wrath at their failure to get hold of any more. Desperate to start repaying the additional $5 million he'd been forced to borrow, Siegel opened the incomplete *Flamingo* too early, only to have to close down after two weeks even deeper in debt. Although the hotel swiftly re-opened, and was soon running at a profit, Siegel's backers had lost patience, and he was shot dead at his girlfriend's home in Beverly Hills in June 1947. Literally within minutes, new Mob-appointed managers announced themselves at the *Flamingo*.

It could be said that Siegel's death was the perfect advertising gimmick; no amount of FBI investigations or congressional committees could mask the fact that the punters who flocked to Las Vegas actually liked the idea that they were rubbing shoulders with murderous gangsters. All through the Fifties and Sixties, as the *Flamingo* grew ever grander and glitzier, Meyer Lansky was still pulling the strings behind the scenes. When Kirk Kerkorian finally bought the *Flamingo* in 1967 – partly to have somewhere to train staff for his projected *International Hotel* – its financial records were in such murky shape that he could only get

THE FLAMINGO HILTON

the tax authorities off his case by selling it on to Hilton in 1970. Since then it's officially been the *Flamingo Hilton*, but no one in Las Vegas ever calls it that.

The *Flamingo* today stakes its patch opposite *Caesars Palace* with a magnificent cascade of neon. Its centerpiece is a bulbous unfurling flower of light, crested by the word "Flamingo" in a flowing, confident script. ("Hilton's" up there too, tacked on like an afterthought.) Around the back of the property, newly landscaped lagoons hold live penguins, tropical fish, and yes, even some genuine flamingos.

As recently as 1990, the *Flamingo* was briefly the largest hotel in the world, with 3530 rooms; it now has 3575, well below that of the *MGM Grand* (see p.30), and pitches itself as a sophisticated upmarket resort, an elder statesman of the Strip too secure of its status to compete head-on with brash modern upstarts. Only a continuing predilection for the kind of pinks and oranges seldom seen outside Barbie's boudoir bear witness to its racy past.

O'SHEAS

Map 2, C2. 3555 Las Vegas Blvd S.

In an unusual twist, the *Flamingo* caters to customers who hanker for the old days by maintaining what looks like a separate, much tackier casino next door. The nominally Irish-themed **O'Sheas** offers lower-stakes gaming and cheap eats, but would be unremarkable were it not for the unlikely **Magic and Movie Hall of Fame**, which fills its entire upper floor (Tues–Sat 10am–6pm; $5). How it could make economic sense to devote so much potential gaming space to this collection of moth-eaten artifacts is the biggest mystery here, but be thankful – it's the best museum in Las Vegas.

Its first displays are devoted to the great magicians of yesteryear, such as Harry Kellar, who devised a "Levitation" stunt since perfected by David Copperfield, and Carter the

Great, whose "Vanishing Elephant" trick is revealed by a scratchy black-and-white film to be a precursor of what Siegfried and Roy get up to in Las Vegas these days. Carter's former assistant Eric Weisz, better known as **Houdini**, is shown performing his "Water Torture Escape" from a crate thrown into the ocean, and you can inspect the equipment that he used.

Next comes a history of **ventriloquism** from 500 BC onward, leading from the Oracle at Delphi to the late Shari Lewis and Lamb Chop. The bizarre "School for Dummies" exhibit – a schoolroom peopled by aging wooden dolls – provides a great photo opportunity, but the most poignant section describes how America's favorite ventriloquist, Edgar Bergen, died in his sleep at *Caesars Palace* in 1978, the self-same night he bade his farewell to his fans, and to his dummy Charlie McCarthy, on the stage downstairs. All this material was gathered by English ventriloquist **Valentine Vox**, whose on-site performances at 4.30pm are included in the entry fee.

The **movie** segment of the museum consists largely of waxworks and costumes from old MGM produtions. As well as one of Rita Hayworth's Seven Veils, there's Clark Gable's costume from *Mutiny on the Bounty*, Charlton Heston's from *Ben Hur*, and Liz Taylor's from *Cleopatra*. A cabinet nearby holds a Panama hat autographed with almost six hundred signatures, ranging from Charlie Chaplin, Errol Flynn, and Knute Rockne up to Ronald Reagan, while Richard Nixon somehow sneaked his name onto a similar sheet of rock stars on the wall, between John Lennon and Johnny Rotten.

THE IMPERIAL PALACE

Map 2, C2. 3535 Las Vegas Blvd S. Hotel accommodation is reviewed on p.137, and the *Legends in Concert* show on p.195.

Despite its small and ultra-tacky checkered exterior, which dragons or not looks more like a makeshift partition in a double-glazing dealership than the facade of a major casino, the **Imperial Palace** is among Las Vegas's largest hotels. Stretching away from its slender frontage on the Strip, it manages to cram in 2700 guest rooms – more than *Caesars* across the street.

Every square inch of the twelve-acre site has been pressed into use. During the 1980s, feeling squeezed between the newly expanded *Flamingo* to the south and the now-defunct *Dunes* to the north, it even reasserted its presence by building over its driveway. That's why, if you stroll off the Strip into what you expect to be the casino, you quickly find yourself either outdoors again, crossing the hotel approach road, or dropping beneath it on an elaborate escalator system.

The emphasis at the *Imperial* remains squarely on gambling. As well as its splendidly old-fashioned **Race and Sports Book**, rising in tiers above a central pit and reached by further escalators straight off the Strip, it also hosts a frenzied daily slot tournament, "Wild Times." Several gaming tables are labeled in Chinese, in deference to its many Asian customers.

Imperial owner Ralph Engelstad's two great passions are revealed in his **Auto Collection**, located in the parking garage at the rear (daily 9.30am–11.30pm; $7, or free with coupon from casino). One, obviously enough, is for cars; he owns more than seven hundred vehicles, of which around a third are exhibited at any one time. The other seems to be for dictators and despots; in among a Rolls Royce made for the Tsar in 1914, and a Packard that belonged to Juan Peron, stands Adolf Hitler's personal armor-plated Mercedes Benz. Engelstad was fined $1.5 million by the Nevada Gaming Control Board in the 1980s for holding a party to celebrate Hitler's birthday, and was also banned from displaying Nazi memorabilia. Less contentious charabancs include Elvis's blue Cadillac and Liberace's cream Zimmer, with onboard candelabra.

More of Liberace's cars are on display in the not-to-be-missed Liberace Museum, p.104.

HARRAH'S

Map 2, C1. 3475 Las Vegas Blvd S. Hotel accommodation is reviewed on p.137.

Until 1997, **Harrah's** was one of Las Vegas' best-known landmarks, kitted out as a proud neon-decked paddlewheeler known as the "Ship on the Strip." Spurred to upgrade by the proximity of mega-rivals like the *Mirage*, *Caesars Palace*, and the *Venetian*, however, it has ditched the supposedly old-fashioned riverboat trimmings in favor of a bland, un-original carnival theme. Gone too are the "party pits" in the casino, where the dealers dressed in party hats and capered like loons.

Its frontage now festooned with trumpeting golden Mardi Gras jesters – quite possibly left over from *Harrah's* abortive mid-Nineties attempt to open a casino in New Orleans – *Harrah's* is a sedate, rather boringly upmarket joint. The large plaza adjoining the *Imperial Palace* at its southern end, one of the few open-air public spaces on the Strip, entices passers-by with live performance on its Carnival Court stage, and goodies from a *Ghirardelli Soda Fountain and Chocolate Shop*.

Inside, *Harrah's* caters to its middle-aged, middle-American clientele by making everything easy to find – not least, an allegorical sculpture called *Virtue Wins*, depicting a glittering waxwork showgirl defeating two bronze gnarled cowboys who are cheating at cards. Upstairs, Jester's Court of Games is a large arcade of kids' video games. The main reasons outsiders might actually bother to pass through are either to catch the comedy shows at the *Improv* (see p.201),

HARRAH'S

53

or to use the spacious parking garage, handy for other nearby Strip attractions.

THE MIRAGE

Map 2, B1. 3400 Las Vegas Blvd S. Hotel accommodation is reviewed on p.138; restaurants include *The Mirage Buffet* (p.154) and *The Noodle Kitchen* (p.167); *Siegfried & Roy* are reviewed on p.197.

Perhaps the best measure of the impact the *Mirage* has had upon Las Vegas is that now, more than ten years since it opened, it's hard to remember quite what was so different about it. Completed in November 1989, it was the first new hotel to be built from scratch on the Strip since 1973. Its high-rise Y-plan design was perfect for its prime position, commanding the point where the Strip curves northeast to parallel the rail tracks toward downtown. Owner Steve Wynn, however, eschewed many of Las Vegas's most time-honored traditions. He spared no expense on fixtures and fittings for the three thousand guest rooms, he neglected neon in favor of plating the entire facade with 24-carat gold stripes, and he even proclaimed that from now on Las Vegas was going to be a family destination.

By common consent, Wynn's $620 million gamble was risky even by Las Vegas standards, and it was no secret that the *Mirage* could only pay its way by making $1 million clear profit from its gaming tables every day of the year. The fact that it succeeded – not in every specific goal, but in the one detail that counts in Las Vegas, financially – transformed the city. Even so, since the opening of *Bellagio* in spring 1999, the *Mirage* has been finding it a little hard to get used to its new status as second-best even within the Mirage Resorts organization. While still holding its own, it no longer stands out from the crowd, and guests who previously stayed here as a matter of course now have half a dozen top-rank Strip casinos to choose from.

One of Wynn's most radical moves lay in recognizing that the increasing numbers of pedestrians on the Strip called for a new kind of architecture. Driving past a casino, however big, you've barely enough time to read the slogans on its signs and billboards; walking past, on the other hand, you're free to stop and stare for as long as you like, and also to change your plans and wander inside. The much-vaunted "**volcano**" outside the *Mirage* was created in order to lure tourists in off the Strip at night – a time when they're in the mood to spend money, but might not otherwise want to venture out of their own hotel. It's basically a lumpy fiberglass island, topped by palm trees and poking from a shallow artificial lagoon, which "erupts" in genteel cascades of water and flame every fifteen minutes between nightfall and midnight. Anything less like a volcano would be hard to imagine, but nonetheless, jostling crowds fill the sidewalk every evening to catch a peek.

The volcano also serves to signal the tropical theme of the *Mirage*, not that you'll need reminding if you go inside. Entering its opulent central atrium, housed beneath a geodesic dome, feels like stepping into a lush garden. Narrow footpaths meander away in various directions, skirting flowerbeds planted with an artful mix of fake and real vegetation. Off to the right, a massive thatched roof shelters the hotel's **registration area**, while the giant fish tank located behind the check-in desks teems with pygmy sharks and stingrays.

Away to the left, a busy corridor leads past a glassed-in environment of molded mock marble that's home at unpredictable times to the **white tigers** that feature in the stage show of illusionists Siegfried and Roy. Seeing them there is free; the alternative is to pay to enter the **Secret Garden and Dolphin Habitat** (Mon–Fri 11am–5.30pm, Sat & Sun 10am–5.30pm; $10, under-10s free). This small zoo, high on camp and low on space, holds the world's greatest concentration of big white cats, including snow leopards and heterozygous white lions, which sleep up to twenty hours per day. On Wednesdays, when only the see-through tank of dolphins is open to the public, the admission fee is reduced to $5.

Siegfried and Roy, incidentally, have been appearing at the *Mirage*'s custom-built theater ever since it opened. Though their image might now perhaps be a little dated, they've always done great business. Suggestions that they'd shortly be joined at the hotel by a Michael Jackson attraction seem to have receded since the allegations of child abuse, some of which mentioned Jackson's stays at the *Mirage*.

All in all, non-gamblers will find that the *Mirage* offers less to see and do than the newer mega-casinos. It's still an efficient moneymaking operation, however. You can buy anything from a fluffy white-plush toy tiger in the logo shop up to an Armani suit in the banally titled "Street of Shops," while the restaurants range from a good-value buffet to exclusive Japanese, Chinese and American options. Use of Steve Wynn's private golf course, Shadow Creek, is reserved for very high rollers indeed, but it's the humble slot machine that keeps the whole place going, earning two thirds of the *Mirage*'s million-plus-a-day bonanza.

TREASURE ISLAND

Map 2, B1 and Map 3, B9. 3300 Las Vegas Blvd S. Hotel accommodation is reviewed on p.141, and the Cirque du Soleil show *Mystère* on p.196.

If you knew no better, you might imagine that the brash-looking **Treasure Island**, next door to the *Mirage*, was a vulgar and possibly unwelcome neighbor. In fact, the relationship is very close, even parental; *Treasure Island* is owned by Mirage Enterprises and was built in 1993 using the first flush of profits from the *Mirage*. They remain umbilically connected, by a monorail that loops between the front of the *Mirage* and the back of *Treasure Island*, and they also share the same approach road from the Strip.

Treasure Island was intended to appeal to a younger audience than the *Mirage*, only a little less affluent but more likely to be traveling with kids in tow. Appropriately enough, given its postmodern blend of ingredients, the theme was suggested by the owner of the *California Pizza Kitchen* chain. Its designers took the volcano concept of the *Mirage* (see p.55) several stages further on. Here, the whole lower facade of the hotel is sculpted into a novelty attraction – an intricate, pastel-pretty seafront village, somewhere on the Spanish Main, that may seem awfully familiar to anyone who's visited Disney's *Pirates of the Caribbean* ride. In addition, the theming extends out onto the sidewalk, which is kitted out with boardwalks and rigging to accommodate spectators (and to obscure the view of drivers who might be tempted to stop). Finally, the diorama also incorporates moving parts and even live actors, in the shape of floating "ships" crewed by pirates and British sailors respectively. Architectural theorists are still arguing whether to call *Treasure Island* a building, a performance space or a theme park.

Amid a great deal of yo-ho-ho-ing and cannonfire, the two vessels slug it out each evening in the **Buccaneer Bay Show**. There was great debate at the planning stage as to which the audience would identify with most, and should therefore win the battle. If you don't want to know which one sinks, look away now – it's the British frigate.

....

The Buccaneer Bay Show takes place daily at 4pm, 5.30pm, 7pm, 8.30pm, 10pm & 11.30pm. Performances are canceled during bad weather or high winds, and in winter, the 11.30pm show only takes place on Fridays and Saturdays.

....

TREASURE ISLAND

The main hotel tower makes little attempt to match the Caribbean clutter below, standing aloof above the ruined battlements and higgledy-piggledy palms. The balconies on this slender, pale orange block are for show only; the whole structure forms a Y-shape, stretching back from the Strip, and holding almost three thousand guest rooms.

Anyone who regards casinos as intrinsically evil will find plenty of evidence in the quasi-Satanic symbolism that permeates *Treasure Island*, from the sign on the Strip depicting a giant skull onward. At ground level, the ornate double gateway across the lagoon-spanning plank bridge boasts a matching pair of skull-shaped doorhandles. Inside the casino, the lobby bar is lit by chandeliers shaped like translucent human bones, while the huge video arcade for kids, "Mutiny Bay," is guarded by two skeletal animatronic pirates who keep up an inane nonstop banter of macabre mutterings.

Beneath its surface fripperies, *Treasure Island* caters very cannily to its yuppie clientele. It offers a top-quality pool area and spa, serious gambling facilities such as a very high-tech Race and Sports Book, and of course a busy *Starbucks* coffee outlet, upstairs near the monorail stop. It also puts on classier entertainment than the *Mirage*, in the form of the over-portentous but nonetheless impressive Cirque du Soleil show *Mystère*.

THE FASHION SHOW MALL

Map 3, C9. 3200 Las Vegas Blvd S. Shopping in the Fashion Show Mall is reviewed on p.227, and the *Dive!* restaurant on p.161.

The Strip's otherwise endless procession of casinos is interrupted between *Treasure Island* and the *New Frontier* by its one large-scale stand-alone shopping mall, the **Fashion Show Mall**. Wandering in is a far less rewarding experience than at the Forum Shops in *Caesars* (see p.46), but at least you'll almost certainly find what you're looking for, with the same major department stores and chain outlets as a million malls nationwide. There's also a large food court, and a handful of restaurants, with Steven Spielberg's glorified sub-shop, the submarine-shaped *Dive!*, positively screaming for attention out on the Strip sidewalk. Note that the mall's underground parking lot is not a good place to leave your car after hours; it turns very quiet and spooky once the sun goes down.

THE VENETIAN

Map 2, C1. 3265 Las Vegas Blvd S. Hotel accommodation is reviewed on p.142; restaurants include *Delmonico's Steakhouse* (p.161), *Pinot Cafe* (p.169), and *Star Canyon* (p.171); and the Grand Canal Shoppes are described on p.228.

The brand-new **Venetian** occupies a legendary Las Vegas location, which as home from 1952 onward to the *Sands* casino played host to the fabled antics of the **Rat Pack**. Although Howard Hughes announced plans for the "new *Sands*" during the late 1960s, the old structure was not demolished until November 1996, and the *Venetian* only just managed to make its debut in the twentieth century. It's the brainchild of one man, Sheldon Adelson, who made his fortune establishing Las Vegas's annual COMDEX exhibition as the world's premier computer-industry trade show, and then selling it for $800 million in 1995.

Unfortunately, however, Adelson's knack for making money seems to be matched only by his ability to put other people's backs up. The *Venetian*'s birth was plagued with complications. As well as antagonizing the local Culinary Union by his refusal to rehire former *Sands* employees or unionize the casino, Adelson battled to protect his vast new Sands Expo and Convention Center by stopping the city from spending tax dollars on its own convention center.

THE VENETIAN

The eventual unveiling of the *Venetian*, in May 1999, has been acclaimed as a textbook example of how *not* to open a casino. After several postponements, it started up with only a handful of restaurants in action and no shops, while a last-minute failure to pass fire-safety inspections meant that celebrity guests had to be housed elsewhere. Further law-suits between the *Venetian* and the company that actually built it drove helpless smaller contractors toward bankruptcy as they awaited payments. The upshot was that the *Venetian* traded initially at a heavy loss, prompting inevitable doubts as to whether its scheduled second hotel tower, the *Lido*, would ever materialize. If at some point it does, the *Venetian* will, with six thousand rooms, become the world's largest hotel – unless of course the *MGM Grand* follows through with any of its expansion plans (see p.30).

So far, construction of the *Venetian* has cost around $1.4 billion – far more than *Paris* or *Mandalay Bay*, and only slightly less than *Bellagio* – and Mr Adelson has in fairness got plenty to show for his money. His dream appears to have been to cram all the snapshots of his real-life honey-moon in Venice, Italy, within a single frame. The Strip facade incorporates loving facsimiles of six major Venice buildings – from south to north, the **Library**, the **Campanile** (allow your eyes to glide over the parking garage at this point), the **Palazzo Contarini-Fasan**, the **Doge's Palace**, the **Ca' d'Oro**, and the **Clock Tower** – as well as the **Rialto Bridge**, the **Bridge of Sighs**, and a small stretch of "canal" kept deliberately muddy to echo the waters of the Adriatic. In yet another example of how Strip rivals feed off each other, the roomy balcony of the Doge's Palace makes a perfect vantage point to watch the volcano at the *Mirage*.

In front of them all stand two **columns**, modeled on a pair brought to Venice's Piazza San Marco from Constantinople in 1172. One is topped by St Theodore, the city's original patron, the other by a winged lion (or chimera) representing St Mark, who became its patron in 1204. The originals were used for public executions – criminals were hanged or even buried alive in the gap – so superstitious Venetians avoid passing between them to this day. In Las Vegas, however, there's little choice, as they flank the main entrance to the casino.

Although Venice was the first European city to have a public gambling house – it opened in 1638, and guests were obliged to wear masks – the challenge of making the casino itself particularly Venetian has been largely ignored. The coolness of its marble floor comes as a welcome relief after the heat of the Strip, but the slot machines and tables in the gaming area beyond are much like any others. Instead, the designers have aimed to propel visitors swiftly upward to the **Grand Canal Shoppes**. The central stairwell is quite magnificent, topped by vivid frescoes copied from yet more Venice originals, and leads to a hallway paved with Escher-like *trompe l'oeil* tiles. Beyond that lies the breathtaking **Grand Canal** itself, a ludicrous re-creation of the waterways of Venice, complete with gondolas and singing gondoliers, that's quintessential Las Vegas, and as such utterly irresistible – for God's sake, it's *upstairs*. The shopping mall is described in detail on p.228, but it's a must-see even if you have no intention of buying anything (and you'll be kicking yourself afterwards if you don't succumb to a $10 gondola ride).

The other major tourist attraction in the *Venetian* is the first US outpost of **Madame Tussaud's** waxwork museum. Set on the second and third floors of the Library, and accessible via moving walkways direct from the Strip, this eschews boring old history in favor of styling itself as the **Celebrity Encounter** (daily 10am–10pm; $12.50). What that means is that visitors can pose with, touch, caress and mock the effigies; some even manage to take home little souvenirs. For all but the rare few visitors, however, the appeal of inspecting Oprah Winfrey as she interviews Michael Crawford, or Larry King with Ivana Trump, is fleeting to say the least; even the few imaginative set-pieces, such as Don King refereeing a bout between the young Muhammad Ali and an ear-less Evander Holyfield, grab your attention only for the time it takes to walk past. On the lower level, in the Las Vegas Legends room, you'll find Siegfried (or is it Roy?) straddling a tiger, and Sammy Davis Jr and Dean Martin serenading Shirley MacLaine, while Frank Sinatra croons to himself in his own tiny Copa room next door. The whole thing culminates in an abysmal performance by Elvis, quite lame compared to the free animatronics across the street at *Caesars Palace*. The Library is incidentally a replica of Venice's Libreria Sansoviniana, whose sixteenth-century architect was imprisoned when its roof caved in during construction.

The *Venetian* is not as much of a change of direction for Adelson as you might imagine. His interests remain firmly rooted in the convention business, and on paper at least building a luxury hotel under the same roof as the world's most extensive convention facilities makes sound financial sense. The main lobby is every bit as opulent as that of *Bellagio*, with its gilded astrolabe and huge colonnaded Galleria adorned with stunning frescoes. The room rates are high, in part because business travelers are notorious for gambling far less than tourists, but each room is an enormous suite, equipped with a private fax and printer.

THE VENETIAN

Sadly, the *Venetian* does nothing to honor its predecessor; the Sands Expo and Convention Center is the only place where the old *Sands* name survives.

THE NEW FRONTIER

Map 3, D8. 3120 Las Vegas Blvd S. Hotel accommodation is reviewed on p.139; restaurants include *Margarita's Mexican Cantina* (p.165).

For all the fuss that surrounds the *Flamingo* (see p.48), the **New Frontier** is the oldest casino still surviving on the Strip. In fact, although it opened in 1942, a year after the long-vanished *El Rancho Vegas*, it incorporated Guy McAfee's *Pair-O-Dice Club*, which had in 1938 become the first gambling joint on Las Vegas Boulevard. Originally named the *Last Frontier*, it started out as a glorified hundred-room motel that milked its desert setting for every possible drop of Old West appeal. The decor was a deliberate combination of crude log-cabin trimmings with glittering neon, marketed under the slogan "the Early West in Modern Splendor." There was even a theme park alongside, Last Frontier Village.

....

The Little Church of the West, now serving as a wedding chapel at 4617 Las Vegas Blvd S (see p.255), was once the centerpiece of Last Frontier Village.

....

The *Last Frontier* reinvented itself as the space-age *New Frontier* in 1955, and played host to Elvis Presley's first disastrous Las Vegas appearance the following year. In 1965, it was bulldozed and completely rebuilt, with a Western theme once again. That wholesale reconstruction did not extend, however, to getting rid of the Mob presence with which it had become permeated, and the Mafia continued in covert control for several years even after the hotel was acquired by Howard Hughes in 1967. Hughes was living in the *Desert Inn* across the street, and is said to have bought the *New Frontier* because he was alarmed that its new sign, at 184 feet the tallest in the world, might blow down and hit his home. Steve Wynn, now the owner of *Bellagio* and the *Mirage*, then held a five percent stake in the *New Frontier*, and was its slot manager.

That same worrisome sign still stands outside the *New Frontier*, looking deeply old-fashioned with its staid movie-theater lettering and tame slogans: "choice beef, poultry and seafood at affordable prices." The *New Frontier* is the last Strip property where it's still possible to park your car in the front lot, though it has finally lost its Strip-side swimming pool. The casino itself – sorry, "Gambling Hall" – remains locked in the Wild West tradition. A chuckwagon waits outside for its owner to return, while you're confronted immediately through the saloon-style doors by vintage slot machines in the shape of John Wayne and other gunslingers.

The *New Frontier* has clearly identified its market as the kind of aging cowboys and cowgirls who get their kicks from knocking back tequila at *Margarita's Mexican Cantina* and paying rock-bottom prices for barbecued chicken in the *Cattleman's Buffet*. Surprisingly, however, the actual hotel behind this down-at-heel veneer is a sleek, new edifice of gleaming reflective glass. Surrounded by tousled palm trees and topped by green roof tiles, it wouldn't look out of place on an exclusive Hawaiian beach. Not all the rooms live up to that promise, but the two-room suites in the Atrium Tower are good by any standards.

THE DESERT INN

Map 3, D8. 3145 Las Vegas Blvd S. Hotel accommodation is reviewed on p.134.

Ever since 1950, the **Desert Inn** has ranked among the top echelon of Strip casinos. While not exactly innovative – the ranch-in the-desert theme was hardly new even then, and a similar *Desert Inn* had long operated in Palm Springs – it was always elegant. Its "Sky Room" in particular caused an immediate sensation; perched atop its three-story porte cochere, with false stars set into its ceiling, it was the highest spot in town. However, it had taken nominal owner Wilbur Clark five years to complete construction, and he paid the heavy price of acquiring some very dubious partners, such as Mob associate Moe Dalitz, along the way.

By welcoming **Howard Hughes** as a guest at Thanksgiving in 1966 – on the express condition that he checked out before the high rollers arrived for New Year – the *Desert Inn* inadvertently spearheaded Las Vegas's move toward corporate domination. Rather than leave, Hughes took over the whole hotel, buying its license to operate until 2002 (although not the casino itself) for $13.2 million. That was seen as a vastly inflated price, but Hughes wasn't worried; he'd sold his 76 percent stake in TWA in 1966 for $546 million, then the largest payment anyone had ever received.

Hughes remained at the *Desert Inn* for exactly four years, living on the ninth floor and keeping the entire eighth floor empty. During that time, he bought enough casinos to become Nevada's largest single operator, despite seldom if ever allowing even his closest associates to see him. Tales of his eccentricity abound: quite apart from storing all his urine in jars in his closet, and having total transfusions of Mormon blood, he canceled the hotel's traditional Easter Egg hunt because he loathed children, and abandoned its pro golf tournaments because he couldn't bear the thought of golfers coming onto his property after putting their hands in those dirty holes.

"Skimming" of the *Desert Inn*'s profits by organized crime probably continued through the Hughes years, and despite its undoubted class it remained financially troubled even after passing first to Kirk Kerkorian and then, in 1993, to ITT Sheraton. Despite comprehensively remodeling the *Desert*

THE DESERT INN

Inn, ITT failed to gain sufficient return on their investment, and put it back on the market. Rumored bidders included Michael Jackson and an Asian consortium that was going to give it an ancient-China theme, complete with four-mile Great Wall. The eventual purchaser, in May 1999 for $275 million, was Sun International, best known for high-profile resort properties in the Bahamas such as *Atlantis*.

Another transformation for the *Desert Inn* is clearly in the offing, even though to the casual observer it seems very nice as it is. Unusually, its hotel and casino segments are very distinct from each other. The main lobby is a sumptuous five-story atrium, its walls and ceiling decorated *a la* Forum with Roman-influenced frescoes. A floor-to-ceiling window at the far end looks out on the hotel's formal gardens and lovely pool, beyond which the lush fairways of the golf course – the *Desert Inn* is the only Strip hotel with its own on-site golf course – stretch as far as the eye can see. A marble corridor to the right leads to the casino itself, renowned for high-stakes gambling on baccarat in particular.

As the *Desert Inn*'s former owners were the main opponents of running a monorail between the Strip and downtown, the project may now go ahead.

GUARDIAN ANGEL CATHEDRAL

Map 3, E8. 302 Cathedral Way.

Immediately north of the *Desert Inn*, just after Desert Inn Road suddenly burrows underground, a small spur road to the right leads to one of the Strip's least likely sights. Though dwarfed to the point of invisibility by the surrounding cathedrals to Mammon, the starkly angular **Guardian Angel Cathedral** is a genuine Roman Catholic cathedral. Looking very spruce, and much newer than its actual construction date of 1963, it's a welcome haven from the frenzy outside its doors, but it does feature some true Las Vegas touches. The baptismal font resembles an over-sized marble Jacuzzi, coin-in-the-slot electric "candles" line the aisles, and of course there's a gift store. Best of all is the stained-glass window to the right of the altar, depicting the *Stardust*, the *Sands* and the *Hilton* rising above a maze of concrete freeways.

Sunday masses at the Guardian Angel Cathedral take place at 8am, 9.30am, 11am, 12.30pm & 5pm.

Ironically, one of the last remaining vestiges of the old, tacky Strip lies just north of the cathedral, opposite the *Stardust*. As well as the grubby **Silver City** casino – remarkable only for being owned by the Mandalay Resort Group (formerly Circus Circus), for whom renovations are clearly not a major priority – it's also the site of the down-market **Las Vegas Shopping Plaza**. A true architectural gem has somehow survived alongside, however, in the shape of the little **La Concha** motel (see p.137), whose gorgeous scalloped arches were designed in 1961 by black LA architect Paul Williams.

THE STARDUST

Map 3, D7. 3000 Las Vegas Blvd S. Hotel accommodation is reviewed on p.140.

Though long since overshadowed by a host of nouveau-riche newcomers, the **Stardust** can look back on a career as a major Las Vegas player. A glittering child of the space age, it burst on the scene in 1958 as the self-proclaimed largest hotel in the world, no more than two stories high perhaps, but boasting more than a thousand rooms.

Cascades of neon color erupted from its Sputnik-inspired Strip facade; it had its own rodeo facility, and soon acquired a Grand Prix racetrack as well.

However, all that dazzling starlight served to conceal some very murky figures lurking in the background. Its true owner at the outset was said to be Chicago mobster Sam Giancana, and control passed during the 1970s to the Midwest Mafia, based in Kansas City. A Federal raid in 1976 revealed the *Stardust*'s role at the heart of the largest ever "skimming" operation in Las Vegas, in which a concealed vault was used to whisk away an estimated $4 million per year in unrecorded slot machine takings. Similar scandals erupted periodically well into the 1980s; Martin Scorsese's 1995 movie *Casino* tells the story in entertaining detail.

Under the ownership of the Boyd Corporation, whose other properties include *Sam's Town*, the *Stardust* is these days entirely legitimate. Its original frontage was supplanted 25 years ago by the more abstract but no less spectacular pink neon starburst sign that still stands today, albeit toned down by a very staid choice of lettering. With its windows tinted a rich, deep purple, the main hotel block looks comparatively upmarket, though the effect is spoiled by the low-rise casino sprawl in front.

For its first 33 years, the *Stardust* was renowned as the home of the French nude revue *Lido de Paris*, Las Vegas's longest-running show of all time. That reputation led to its use as the fictional location for the movie *Showgirls*, and continues to draw in customers to its current after-hours show, *Enter The Night*. Otherwise, in the absence of the usual modern frivolities and distractions, people tend to visit the *Stardust* specifically in order to gamble. The very large, high-tech Race and Sports Book, which has its own separate entrance straight off the Strip at the northern end of the property, stages regular $10,000 football and handicapping contests.

THE RIVIERA

Map 3, E7. 2901 Las Vegas Blvd S. Hotel accommodation is reviewed on p.140; shows include *Crazy Girls* (p.192) and *Splash!* (p.198).

In 1955, the new **Riviera** held considerable novelty value. Merely by remaining erect, it confounded skeptics who predicted that the sands of Las Vegas could never bear the weight of its unbelievable nine stories. Furthermore, its style, derived in theory from the French Côte d'Azur, seemed both exotic and romantic – even if in practice the decor owed more to the Florida resorts already run by its Miami backers.

Any attempt at creating a Mediterranean ambience having long been abandoned, the *Riviera* today touts for custom with one of the Strip's most exuberantly garish facades. The towering curved wall that faces south toward the *Stardust* consists in its entirety of a multilayered mirror, across the parallel planes of which swirl extravagant neon patterns of stars, stripes and curlicues. After that, the interior comes as a disappointment; while the *Riviera* claims to devote more floor space to gambling than any of its rivals, the casino area into which you're plunged straight off the Strip is relentlessly mundane. Immediately across from *Circus Circus*, and with its own sidewalk entrance, it even has a separate arcade known as **Nickel Town**, devoted exclusively to nickel slots and cheap snacks. Much further back, behind the whole casino caboodle, you come to the hotel lobby and the *Riviera*'s own convention center, which is now the basis of its prosperity.

Ever since the *Riviera* began, it has stuck to the old formula of enticing in gamblers with traditional semi-sexy entertainment. When it first opened, it set new records by paying Liberace $50,000 per week – by no coincidence, it went briefly broke within three months – and it still has four showrooms in nightly operation.

THE RIVIERA

CIRCUS CIRCUS

Map 3, E6. 2880 Las Vegas Blvd S. Hotel accommodation is reviewed on p.134.

> *"The aspect of* Circus *that has me disturbed is the popcorn, peanuts and kids side of it. And also the Carnival Freaks and Animal side of it . . . The dirt floor, sawdust and elephants . . . After all, the Strip is supposed to be synonymous with a good-looking female all dressed up in a very expensive diamond-studded evening gown and driving up to a multimillion dollar hotel in a Rolls-Royce. Now you tell me what, in that picture, is compatible with a circus in its normal raiment, exuding its normal atmosphere and its normal smell ?"*
> **Howard Hughes**

These days, **Circus Circus** effortlessly exemplifies Las Vegas's most surefire money-spinning formula – to combine children's entertainment with casino gambling under a single roof. Back in the 1960s, however, that was a pretty radical concept, and it took a while to work out quite how to go about it.

Circus Circus began life as Jay Sarno's follow-up to his mega-hit *Caesars Palace* (see p.44), reinvesting the profits from the sale of *Caesars* to create a new property that would appeal to fun-seeking families and high rollers alike. The basic theme, of a hectic, spit-and-sawdust gaming area at street level overlooked by a carnival-style "midway" on the mezzanine, featuring sideshows and circus performers, was much as it remains today. The flaws were in the details. Not only did the original *Circus Circus* lack any hotel accommodation, but it even charged an admission fee to visitors. On top of that, Hughes' revulsion had some basis in fact. The midway was at first the sleazy preserve of unsavory independent operators. One sideshow, for example, "Bed Toss," invited patrons to throw softballs in the hope of spilling

naked showgirls out of giant satin beds. At least Sarno was
forced to abandon his experiments with propelling "flying"
elephants along a concealed monorail system, when it
became clear that his would-be Dumbos couldn't contain
their excitement and would have to wear diapers. Only
once Sarno sold his stake to William Bennett, in 1974, did
Circus Circus turn both wholesome and profitable, so much
so in fact that Circus Circus Enterprises (now known as the
Mandalay Resort Group) went on to become the leading
casino operator in the country.

Though the main building of *Circus Circus* is very low-
rise by Las Vegas standards, its presence on the Strip is
unmistakable, thanks both to its gigantic Lucky-the-Clown
neon sign and its marquee-like Big Top canopy. Trapeze
artists and acrobats still strive to distract the gamblers by
flipping and flaunting themselves above the principal casino
floor between 11am and midnight daily, while the ramp
that leads up to the now more consistently child-oriented
midway is open during those same hours. With new hotel
towers being added year after year, the whole *Circus Circus*
complex stretches so far back that there's even an in-house
monorail link to help lost or exhausted guests return to
their rooms.

No one could mistake *Circus Circus* for a sophisticated
joint. Even the most gung-ho apologist for the gaming
industry would be hard pressed to find anything glamorous
about its three low-stakes, high-volume casinos. What's
more, while *Circus Circus* may have pioneered the provision
of no-smoking areas, its low ceilings actually make it one of
the most claustrophobic and smoky places to gamble in
town.

Circus Circus continues to lure in tourists with children –
even those staying elsewhere in Las Vegas – largely because
of its theme park, **Grand Slam Canyon** (Sun-Thurs
10am–6pm, Fri & Sat 10am–midnight), which was tacked

CIRCUS CIRCUS

onto the back of the property in 1993, at the same time as its more ambitious rival at the *MGM Grand* (see p.30). It has been much more successful, too – not least because its full five-acre extent is protected from the extremes of the local climate beneath a huge bubble of pink glass. Entered only through the casino proper, this "Adventuredome" encloses a Disney-esque melange of rides and sideshows. Around its central feature, a big red-rock mountain that reaches almost to the artificial sky, race both a roller coaster and a water-flume ride, passing such dioramas as an Indian pueblo village and a herd of animatronic dinosaurs. Visitors can choose whether to pay for each individual attraction, or to buy an all-day wristband priced at $16 if you're over four feet high, $12 if you're not.

GUINNESS WORLD OF RECORDS

Map 3, F5. 2780 Las Vegas Blvd S. Daily 9am–6pm; $5.
Set back slightly from the Strip just north of *Circus Circus*, one of Las Vegas's dullest-looking sheds houses the eminently missable **Guinness World of Records** museum. As well as waxworks, film clips and photos depicting the gamut of weirdness and extremity, it also maintains a databank of Las Vegas superlatives.

WET'N'WILD

Map 3, F5. 2601 Las Vegas Blvd S. Early May to Sept daily 10am–8pm; adults $24, under-10s $18.
If you've been to a water park before, you'll need no persuading to spend a half-day at **Wet'n'Wild**, immediately south of the *Sahara*; if you haven't, you're in for a real treat. The ideal place to cool off during the long hot Las Vegas summer, or release the tension you've accumulated at the gaming tables, it offers an exhilarating array of flumes and

chutes, plus a huge wave pool. Having paid the hefty admission fee – look beforehand for discount coupons in local magazines – you're free to pad around in your swim-suit for the rest of the day, repeating your favorite rides until the novelty wears off. Stand-outs include the seven-story **Der Stuka** plummet; **Bomb Bay**, in which the floor suddenly gives way to drop you 76 feet; and the **Black Hole**, a flume ride through interstellar darkness that's reminiscent of Disney's Space Mountain. Lines are longest during school vacations.

THE SAHARA

Map 3, G5. 2535 Las Vegas Blvd S. Hotel accommodation is reviewed on p.140.

Revitalized by an injection of capital from new owner William Bennett, the former chairman of Circus Circus, the **Sahara** is the last bastion of a once-ubiquitous Las Vegas tradition. There was a time when Strip casinos relished the city's desert setting, but with the demise of long-standing soulmates such as the *Dunes*, the *Sands*, and the old *Aladdin*, only the *Sahara* still caters to those who nurture Arabian Nights fantasies of sheiks at play in the shifting sands.

Though almost fifty years have elapsed since December 1952, when the combined efforts of LA jeweler Milton Prell and Phoenix developer Del Webb went into replacing the bankrupt *Bingo Club* with the gleaming new *Sahara*, surprisingly little about the hotel has changed. Sadly, the trademark camels above the main entrance have been put out to pasture, in favor of a glittering golden dome encircled by Moorish arches. Inside, however, the theming was always pretty rudimentary, and it still resembles a Third World airport lounge more than a sultan's palace. At least the venerable *Congo Showroom*, the *Casbar Lounge*, and the

Caravan Restaurant are still going strong. All would have been familiar to Elvis Presley and his entourage, for whom the *Sahara* was a second home throughout the 1960s – notably during the shooting of *Viva Las Vegas* in the summer of 1963, which kickstarted his hectic off-screen romance with co-star Ann-Margret – and to the Beatles, who performed here in 1964.

Elvis would no doubt have been unable to resist the Sahara's latest crowd-pleaser, the indoor **Sahara Speedworld** (Sun–Thurs 10am–10pm, Fri & Sat 10am–11pm), where two distinct virtual-reality rides aim to reproduce the thrill of Indy car racing. In the first, $8 entitles you to "drive" a three-quarter-size replica car, which bucks and surges in response to the slightest touch of the controls as you face your own private screen. At any one time, eight cars race each other around a video rendition of the Indianapolis racetrack; printouts at the end reveal which driver beat the rest. The more you do it, the more likely you are to win, so the whole experience is fiendishly addictive. By way of alternative, you can also pay $3 for the much less heart-thumping experience of watching a 3-D movie of the real thing.

THE STRATOSPHERE

Map 3, G3. 2000 Las Vegas Blvd S. Hotel accommodation is reviewed on p.140; restaurants include the *Stratosphere Buffet* (p.155) and *Top of the World* (p.171).

The stretch of Las Vegas Boulevard that runs north from Sahara Avenue, dominated by the mighty **Stratosphere Tower**, is not traditionally regarded as part of the Strip – not least because it lies within the city limits of Las Vegas rather than Clark County. This area was long known as Naked City, at first because the showgirls who lived here in the 1940s were said to sunbathe in the nude, but later to denote its status as one of Las Vegas's poorest and most crime-ridden neighborhoods.

In 1979, one of the great Las Vegas hucksters, Bob Stupak, opened the immensely tacky **Vegas World** casino where the *Stratosphere* now stands, half a dozen short blocks up from the *Sahara*. His promotional genius, expressed in advertisements and direct mailings that promised "virtually free Las Vegas vacations," filled the place with first-time Vegas visitors. An inveterate gambler himself, he also specialized in bargain deals for gamblers, offering games such as no-zero roulette, crapless craps, and "Double Exposure" blackjack, in which the dealer's cards were dealt face up. Stupak's dream was to erect the world's tallest tower alongside *Vegas World* – what could be more perfect than owning a building where people will wait in line to pay for the privilege of riding up the elevators?

Construction costs, however, proved wildly expensive, and plans had to be scaled down. Thanks to the strong desert winds, and the fact that the foundations could only be twelve feet deep, the tower ended up as not the tallest structure in the world, but simply the tallest west of the Mississippi. Similarly, the projected King-Kong-shaped elevator that would climb its exterior was quietly shelved. A harmless but all-too-visible electrical fire that lit up the half-completed edifice like a Roman candle did nothing to help, and panic among his co-investors all but forced Stupak to sell his soul. To persuade the Minneapolis-based Grand Casinos company (no relation to MGM Grand) to buy a three-quarter stake in the project, he agreed that *Vegas World* itself would have to go and be replaced by a higher-class hotel to match the tower.

When the *Stratosphere* finally opened, in 1996, foot traffic turned out to be even lower than worst-case scenarios had dared to contemplate. The stewards employed to shepherd the crowds toward the tower were swiftly laid off, and the place

THE STRATOSPHERE

was widely reported to be empty for the first ten months. In the longer run, however, it has done surprisingly well, kept busy particularly by European tour groups, who may perhaps be less sensitive than Americans to the fact that it's not really on the Strip, but are also attracted by the low rates for its no-nonsense rooms. It has also maintained the Stupak tradition of low-cost gambling with eye-catching gimmicks.

Bob Stupak has an eye for a disaster; he's currently battling to obtain zoning permission for a new hotel just north of the *Stratosphere* to be called *The Boat*, and themed on the *Titanic*.

At ground level, the *Stratosphere* is far from enthralling. It's hard to tell quite what its theme is supposed to be: a hot-air balloon here, a chunk of the Eiffel Tower there, stray slices of general Americana elsewhere. For sightseers, the only reason to come is the 1149-foot **tower** itself. While the drabness of the main shaft means that it's not a great piece of architecture, the multicolored flashes and spirals of light around its base provide one of Las Vegas's finest displays of neon, and the "pod" at the summit fully lives up to expectations.

Tickets to reach the top are sold in the hotel lobby, just to the right of the main entrance, but the elevators start from the far end of the second floor (Sun–Thurs 10am–midnight, Fri & Sat 10am–2am; $6, or $10 including one free meal at the casino buffet; see p.155). At the end of the 75-second ascent, you emerge outdoors, on the 109th floor, to be confronted by an astounding 360° panorama of the city. The views are even better from the floor below, where the windows of the indoor gallery are angled out over the edge, and detailed captions and photographs explain every discernible detail. The next floor down holds the *Top of the World* restaurant, reviewed on p.171.

Most visitors come this high, however, in order to go another few steps closer to heaven on the two utterly demented **thrill rides** that occupy the uppermost level of the pod ($5 each, $3 per re-ride). The **High Roller**, the world's highest roller coaster, rumbles its way around the outside at what might seem an innocuous speed were you not a quarter of a mile up in the sky, while the ludicrous but terrifying **Big Shot** is a four-person open-air couch on which you're shunted to the very top of an additional 160-foot spire, and then allowed to free-fall back down again.

Downtown Las Vegas

Downtown Las Vegas has never been a "downtown" in the conventional sense of the word. True, it does stand on the site where the city was founded, less than a century ago. Having just laid its tracks across the valley, the San Pedro, Los Angeles & Salt Lake Railroad established Las Vegas in May 1905 by auctioning parcels of land close to the railroad station. A simple grid was mapped out, with the station itself on Main Street at the head of the principal thoroughfare, **Fremont Street**.

However, the city never grew to any size before the legalization of gambling in the 1930s; even in 1940, it had a population of just eight thousand. Fremont Street failed to develop a significant infrastructure of stores and other businesses, and those few it did acquire were in any case to be supplanted by the advent of the casinos. In time, the neighboring streets filled up with the offices of state and city administrators, but downtown as a whole remains much like the Strip, in that the only conceivable reason to come here is to visit the casinos.

Las Vegas has always had the strongest of incentives to

promote downtown at the expense of the Strip; the Strip is not in fact in the city at all (but in Clark County), so only the downtown casinos pay city taxes. In the 1940s, it officially baptized Fremont Street as "**Glitter Gulch**," and for several decades downtown more or less kept pace with the burgeoning Strip. At the time the *Mirage* opened on the Strip in 1989, for example, the veteran *Horseshoe* downtown remained the city's most financially successful casino.

The downtown area is shown in full detail on color map 4, at the back of this book.

However, as the Strip raced ahead during its building boom in the first half of the 1990s, downtown appeared to be in terminal decline. It was clear that something drastic had to be done. One proposal, put forward by Steve Wynn of the *Golden Nugget*, was to turn Fremont Street into a Venetian-style canal. The ultimate solution was almost as absurd; instead, they put a **roof** on it. As the **Fremont Street Experience**, it has become the scene of banal but undeniably spectacular nightly light shows. These have done much to entice the crowds back, although many visitors are disappointed to find that there's nothing to do once the show's over – except gamble, of course, which was the point of the thing. The bottom line, however, is that while downtown is showing signs of recovery, with its hopes pinned on the forthcoming Neonopolis shopping and entertainment complex, it's currently operating at an overall loss.

Fremont Street today is downtown restyled as a sanitized suburban mall, its block-spanning casinos now seeming like little more than identical department stores. It has to be said that nothing downtown, not even the much-vaunted *Golden Nugget*, would merit a second glance on the Strip. If you come to Las Vegas specifically to gamble, there's a strong case for spending time downtown – the odds tend to be better, the room rates cheaper and the atmosphere a bit more casual – but otherwise you miss little by avoiding it altogether.

Downtown used to be seen as an area where you could walk around, in contrast to the Strip where you were forced to drive. Nowadays, however, the gaps that formerly peppered the Strip have all but disappeared, and most visitors explore sizable stretches of it on foot. Downtown, on the other hand, offers little scope for strolling anywhere other than the few central blocks of Fremont Street. The streets

The Fremont Street Experience

The gigantic metal mesh of the **Fremont Street Experience**, completed in 1995, stretches for four entire blocks of Fremont Street, from Main Street to Fourth. Ninety feet high, this "Celestial Vault" shades the pedestrianized street during the day, but comes into its own at night. It's studded with over two million colored lightbulbs, which effectively turn into a giant movie screen. Specially designed light shows are controlled by 121 computers, which run what are claimed to be among the most complicated programs ever written. Some simply consist of colorful patterns; others transform the quarter-mile length of Fremont Street into a virtual-reality theater. The spectators below gasp, stagger and applaud as they're catapulted into space or menaced by colossal swarming snakes. There's no plot or content, just pure eye-catching spectacle; in essence, it's an updated version of downtown's traditional neon signs.

Free performances of the Experience take place every night, hourly from 8pm until midnight. It's jointly sponsored by ten downtown casinos, which turn off all their external lights while it's happening. Each show lasts a mere six minutes; the idea is that at the end you'll find yourself milling around on the street with nowhere to go except into the nearest casino.

to the south hold the occasional interesting shop, like the *Attic* (see p.233) or the *Gamblers General Store* (see p.235), or budget restaurant, but although they may seem close enough on the map, they're grim and unsettling places to walk, and unbearably hot in summer.

THE GOLDEN GATE

Map 4, E3. 1 E Fremont St. Hotel accommodation is reviewed on p.144.

What's now the **Golden Gate** is unique for Las Vegas in being genuinely old, rather than simply themed to look old. The city's most venerable establishment, it has occupied its prime position at the west end of Fremont Street since 1906, when Las Vegas itself was just a year old. It started out as the *Nevada Hotel*, catering to travelers who arrived at the railroad station opposite, and was styled on the grand hotels of San Francisco, many of which were destroyed in that year's earthquake. As the first hotel in southern Nevada, it boasted a distinguished phone number: 1. It later became first the *Sal Segav* (Las Vegas spelled backwards), and then, in 1955, the *Golden Gate*. Having barely grown since it added its third story in 1931, it's now so small that it thinks of itself as a B&B, and its casino area is tiny and unexciting. Many repeat Las Vegas visitors, however, make a special pilgrimage to its *San Francisco Shrimp Bar and Deli*, which claims to have originated the 99¢ shrimp cocktail in 1959 and to have served more than 25 million of them since then.

THE GOLDEN NUGGET

Map 4, F4. 129 E Fremont St. Hotel accommodation is reviewed on p.144; restaurants include the *Golden Nugget Buffet* (p.156) and the *California Pizza Kitchen* (p.173).

The **Golden Nugget** is generally described, not least in its own brochures, as being the one downtown casino that matches the extravagance and splendor of the Strip. It doesn't. It's a bright, glittery place that attracts a much more upmarket clientele than any of its neighbors, but it's also deeply boring, and very far indeed from counting as a must-see destination.

The *Golden Nugget* has always regarded itself as a cut above its downtown rivals. It opened in 1946, the same year that the *Flamingo* was unveiled on the Strip, with a decor modeled on the opulent saloons of nineteenth-century San Francisco. Its significance today, however, is as the place where Las Vegas's premier gaming entrepreneur, **Steve Wynn**, gained his first foothold in the casino business. During the early 1970s, the young Wynn – then a liquor distributor and real-estate speculator – accumulated enough shares in the ailing *Nugget*, together with inside knowledge of corruption among its staff, to engineer a boardroom coup in 1973. The *Nugget* swiftly prospered under his control, aided by the addition of its first hotel rooms in 1977. That enabled Wynn first to develop another *Golden Nugget* in Atlantic City, and then to build the *Mirage* on the Strip. His Mirage Resorts has since been responsible for *Bellagio*, while Wynn himself is said to be the highest paid executive in the US.

Although successive remodelings have ensured that the *Nugget* gleams like new, it still looks very much like a product of the 1970s, with more than a hint of Graceland about its long, neat rows of gold-painted lightbulbs, little white leatherette stools for slots players, and plump white padded chairs at the gaming tables. On the plus side, at least the casino proper is well lit and high ceilinged, and much less gloomy than most.

Those parts of the *Golden Nugget* that lie closest to Fremont Street are devoted to gambling, with the exception of the small *Buffet*. In adding its two hotel towers, further back, the *Nugget* simply swallowed up and built over Carson Street for the length of an entire block, replacing the road with the disappointing *Carson Street Café* coffeeshop.

A surprisingly inconspicuous case near the elevators for the North Tower shows off the hotel's collection of genuine golden nuggets. Pride of place goes to the Hand of Faith nugget, found in Australia in 1980 and said to be, at 61 pounds 11 ounces the largest "on public display" in the world. At current prices, it's worth $252,672. Alongside are several sizable Alaskan lumps, including one worn smooth from being carried in the pocket of its owner as a good-luck charm for 25 years. In that time, a full two ounces were rubbed off.

BINION'S HORSESHOE

Map 4, F3. 128 E Fremont St. Hotel accommodation is reviewed on p.143; restaurants include the *Coffee Shop* (p.173).

If the *Golden Nugget* represents downtown at its most pretentious, then **Binion's Horseshoe** goes to the other extreme, resolutely promoting itself as the definitive downtown gambling hall and nothing more. That ethos dates back to its founder, Benny Binion, affectionately remembered as one of the great Las Vegas characters. Benny's record for violence was exceptional even by local standards: an itinerant Texan horse trader with at least two killings to his name, he ran the criminal underworld in Dallas during the 1940s, before a bloody gang feud persuaded him to relocate to Las Vegas. Acquiring two faltering Fremont Street casinos, he replaced them with the *Horseshoe*, which opened as downtown's first "carpet joint" in 1951.

Binion himself lost control of the casino when he was jailed for tax evasion in the 1950s – he took advantage of the interlude to learn to read and write – and never regained his gaming license. However, his family bought it

BINION'S HORSESHOE

back in 1964, with Benny very much in charge behind the scenes. By the time he died, on Christmas Day 1989, the *Horseshoe* was the most profitable casino in Las Vegas. To Benny, the explanation was simple: "We got a little joint and a big bankroll, and all them others got a big joint and a little bankroll." The *Horseshoe* had in 1988 taken over the legendary *Mint* next door, simply bashing down the party wall, and in the process finally acquired a significant number of hotel rooms.

Such was Benny's single-minded focus on gambling that he refused to put on live music, saying "I'm not going to let some S.O.B. blow my bankroll out the end of a horn." His greatest coup was to establish the *Horseshoe* as the permanent home of the **World Series of Poker** in the late 1970s. At that time, few casinos offered poker, which was seen as having too much potential for fraud and other trouble. Since then, the high profile of the three-week tournament, which takes place in late April and May each year, has encouraged others to follow suit (though none as successfully), while cementing the *Horseshoe*'s reputation as being, in their words, "where real gamblers hang their hats." It continues to operate the highest limits of any casino in town, and possibly the world; you can bet as much as you like, so long as you bet it as your very first stake.

Once you get past the *Horseshoe*'s enormous neon sign, its dim, smoky and intensely serious interior holds little appeal to non-gamblers, though its downstairs coffeeshop ranks among the best bargains in town, with a long-running $2 (sometimes $3) steak deal. As you approach it, you also get the chance to pose for (free) photos in front of a display case containing a million dollars in banknotes. Incidentally, the Binion name hit the headlines again in 1999, following the alleged murder of Benny's son Ted by a former girl-friend.

Nothing to lose

One million dollars – the winner's take at the yearly **World Series of Poker** – likely seems a good haul to most, but it can disappear overnight in Las Vegas. Such was the (near perpetual) luck of three-time Series champion **Stu Ungar**, known to have won untold millions during his poker-playing career yet to have been more than willing to gamble it away on a sports bet, a golf putt, or pretty much anything that brought with it the thrill of having "action." Considered a poker player nonpareil at No Limit Texas Hold 'Em (see p.215), a high-stakes guts test that serves as the official game played at the World Series, Ungar was by his own account a better gin rummy player – which also netted him plenty of money in his time, if not necessarily the thrill associated with high-risk poker. Belying his nothing-to-lose attitude was the fact that he was no husky, cigar-chomping cardplayer from the Wild West, rather a slight Jewish kid from New York's Lower East Side, who thralled in hanging around the company of Mafioso. Sadly, and not at the hands of some beaten or cheated opponent, Ungar was found dead at age 45 with but $800 to his name in a seedy "adult-movie" motel, the *Oasis*, north of the Strip proper at 1731 Las Vegas Blvd S, on November 22, 1998. The cause of Ungar's death remains a mystery, most often attributed to a hard and fast life mixing drugs and gambling. He died just one and a half years after his last Series title, and weeks before he was to have played in an Atlantic City tournament meant to get him back on his feet, backed by the money of the *Stratosphere* owner and longtime friend Bob Stupak.

Coincidentally, the low-rent *Oasis* was the site just a few months later of another bizarre tragedy, the suicide of actor David Strickland, a cast member of Brooke Shields' sitcom *Suddenly Susan*.

THE FOUR QUEENS

Map 4, F4. 202 E Fremont St. Hotel accommodation is reviewed on p.144.

Named not for a poker hand but for the four daughters of its original owner, the **Four Queens** has been a fixture on the downtown scene since 1966. In recent years it has prospered along with the three better-known neighbors with which it shares Fremont Street's busiest intersection, adding two nineteen-story hotel towers and sprucing up its lobby away from its old New Orleans theme in favor of matching the sparkling lights of the *Golden Nugget*.

The one unusual feature of the *Four Queens* is that it's the only casino in Las Vegas that allows you to take **photographs** in its gaming area. If you've been dying to take snaps of gamblers in action, this is the place to do it; just be sure to check with security personnel before you start.

SAM BOYD'S FREMONT HOTEL

Map 4, G3. 200 E Fremont St. Hotel accommodation is reviewed on p.146; restaurants include the *Second Street Grill* (p.174) and the *Fremont Paradise Buffet* (p.156).

Hard though it is to imagine, the **Fremont Hotel** was at fifteen stories the tallest building in Nevada when it was completed in 1956. The still-visible concrete facade of its main hotel tower was seen as shockingly modern and marked a deliberate eschewal of downtown's previously universal Wild West style of architecture. These days the *Fremont*, which has been owned by Sam Boyd of *Sam's Town* fame since 1985, is just another downtown gambling palace, not quite as fashionable as the *Golden Nugget* despite boasting the excellent *Second Street Grill* restaurant, but with its bright lights and purple baize tables jazzier than the rest of the pack.

FITZGERALDS

Map 4, G4. 301 E Fremont St. Hotel accommodation is reviewed on p.143.

Fitzgeralds, which supplanted the former *Sundance* during the 1980s and is now run as a Holiday Inn, occupies an entire block of Fremont Street. It's the most fully themed of the downtown casinos, but unfortunately the theme is so dismal that they might as well not have bothered. Every Irish cliche imaginable is brought to bear in the bid to part fools from their money, including the opportunity as you go in to rub a piece of the genuine Blarney Stone at the feet of "Mr O'Lucky." Further leprechauns, shamrocks and pots of gold abound inside. A small balcony adjoining the second-floor lounge makes a good vantage point for watching the evening light show outside, but that's about it.

THE NEON MUSEUM

Map 4, G4.

Las Vegas is seldom sentimental about erasing the traces of its past, but as casino after casino upgrades its image, eschewing "vulgar" neon in favor of "classy" gilt trimmings, dewy-eyed preservationists have campaigned to save its abandoned neon glories. As a result, the block between the end of the canopied section of Fremont Street at Fourth Street, and Las Vegas Boulevard to the east, has been grandly designated as the **Neon Museum**.

This open-air neon graveyard displays restored and fully functional signs gathered from all over the city. Some of these winking, blinking, garish delights are perched on street-level pedestals; larger examples cling to the corners of adjacent offices or parking lots. The oldest piece is a classic "Red Indian" motel sign that adorned the *Chief Hotel Court* in 1940; others include the Horse and Rider from the *Hacienda*, demolished to make way for *Mandalay Bay*, and the giant lamp that advertised the *Aladdin* until 1997.

You might expect the intersection of Fremont Street and Las Vegas Boulevard to be one of the busiest, most vibrant locations in the city. If so, you'll probably be bemused by its current seedy and run-down state, but you can console yourself with the thought that someone shares your vision. As this book went to press, World Entertainment Centers of Miami were committed to turning an entire block of Fremont Street here into **Neonopolis**, a complex featuring around fifty stores, five restaurants, an eleven-screen movie theater, and a food court.

EL CORTEZ

Map 4, H4. 600 E Fremont St. Hotel accommodation is reviewed on p.143.

Surrounded by pawn shops and T-shirt stores, a couple of rather uneasy blocks' walk east of the Fremont Street Experience, the shabby, quasi-Moorish **El Cortez** has allowed half a century to slip by since its brief 1940s heyday. In 1941 it was the largest downtown hotel – albeit with a mere 59 rooms – while in 1946 it served as a stepping stone for early investor "Bugsy" Siegel en route to the *Flamingo*. Since 1963, however, it has been owned by Jackie Gaughan, who lives in a penthouse flat upstairs and has barely changed a thing – according to scurrilous popular legend, not even the ashtrays, let alone the carpets. Its cut-rate rooms and suites make it a haunt of budget travelers, but the bottom dollar lies in its appeal to local low-rollers. As well as offering some of the lowest-stakes gambling in town, Gaughan continues to stage regular drawings of Social Security numbers, with prizes of up to $50,000 for matching all nine digits.

JACKIE GAUGHAN'S PLAZA

Map 4, E3. 1 Main St. Hotel accommodation is reviewed on p.145.

The giant **Plaza** hotel and casino faces the west end of Fremont Street from the site of Las Vegas's now-defunct railroad station. Originally a railroad-company project, it began life in 1971 as the *Union Plaza*. The Union Pacific Railroad held a 75 percent stake, while a consortium of downtown casino operators had the rest. In time, as Union Pacific gave way to Amtrak, the partners consolidated, until Jackie Gaughan finally acquired the whole thing in 1993. Though Amtrak abandoned rail service to Las Vegas in 1997 – whereupon its facilities were swallowed up into the *Plaza*'s capacious bowels – Greyhound buses still use the adjoining depot.

With its threadbare carpets and smoke-laden air, the *Plaza* is even tackier and more downmarket than Gaughan's *El Cortez* (see opposite). As well as offering some of the last penny slots left in Las Vegas, the lone dollar blackjack table on Fremont Street and a dining counter that sells bowls of Campbell's soup for $1, it has a large Race and Sports Book that's forever busy with off-duty downtown employees and Greyhound passengers.

MAIN STREET STATION

Map 4, F2. 200 N Main St at Ogden. Hotel accommodation is reviewed on p.145; restaurants include the *Garden Court Buffet* (p.156); the *Triple Seven Brewpub* is reviewed on p.186.

Despite very unpromising beginnings, **Main Street Station** has turned into one of the principal downtown success stories of the 1990s. It started out in 1991 as an offshoot of the money-spinning Church Street Station development in downtown Orlando, but the Florida formula of paying a single admission fee to gain access to a complex of nightclubs and entertainment venues failed to transfer to Las Vegas. An unpromising location, two blocks off Fremont Street, did nothing to help, and *Main Street Station* went broke within a year.

Once it was acquired by the Boyd Corporation, however, and brought back to life as a conventional hotel-casino in 1996, *Main Street Station*'s distinctive and tasteful design began to pay dividends. The general concept is intended to evoke New Orleans in the 1890s, with an abundance of authentic antiques ranging from wrought-iron fences to Teddy Roosevelt's private railroad car and even bronze chandeliers from Buenos Aires. Thanks to the very high ceilings and natural lighting, all that period detail is never oppressive, and a well-thought-out array of good-value, down-to-earth restaurants and other facilities have put *Main Street Station* firmly on the tourist map. The *Triple Seven Brewpub* is a particularly good spot for a downtown drink.

Confusingly, *Main Street Station* is not part of what's known as the Stations chain, whose four casinos are scattered across outlying neighborhoods of Las Vegas (and described in Chapter Four of this book).

CALIFORNIA HOTEL

Map 4. F2. 12 Ogden Ave at First St. Hotel accommodation is reviewed on p.143.

Of the various Boyd Corporation properties in Las Vegas, which include *Sam's Town*, the *Stardust*, and the *Fremont Hotel*, the **California Hotel** probably has the lowest profile of all. Stretching between Main and First streets a block north of Fremont Street, and connected by a mezzanine-level footbridge with the neighboring *Main Street Station* –

also Boyd-owned – it was, however, the first member of the group.

Sam Boyd, who had previously managed the now-vanished *Mint* on Fremont Street and held a stake in the *Plaza*, constructed the *California* in 1975. He named it in the understandable belief that most of its clientele would be Californian, but after initial occupancy levels proved disappointing he turned his attention to Hawaii, where he had spent five years running bingo games in his youth. Amazingly enough, sixty years on from that sojourn in Paradise, the casino remains dominated by Hawaiian customers. It advertises itself with the slogan "whether you are from Hawaii or just homesick for her aloha spirit," and the majority of its eight hundred guestrooms tend to be taken by Hawaiian tour groups. Hawaiian menu items are prominent in the bars and restaurants, and there are even slot machines labeled in Hawaiian. All that makes for quite a pleasant atmosphere, though there's no real reason for non-guests to pass this way.

CALIFORNIA HOTEL

The rest of the city

Las Vegas may look enormous on the map, but as far as tourists are concerned the only significant neighborhoods are the Strip and downtown. Nowhere else even deserves to be called a "neighborhood," in the sense of having a distinctive identity, a variety of attractions, and being explorable on foot. If you think the individual blocks along the Strip are large, wait until you drive into the rest of the city. Soon the streets start to be spaced half a mile or more apart, and often there really is nothing between one and the next. As it has grown, the city has repeatedly vaulted across swathes of empty space, and sizable portions of the grid remain completely undeveloped.

Certain districts of Las Vegas are known for their **shopping**, as detailed in Chapter Ten – Maryland Parkway close to the University, for example – and there's the odd concentration of restaurants, such as on Paradise Road south of Twain. However, no area of the city ranks as a destination in its own right, nor is likely to tempt you out of your car should you happen to pass through. Instead, your only ports of call away from downtown and the Strip are likely to be specific individual attractions, either the scattered **casinos** that cater primarily to local residents or the handful of **museums**. And if you're not driving, none of the latter, with the possible exception of the **Liberace Museum**, merits an excursion on public transport.

Note that Las Vegas has fewer **public parks** than any major city in the US. If you want to get out into the open air, your best bet is to head for nearby Red Rock Canyon, as described in Chapter Five, Out of the city.

Other casinos

Not all the gamblers in Las Vegas are tourists. Now that the city has well over a million inhabitants, casinos intent on capturing local customers are springing up throughout the valley. Known as **locals casinos** – though all those reviewed here do have at least a few hotel rooms for guests from further afield – they specialize above all in slot machines, and video poker in particular. Even at their best, most resemble community centers rather than glamour palaces, offering bowling or skating facilities and movie theaters as opposed to white tigers and sphinxes, but with their good-value restaurants and low-stakes gambling they do have something to offer the out-of-state visitor.

BOULDER STATION

Map 1, E5. 4111 Boulder Hwy.

Boulder Station stands roughly five miles east of the Strip along Desert Inn Road, at the point where Fremont Street passes under US-93/95 and becomes Boulder Highway. Though its presence is flagged by the world's largest full-color "message board," the second of the four casinos in the Stations chain has little to boast about. Customers are lured in by the usual combination of cheap, cheerful restaurants and childcare facilities (at $5–6 per hour), but the business of betting is taken very seriously. The huge Race and Sports Book has a positively Dickensian atmosphere, with rows of pencil-chewing gamblers overlooked by dark Victorian "stained glass" as they scan the news from far-off racetracks. Railroad motifs permeate the whole place, especially in the *Railhead* lounge (see p.200), where the sizable stage plays host to nationally known country stars plus a smattering of R&B musicians.

GOLD COAST

Map 1, C5. 4000 W Flamingo Rd. Hotel accommodation is reviewed on p.146.

Standing just across Valley View Boulevard from the *Rio* (see p.99), half a mile west of the Strip, the **Gold Coast** is overshadowed both literally and metaphorically by its enormous neighbor. Though built only four years before the *Rio* – it was opened in 1986 by Michael Gaughan (son of Jackie), who made his money running the slot concessions at the airport – it has the feel of a much earlier era. Only diehard old-timers pause to admire the dull rodeo memorabilia in the lobby, but it's not a bad little place, with the 72-lane Brunswick bowling center upstairs and the two-screen Twin Movie Theaters downstairs. Free shuttle buses connect it with Michael Gaughan's other properties, the *Orleans* to the south and the *Barbary Coast* on the Strip.

HARD ROCK HOTEL

Map 3, G4. 4455 Paradise Rd. Hotel accommodation is reviewed on p.147; restaurants include *Mr Lucky's 24/7* (p.178).

If you don't already share the widespread delusion that the *Hard Rock Cafe* is by definition the coolest place in any city worldwide, nothing about the **Hard Rock Hotel**, a mile east of the Strip, is likely to convince you. Its own brochures drone on about how "hip" the place is, how it's "the first ever rock'n'roll resort," and that "this is not your father's Vegas any more," but it's really not a patch on the current generation of Strip giants. Yes, guitars signed by the likes of Bob Dylan and George Michael hang above the check-in desk, and the cashier's cage bears the slogan "In Rock We Trust." Elsewhere, display-case mannequins sport Prince's spangly jumpsuit and Madonna's pointy corset, while motorcycles and drum kits stand atop banks of slot machines. It's just that the whole thing is so lame. Not even the background music is "hard rock"; it remains consistently soft and soothing.

The casino itself occupies the sunken central floor space of this circular building, so it's easy to find your way around. Much smaller than its Strip counterparts, it's also as a rule much less busy. There are so (relatively) few rooms in the hotel, and they're so expensive, that the only time the place really comes alive is when there's a big-name gig in its live-music venue, *The Joint* (tickets can cost over $100; see p.199).

Peter Morton, the co-founder of the *Hard Rock* franchise – though the *Hard Rock Hotel* is the only one he still owns – is the son of Arnie Morton, who set up the steakhouse chain *Morton's of Chicago*. Hence the presence of *A.J.'s Steakhouse*, recently added as part of a general upgrading of the hotel's restaurants that will also see the arrival of an official *Morton's* outlet.

THE LAS VEGAS HILTON

Map 2, G7. 3000 Paradise Rd. Hotel accommodation is reviewed on p.148.

The **Las Vegas Hilton** stands a full half-mile east of the Strip, set back behind the *Riviera* on Paradise Road.

However, its location alongside the Convention Center enables it to compete on equal terms with the major Strip casinos. In the late 1960s, Kirk Kerkorian hoped that building the largest hotel in the world on this site would spur the development of Paradise Road as a second, parallel Strip. Existing Strip owners felt threatened enough to attempt to prevent his *International Hotel* project ever breaking ground. When it finally went ahead, Howard Hughes tried to spoil things by buying up the *Landmark Hotel* nearby – a miniature *Stratosphere* – and reopening it as a casino on the selfsame weekend, in July 1969.

In any event, the *International* was an instant success, perhaps best remembered as the venue for **Elvis Presley**'s triumphant return to live performance. Elvis wisely allowed Barbra Streisand to inaugurate its untested showroom, profiting from her less than happy experience when he replaced her a month later. Kerkorian himself swiftly tired of his creation, and after just a year he sold his stake to Hilton, who made it a condition of the sale that they took over Elvis's contract as well as the hotel itself. In his eight-year run at the *Hilton*, Elvis went on to sell out 837 consecutive shows, appearing in front of 2.5 million people. The Hilton people remain grateful; a statue of Elvis in the main lobby commemorates the King's achievement, and a memorial service was held here for his manager Colonel Tom Parker in 1998.

....

Note that referring to the "Hilton" in Las Vegas always means this, the *Las Vegas Hilton*, and not the *Flamingo Hilton* (see p.48).

....

The *Las Vegas Hilton*'s symmetrical trefoil shape made it easy to double its initial 1500 rooms to more than three thousand in 1973, simply by extending each of its three wings (if you look closely you can see the joins). However, it had to wait 25 years before Paradise Road acquired its second casino, the *Hard Rock*, about two miles south. It remains primarily a business travelers' hotel, complementing the city's convention facilities next door with more convention space under its own roof than any other hotel on earth. Pedestrians being the rarest of species on Paradise Road, it's a place you're only expected to reach by car, and it doesn't even bother to present an enticing facade to the sidewalk. In theory, it's enough of a self-contained resort that guests need never leave the premises.

It seemed oddly out of character for the somewhat staid *Hilton* to open the **Star Trek Experience** in its north tower in 1998, which has quickly established itself as one of Las Vegas's most popular themed attractions (daily 11am–11pm; $15, or $13.50 should you happen to have a Star Trek Mastercard). The Experience is roughly equivalent to a top-echelon ride in the theme parks of LA and Orlando; it's not at all bad, but it is expensive for a one-off. Visits start from the **Space Quest Casino**, a sort of Enterprise with slots, to which access is free. If you're lucky enough to arrive when the lines are short – expect to wait up to two hours on summer weekends – you might not even realize that the ramp that spirals up from the ticket booths is a glorified queuing area. Glossy display panels on both sides recount a very wordy episode-by-episode Star Trek chronology that features highlights such as World War III in 2053, the colonization of Mars in 2103, and the birth of Spock in 2230. Museum-like artifacts and costumes abound, and diminutive Ferengi stroll among you.

The whole thing culminates when you're caught up in a dramatic plot to prevent Jean-Luc Picard ever being born (you'll know by now that he's due in 2305), and sent on a potentially vomit-inducing motion-simulator ride through deep space. Visitors with conventional human digestive systems can opt to sit out this portion. You emerge in due course in a shopping area you could have reached without

THE LAS VEGAS HILTON

97

paying anyway, where memorabilia prices boldly go to well over $2000 for a customized leather jacket.

ORLEANS

Map 1, C5. 4500 W Tropicana Ave. Hotel accommodation is reviewed on p.146; restaurants include the *French Market Buffet* (p.158).

Two miles west of the Strip on Tropicana Avenue, a stylish fake facade of pastel-painted townhouses and intricate balconies conceals the warehouse-like **Orleans** casino. When it opened, at the end of 1996, this previously untested location seemed destined to drive it into rapid bankruptcy, but owner Michael Gaughan managed to turn things around, and its extensive outdoor parking lots are now almost permanently full. Don't expect too much, however, from its New Orleans theme. The three jazz-playing alligators that greet you just inside the plate-glass doors typify its half-hearted nods to the ambience and character of the Crescent City, and there's disappointingly little New Orleans music on offer in its lounges and showrooms.

As a casino, however, it's quite exciting, with the loud broadcast commentaries in its Race and Sports Book matched by the enthusiasm of the clientele. Low stakes are offered on all table games, there's video poker galore and penny slots – just like in Gaughan's father's *Plaza*, downtown – and the croupiers are even decked out in Mardi Gras beads. Most of the customers are local, though busloads of tourists arrive from the Strip via free shuttle buses from the Gaughan-owned *Barbary Coast*.

The *Orleans' Mardi Gras* ballroom regularly hosts middle-of-the-road stars for short engagements, but Friday nights are kept free for bills of men's and women's boxing (see p.246). Other features that were hastily added to lure in the crowds include a 70-lane, 24-hour bowling arcade upstairs, and the twelve-screen Century Theatres, equipped with love seats and rockers.

PALACE STATION

Map 1, C4. 2411 W Sahara Ave.

The oldest of the four members of the Stations chain, **Palace Station** is also the closest to the Strip, standing less than a mile west along Sahara Avenue. Originally known as simply *The Casino*, it opened in 1976 and was renamed in 1983. It now feels more claustrophobic and less appealing than its younger siblings, but with its inexpensive restaurants and emphasis on slots it established the formula for their common success.

RIO

Map 1, C5. 3700 W Flamingo Rd. Hotel accommodation is reviewed on p.147; restaurants include *Napa* (p.175) and the *Carnival World Buffet* (p.157).

In becoming the first off-Strip casino to gain respect as a major Las Vegas player since the *Las Vegas Hilton* did it thirty years ago, the **Rio** has pulled off a remarkable achievement. What's more, the *Rio* did it by playing the Strip at its own game – building the city's most dazzling display of neon to catch the eye of motorists on the adjoining I-15 interstate, spending top dollar to attract high-class restaurants while also offering great-value buffets, and gaining a reputation for big-name entertainment.

Things were far from easy for the infant *Rio* in 1990, stranded half a mile west of the Strip on sleepy Flamingo Road, but successive upgradings and extensions over the course of the decade have seen it grow to become a true Vegas behemoth. Its interior is now almost as large and confusing as that of *Caesars Palace*, while the shops in its newest section, **Masquerade Village**, added in 1997, have made a start at rivaling *Caesars'* Forum. New owners *Harrah's*, who bought the *Rio* in 1998, have pledged to expand even further, with plans including the construction of a 1700-seat theater.

Free shuttle buses connect the *Rio* with the Strip, leaving from the northeast corner of Harmon Avenue, near the new *Aladdin*.

The most impressive feature of the *Rio* is its dramatic black-glass exterior. A stunning purple light show plays across both its original building and its more recent hotel tower, and is visible from all over the city. The top of that tower is also a fantastic vantage point for viewing the Strip; the outdoor terrace of the *VooDoo Lounge* (see p.182) makes a perfect spot for an evening cocktail.

Inside the *Rio*, you can't tell where the older section ends and the newer tower begins. The high-octane, high-stakes casino itself twists and turns in all directions and incorporates a huge, lavishly appointed Race and Sports Book. The "Rio" theme is also quite hard to pin down, having mutated from being specifically Brazilian to incorporating pretty much anything that's either tropical, carnival-related, or at the very least colorful.

Masquerade Village stages its own "carnival" every two hours between midday and midnight, in which parade "floats" suspended from overhead rails pass above the casino floor while costumed loons cavort on the central stage. Each "Show in the Sky" lasts for twelve minutes; as ever, it's carefully calculated not to distract you from the slots and tables for too long. Exact timings vary, but there are usually no shows on Wednesdays. Members of the public can ride on the floats for a small fee.

RIO

—

SAM'S TOWN

Map 1, F5. 5111 Boulder Hwy. Hotel accommodation is reviewed on p.148; restaurants include *The Great Buffet* (p.158).

One of Las Vegas's few surviving hold-outs of the city's once-ubiquitous Wild West theme, **Sam's Town** stands roughly six miles east of the Strip by way of Flamingo Road, at the point where Nellis Boulevard meets Boulder Highway. It's the quintessential locals casino, not least because after years of low-profile prosperity providing bargain-basement grub-and-gambling, it has suddenly blossomed into a genuinely appealing place.

Though the "Sam" of the name is veteran casino operator Sam Boyd, *Sam's Town* was the brainchild of his son, Bill Boyd. During his daily drive to work in 1979, he was struck by the sheer volume of traffic along this hitherto uncommercialized stretch of highway. *Sam's Town* was soon drawing in crowds of thrill-seeking commuters, giving them hearty old-style Western meals then clawing back their wages via its endless banks of slots.

While its general decor is still bursting with boots 'n'spurs'n'cactuses, *Sam's Town* transformed itself in 1994. It now centers on a large glass-roofed atrium, overlooked on all four sides by the high-rise brownstone facades of its hotel towers. Officially known as Mystic Falls Park, and kitted out with fiberglass mountains, waterfalls, real trees, recorded birdsong, and even animatronic beavers, it's reminiscent − if you're in the right mood − of New York's Central Park. A free "Sunset Stampede" laser and light show takes place four times daily (2pm, 6pm, 8pm & 10pm).

The main hotel registration desk is in the park, as is a *Java in the Park* espresso stand, while the massive Western Emporium in one corner (see p.233) stocks a vast range of Westernwear and associated paraphernalia. Elsewhere, there's usually some kind of Western or country-music-related activity going on, and there's a 56-lane 24-hour bowling center downstairs.

Free shuttle buses run between *Sam's Town* and other Boyd Corporation properties, including the *Stardust* on the Strip and the *Fremont* downtown. It is a surprisingly long way out; if you feel like dropping in, it makes sense to do so as part of the trip to or from Hoover Dam.

The Hoover Dam is covered in detail on p.121.

SANTA FE HOTEL AND CASINO

Map 1, B2. 4949 N Rancho Drive.

Only tourists who make the excursion to Mount Charleston (see p.115) are likely to stumble across the **Santa Fe**, eight miles up Rancho Drive in the far northwestern corner of town. Even then, there's little reason to stop, though it does offer the usual good-value buffet and restaurants.

For Las Vegas residents, however, it's a different story. As the only casino to have its own public **ice rink** (see p.228), the *Santa Fe* is literally the coolest place in the city. Local kids fill the Ice Arena on weekends, while their parents while away the hours either in the adjoining 24-hour bowling center, or watching from the buffet or casino. The Southwestern theming is minimal, but the dealers do at least wear bolo ties.

SUNSET STATION

Map 1, F6. 1301 W Sunset Rd, Henderson. Hotel accommodation is reviewed on p.149; restaurants include the *Costa del Sol Oyster Bar* (p.176) and the *Feast Around The World*

Buffet (p.157).

Eight miles southeast of the southern end of the Strip, in suburban Henderson, **Sunset Station** is a long drive from the center of Las Vegas. En route to Hoover Dam, however, and opposite the Galleria Mall (see p.230), the newest and largest of the Stations chain is not exactly off the beaten track, and it's worth seeing in its own right.

Completed in 1997, *Sunset Station* was designed to look something like an old Spanish mission. The attempt is enjoyable enough, even if it's not all that coherent, and some of the interior trimmings are truly spectacular. An extraordinary adobe-styled and mushroom-shaped canopy of stained and colored glass undulates above the gaming area, reaching a climax in the central *Gaudi Bar* (see p.181). A fantastic mosaic-enhanced tribute to the Catalan architect Gaudi, it's Las Vegas at its most surreal. Running at a close second, perhaps, is the nearby bakery, *Kenya's Cakes of the Stars*, which believe it or not is co-owned by soul sisters Gladys Knight, Patti LaBelle, Dionne Warwick and Natalie Cole.

Sunset Station also features a thirteen-screen movie theater, some good restaurants and an excellent buffet, childcare facilities, and a Sega games arcade, plus free shuttle buses to the Strip.

TEXAS STATION

Map 1, C3. 2101 Texas Star Lane. Hotel accommodation is reviewed on p.147; restaurants include *Laredo del Mar* (p.175) and the *Feast Around The World Buffet* (p.157).

"Texas" might not sound like a wildly exciting concept for a casino, and in truth **Texas Station** doesn't exactly pick it up and run with it. Its carpets may be adorned with assorted lone stars, state maps and spurs, but really the theming doesn't extend beyond enabling its guests to eat well, drink a lot, and gamble themselves into penury in cheerful surroundings. The third in the Stations chain, built two miles northwest of downtown in 1995, it offers no outstanding novelties or gimmicks, but as locals casinos go it's definitely one of the best.

Texas Station's buffet and conventional restaurants are top-notch, while fast-food outlets include every Southerner's favorite donut chain, *Krispy Kreme*, plus the much-loved *Fatburger*. There's also an eighteen-screen movie theater, an enormous play area for kids (prices from $5.25 per hour; see p.200), and a separate and very serious Bingo Hall, but the real highlight for country-mad hoe-downers is the *Armadillo Honky Tonk Lounge*, complete with 200-pound mirrored disco armadillo.

Other attractions

LIBERACE MUSEUM

Map 1, E5. 1775 E Tropicana Ave ⓒ798-5595, *www.liberace.org*. Mon–Sat 10am–5pm, Sun 1–5pm; minimum adult donation $6.95, under-12s free.

The finest of Las Vegas's handful of museums is, not surprisingly, the one most in keeping with the city's sheer exhibitionism. The **Liberace Museum**, two miles east of the Strip, is a fabulous romp through the life and times of the former Walter Liberace (1919–87), who changed his name to a single word on the advice of fellow-Polish musical maestro Paderewski.

Liberace originally wanted to have his museum in his hometown of Wauwatosa, Wisconsin, but couldn't buy the house he had in mind, and plumped for scattering it across three separate buildings in a small Las Vegas mall instead. A framed contract from 1940 shows how he started out, playing five hours a night, six nights a week for $45 in Milwaukee's *Plankington Red Room*. Yellowing newspaper cuttings and family photographs trace his subsequent progress from sensitive youth to a caped Dracula, concealed beneath layers of pancake makeup. Alongside pictures of Liberace with Elvis at the *New Frontier* in 1957 and of showbiz pals ranging from Cary Grant to Bill Cosby, hang a fine collection of images of the Pope, the Queen, and Charles and Diana *not* with Liberace. You can also enjoy film of Liberace on stage with Debbie Reynolds, performing a frighteningly soulless rendition of "Your Love Is Taking Me Higher," and admire the conviction with which he advertised Blatz Beer in 1951.

With success came scandal – he was ruthlessly hounded by the press – but also phenomenal wealth. His collection of pianos ranges from an instrument dating from 1788, via one thought to have been played by Chopin for Liszt, to a giraffe-shaped piano with an upright harp-like frame, and there's also a fine array of cars, including a white hounds'-tooth London cab driven by an oversized white teddy bear. Home furnishings on display include a horrendously vulgar desk that belonged to the last czar of Russia, and Liberace's personal bedroom suite, equipped with two single beds.

If Liberace is remembered for just one thing, however, it wouldn't be his music – which, piped into the scented restrooms, has sadly not improved with age – but his costumes. He called them "a very expensive joke"; confronted by rhinestone-studded stage furs valued at $500,000, $600,000, and even $750,000, it's hard to disagree. The pièce de resistance is the red, white, and blue hot pants set he wore for the Bicentennial in 1976. Said to have cost a million dollars, it looks worth ten bucks at the most.

LIED DISCOVERY CHILDREN'S MUSEUM

Map 1, E3. 833 Las Vegas Blvd N ☏384-3445. Daily except Mon 10am–5pm; adults $5, ages 12–17 $4, ages 3–11 $3.

The **Lied Discovery Children's Museum**, a bit less than a mile north of downtown on a very pedestrian-unfriendly stretch of Las Vegas Boulevard, is a rather poor specimen of the modern breed of hands-on children's museums. Occupying a few rooms of a city library building, it's far less likely to stimulate childish imaginations than the wonders on the Strip. Local kids on school trips enjoy the chance to paint, draw and sculpt, but even the youngest tourists may resent being dragged away from *Luxor* or *Circus Circus*. There are a few typical Las Vegas touches, like the fact that infant artists are rewarded for each work of art that they create with forty "Discovery Dollars," which they can withdraw from the Discovery ATM. However, a significant proportion of the more sophisticated displays tends to be broken at any one time, and unless a good temporary exhibition is taking place (call ahead) there's not a lot of point coming.

LAS VEGAS NATURAL HISTORY MUSEUM

Map 1, E3. 900 Las Vegas Blvd N ☏384-3466. Daily 9am–4pm; adults $5, ages 4–12 $2.50.

A mile or so north of downtown, a block beyond the children's museum, the **Las Vegas Natural History Museum** has been making efforts to move beyond its traditional dioramas of stuffed animals. Thus the Marine Life Room features a small-ish tank of live sharks alongside its mounted specimens, while the Prehistoric Room now offers three large animatronic monsters, including a roaring Tyrannosaurus Rex. Even the old-fashioned exhibits in the International Wildlife Room are a bit less static than you might expect; note the zebra frantically trying to fend off two lions.

NEVADA STATE MUSEUM

Map 1, B4. 700 Twin Lakes Drive ©486-5205. Daily 9am–5pm; $2, under-18s free.

The world can hold few quieter, emptier museums than the **Nevada State Museum**, three miles west of downtown. That's partly due, no doubt, to the fact that it's fiendishly difficult to find – follow the signs to Lorenzi Park from the intersection of Washington Avenue and Valley View Boulevard. It might also be because Las Vegas has a shorter history than any other major city; and yet despite ample floor space the museum seems to make so little of it. Las Vegas is unique in having grown up entirely since the invention of the camera – one image shows Paiute Indians toting bows and arrows in the valley in 1873 – but rather than celebrating its extravagantly photogenic flowering, the displays peter out altogether in the 1950s.

Things do seem reasonably promising at first. Galleries devoted to regional prehistory hold the skeletons of a Pacific horse – the horse evolved in North America and migrated through Alaska to populate Asia, but was extinct in America until the Spaniards reintroduced it – and a Columbian (not woolly) mammoth, which was found in Utah but may have been hunted by humans in the Las Vegas area.

Perfunctory captions and lifeless dioramas soon start to reveal the museum's intended audience as school parties with very short attention spans, however, and it barely touches upon the glitz and glamour, vice and viciousness of the early casino years. There's a tasty little account of the gangland feudings that surrounded the construction of the *Flamingo*, but the main exhibit to accompany it is the origi-

NEVADA STATE MUSEUM

107

nal door to Bugsy Siegel's suite – quite the dullest door you ever saw. Next up is some tantalizing material about atomic tests during the Fifties; and then, suddenly, it's all over, with not a word about modern Las Vegas.

Lorenzi Park, outside the museum and centered around a small lake, is perhaps the nicest of the city's rare public spaces. Its other significant feature is the **Sammy Davis Jr Festival Plaza**, a walled auditorium used for open-air concerts.

Out of the city

Spend more than a day or two in Las Vegas and you'll soon find yourself gasping for a blast of sunlight and fresh air away from the casinos. A glance at the horizon makes it clear that you'll have to cross a significant expanse of empty desert before you reach anywhere interesting, but exhilarating day-trip destinations do exist.

Perhaps the most obvious targets lie in the eye-catching **Spring Mountains** to the west. At their base, monumental walls cradle the desert fastness of **Red Rock Canyon**, while further north their wooded slopes rise toward the summit of **Mount Charleston**. If Red Rock Canyon whets your appetite for other-worldly desolation, you'll also enjoy the longer excursion to the incandescent moonscape of the **Valley of Fire**, northeast of the city. Finally, neither **Hoover Dam** nor **Lake Mead** counts as a natural wonder, but both are in their own ways every bit as breathtaking.

For day-trip tours to the Grand Canyon, see p.122.

This chapter only includes places that can be reached and explored in a day's round-trip drive from Las Vegas. It does not, therefore, cover the awe-inspiring national parks of southern Utah, such as **Zion**, which is 160 miles distant, and **Bryce Canyon**, eighty miles beyond that. On the basis

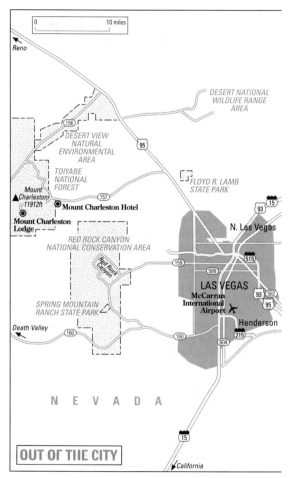

OUT OF THE CITY

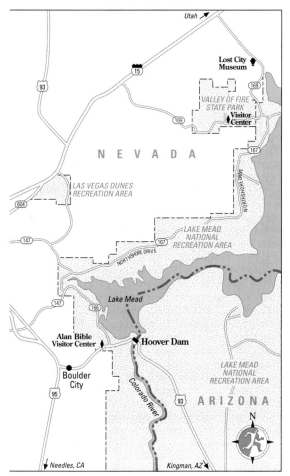

that Las Vegas holds enough casinos to last any sane human being a lifetime, neither does it include the nearby state-line gambling resorts of **Primm**, **Mesquite**, or **Laughlin**.

Red Rock Canyon

The closest concentration of classic Southwestern canyon scenery to Las Vegas lies a mere twenty miles west of the city center. The sheer 3000-foot escarpment that towers above **Red Rock Canyon National Conservation Area** is clearly visible from hotel windows along the Strip, with every fiery detail picked out each morning by the rising sun. What you can't see until you enter the park, however, is that there's a cactus-strewn desert basin set deep into those mighty walls, surrounded by stark red cliffs that are pierced repeatedly by narrow canyons accessible only on foot.

Run by the Federal Bureau of Land Management, Red Rock Canyon covers almost 200,000 acres of wilderness. Like other such BLM areas, it's less groomed for tourists than a national park or monument. Thus while it includes over thirty miles of hiking trails, they're not as well signed or maintained as you might expect, and it's all too easy for novice walkers to get lost.

To reach the canyon, just keep going west on Charleston Boulevard, from the extreme north of the Strip. The pink leaves of the trees lining the road perfectly complement the pink strata of rocks on the mountains straight ahead, though this scene has been somewhat spoiled by the construction of the **Summerlin** residential and resort development at the west end of Charleston, of which the first phase opened in 1999.

Having continued due west for the entire width of the valley, Charleston eventually veers south to follow Red Rock Wash. You soon reach Red Rock Canyon's **visitor center** (daily 8.30am–4.30pm; ©363-1921), to the right of the highway at the start of the Scenic Drive. Displays and models here explain the geological formation of the canyon, while a window commands a panoramic view of its main features.

At the visitor center, you're facing into a natural amphitheater of Aztec sandstone that soars on three sides of the central basin. The **Wilson Cliffs** to the left are topped by a layer of gray limestone, which has preserved them from erosion and left them taller than the rounded **Calico Hills** to the right.

Gray Line (©384-1234) runs full-day bus tours from Las Vegas, combining visits to both Red Rock Canyon and Mount Charleston, for around $30.

THE SCENIC DRIVE

Red Rock Canyon's **Scenic Drive** (daily 7am–dusk; $5 per vehicle) is a one-way loop road that meanders for thirteen miles around the edge of the basin before rejoining the main highway a couple of miles southwest of the visitor center. As the name implies, it's designed for drivers not pedestrians, but it's also popular with cyclists, for whom its gradients are never too demanding. Along the way, it passes a number of overlooks, many of which also serve as trailheads for hikes of varying lengths.

If you plan to hike, buy a good **map** in the visitor center before you set off; the free handouts aren't up to the job. Be warned also that the desert is home to mountain lions, rattlesnakes, and even Gila monsters, which, should you permit one to chew on you for several hours, are poisonous.

The Calico Hills

The most dramatic views along the Scenic Drive come early on, as you head straight toward the **Calico Hills** that form the basin's northeastern wall. From two successive overlooks, Calico Vistas 1 and 2, it's possible to scramble short distances down from the road to find yourself dwarfed amid these crumbling domes of cream and red sandstone.

Further along, the **Calico Tanks Trail**, a 2.5-mile round trip, heads up from Sandstone Quarry and beyond the visible rim to reach the largest of the area's natural "tanks." The rainwater collected and stored in such depressions was once a valuable resource for nomadic desert peoples. On a clear day, you should be able to see the Strip from up here.

Willow Spring

The easiest trail in the canyon starts at **Willow Spring**, a short way up a spur road seven miles from the visitor center. Designated the **Red Rock Canyon Discovery Trail**, it follows the tree-filled minor canyon formed by Lost Creek, passing rock shelters used by ancient Indians. Children who complete this 1.5-mile stroll can claim a certificate and badge at the visitor center, which provides full details on request.

Pine Creek Canyon Trail

Energetic hikers who lack the urge to do out-and-out rock climbing should enjoy the **Pine Creek Canyon Trail**, which sets off a little less than eleven miles from the visitor center. From the trailhead, look down and to the left to see the row of ponderosa pines that reveals the presence of Pine Creek. Reaching the ruined homesite beside it takes around twenty minutes, along a sandy red footpath fringed with cactuses.

The clear stream itself, rippling over red-rock boulders and lined with lush flowers, can be accessed via various imprecise trails. The main trail, on the other hand, continues up to the right. Keeping going all the way to the foot of a red-capped monolith that divides two forked canyons will give you a total round-trip hike of roughly five miles.

Mount Charleston

Las Vegas residents desperate to escape the desert heat flock in summer to the **Spring Mountain Recreation Area**. Thirty miles northwest of the city and forming part of the Toiyabe National Forest, it's more widely known as **Mount Charleston**, on account of its highest point, the 11,918-foot Charleston Peak. Ten thousand years ago, this isolated range formed a natural refuge for wildlife from the lakes that filled the Las Vegas valley, and it retained its own unique ecosystem as the rest of the region dried out. Many of its plants and animals, including one species of chipmunk, are found nowhere else on earth.

The cool wooded slopes of Mount Charleston are much less of a novelty for most tourists, of course, but they do offer some great **hiking**, and in winter you can even drive out for a day's **skiing**. Higher elevations usually remain covered by snow between mid-October and mid-May each year, while the streams and waterfalls only have substantial flows during the thaw in spring and early summer.

To reach Mount Charleston, follow US-95 six miles northwest of the intersection of Rancho Drive and I-515, making a total of fifteen miles from the Strip. At that point, head west along Hwy-157, **Kyle Canyon Road**, which for its first ten miles continues to cross flat, barren desert. Shortly

MOUNT CHARLESTON

after dipping through a jagged rocky "reef" that pokes from the valley floor, the highway enters Kyle Canyon.

KYLE CANYON

As it penetrates the Spring Mountains, Hwy-157 itself remains relatively level; the hills rise on either side. When it begins to climb, the ascent is gradual and not all that dramatic. Only as you feel your ears popping do you realize you've left the valley behind. As the closest part of the mountains to Las Vegas, **Kyle Canyon** is the main day-trip destination, and offers a hotel and year-round restaurant, though other practicalities are lacking: there's nowhere up here to buy gas or basic groceries.

Mount Charleston Hotel

Set below the highway on the left, seventeen miles up from US-95 and facing a towering rocky outcrop, the 63-room **Mount Charleston Hotel** is the only accommodation option in the mountains (☎872-5500 or 1-800/794-3456; Jan–Oct ③, Nov & Dec ④). Despite its somewhat forbidding facade, on the inside it resembles an old-fashioned national park lodge, with lots of wooden furnishings, a high vaulted ceiling, a 360-degree open fireplace, and an attractive sculpted tree with bronze leaves. It even has a few discreet slot machines, if you're pining for the city. The rates indicated above are for first-floor rooms; the second floor costs $10 extra, the third $20 extra. Downstairs, the *Canyon Dining Room* serves very inexpensive burger or salad lunches, and pricier steak, chicken, and seafood dinners.

**Accommodation price codes are explained on p.132.
For details of campgrounds in the vicinity of Mount Charleston, call ☎1-800/722-9802.**

Kyle Guard and Information Station

Beyond the hotel, you pass from the lower "life zone" of yuccas and cactuses into forests of pine, fir and mahogany. Hwy-158, described on p.118, branches right in less than a mile, and then half a mile beyond that the **Kyle Guard and Information Station** (Mon & Thurs–Sun 9am–4pm; ℂ872-5486) is tucked amid the trees on the left. Rangers here can supply trail guides and up-to-date weather forecasts.

Mary Jane Falls Trail

A mile or so past the ranger station, Hwy-157 doubles back sharply on itself and starts back along the other side of Kyle Canyon. However, a short spur road, **Echo Road**, keeps going straight on for a few hundred yards up to the trail-head for the **Mary Jane Falls Trail**. This 2.5-mile round-trip hike follows a disused road for a little under a mile, before requiring hikers to ascend a series of exhausting switchbacks to reach the twin Mary Jane Falls at the head of the canyon. Fed by separate springs, the falls are at their strongest in early summer, but that's not a good time to enter the caves immediately behind them, which remain icy until later in the year.

Cathedral Rock Trail

Half a mile further along Hwy-157, the **Cathedral Rock Trail** sets off from a roadside parking lot. Starting at 7600 feet and climbing a further thousand feet along a rough but not very steep footpath, the three-mile round trip can be pretty grueling for anyone unused to such elevations. En route to the top of the promontory known as **Cathedral Rock**, you have to circle around Mazie Canyon, by way of denuded hillsides cleared by countless winter avalanches. You're eventually rewarded with views all the way back down Kyle Canyon – though not as far as Las Vegas – as well as onward to **Charleston Peak**. Its smooth bald dome is the only point in the mountains that pokes out above the treeline.

Mount Charleston Lodge

Hwy-157 comes to a dead end shortly after Cathedral Rock, looping around the parking lot of **Mount Charleston Lodge** (✆872-5408). This large and utterly unexciting Southwestern restaurant is usually packed with daytrippers, but if you can get a table on the terrace you'll be treated to fine views over the canyon and up to Charleston Peak.

As detailed on p.243, it's possible to go horse-riding from the stables adjoining *Mount Charleston Lodge*.

HWY-158

The most scenic stretch of road in the Spring Mountains has to be **Hwy-158**, which runs for nine miles across the face of the mountains to connect Kyle Canyon with Lee Canyon to the north. Unmarked pullouts along the way provide opportunities to survey the desert far below. You may even spot caves said to be have been used by bandits who preyed on travelers using the old Mormon Trail across the valley.

Desert View Trail

Not far short of Lee Canyon, the clearly signed **Desert View Trail** is a short, paved footpath with an unlikely history. During the A-bomb test of the 1950s – see p.270 – the Mount Charleston area was designated by the Atomic Energy Commission as being the best vantage point for spectators. On eight separate days in 1957, announced far enough in advance for tourists to plan their vacations to coincide, vast crowds assembled up here to watch the explosions. Metal poles erected to hold official cameras recording the events still stand just below the viewing platform. These days, you have to settle simply for a vast desert panorama, which doesn't extend as far as Las Vegas itself.

LEE CANYON

From the north end of Hwy-159, Hwy-156, also known as Lee Canyon Road, runs eighteen miles northeast to re-join US-95 thirteen miles up from the Kyle Canyon turn-off. Heading three miles southwest instead brings you into the heart of **Lee Canyon**. Like Kyle Canyon, this was once the scene of commercial logging; more recently, the trees have been cut back to create southern Nevada's only **ski** area.

Las Vegas Ski and Snowboard Resort

Just under fifty miles from the Strip, the **Las Vegas Ski and Snowboard Resort** at the head of Lee Canyon functions each winter between late November and early April, with snowmaking equipment to prolong the season. Three chair lifts lead to ten different slopes, graded from novice to advance; lift passes cost $28 per day, and equipment is available to rent. There's no accommodation on site, but it does hold a coffeeshop and a ski school. For more details, or to arrange a free shuttle bus from town, call ©385-2754.

LEE CANYON

Lake Mead and Hoover Dam

The single most popular day-trip for Las Vegas visitors is the thirty-mile drive southeast to the vast artificial reservoir of **Lake Mead**, and to mighty **Hoover Dam** that created it. In many ways, the dam is also responsible for modern Las Vegas's very existence, not so much as a source of energy but because the workers who built it triggered the city's first gambling-fueled boom. As for the lake, it makes a bizarre spectacle, utterly unnatural yet undeniably impressive, with its blue waters a vivid counterpoint to the surrounding desert. Both the lake and its 550-mile shoreline, however, can be excruciatingly crowded all year round.

As the crow flies, the western edge of Lake Mead is barely fourteen miles east of the Strip, but no road follows that route. Although two minor highways provide the most direct access, most visitors choose instead to take **Boulder Highway**, climbing out of the valley at Railroad Pass and reaching **Boulder City** thirty miles out from the Strip. The first surreal vista of the lake arrives as you drop out of Boulder City on Business-93.

Contrary to popular belief, only four percent of Las Vegas's electricity comes from hydroelectric power.

LAKESHORE SCENIC DRIVE

On a stark sandstone slope beside US-93, four miles northeast of Boulder City, the **Alan Bible Visitor Center** (daily 8.30am–4.30pm; ☎293-8990) is the main source of information on the Lake Mead National Recreation Area.

Even if you don't need details of how to sail, scuba-dive, water-ski, or fish from its six separate marinas, it's worth calling in to enjoy a sweeping prospect of the whole thing. Pick up some safety advice, too – the lake averages three fatal water accidents per month.

Though the lake straddles the border between Nevada and Arizona, the best views come from the Nevada side. From the visitor center, Hwy-166, better known as **Lakeshore Scenic Drive**, parallels the western shore of the lake as far as Las Vegas Bay. In places it's set back far enough that the water is not visible, but spur roads lead down to **Lake Mead Marina** and **Las Vegas Bay Marina**. As well as boat and jetski rental – see p.245 – both marinas offer restaurants and stores, but they're functional rather than pleasant places to stop. In between the two, **Lake Mead Cruises Landing** is the base of operations for the *Desert Princess*, an imitation paddlewheeler that makes up to three excursions daily, calling at Hoover Dam ($21–43; ✆293-6180).

HOOVER DAM

Staying on US-83 beyond the visitor center takes you through the rocky ridges of the Black Mountains to reach **Hoover Dam**. Designed to block the Colorado River and supply low-cost water and electricity to the cities of the Southwest, it's among the tallest dams ever built (726ft high), and used enough concrete to build a two-lane highway from San Francisco to New York. It was completed in 1935, as the first step in the Bureau of Reclamation program that culminated in the Glen Canyon Dam at the far end of the Grand Canyon, and the creation of Lake Powell.

If you're happy enough just to get a general view of the scale of the thing, keep driving across the top of the dam into Arizona, and try to squeeze into one of the parking lots as the road climbs on the far side. To get a close-up

Grand Canyon tours

Whatever impression you may have, the **Grand Canyon** is not close to Las Vegas. The **South Rim**, the most famous tourist area, is 290 miles away by road, and the quieter **North Rim** only a little less. A Colorado River viewpoint on the Hualapai Indian Reservation, 130 miles from Las Vegas, calls itself the **West Rim**, but the views are not on the same scale.

Trying to see the South Rim on a day-trip by **bus** involves at least a ten-hour ride, and is not recommended. Competition on **air tours**, however – all of which also include an overflight of Hoover Dam – has brought prices below $100 per person, which isn't bad for a once-in-a-lifetime experience. The prices listed below are typical of those advertised in free magazines like *What's On*. Trips that don't land usually take just a couple of hours or so.

Gray Line ☏384-1234. West Rim by bus ($79) or air ($135 with landing, $89 without); South Rim by bus ($135) or air ($155 with landing).

Las Vegas Tour and Travel ☏739-8975. West Rim air tour ($55), or with landing ($129); South Rim by bus ($49), by air ($90 with landing, $85 without), and by helicopter ($229).

Magic Tours ☏380-1106. South Rim by bus ($46), airplane with ground tour ($90), or helicopter ($225).

Maverick Helicopter Tours ☏261-0007. Deluxe helicopter tours of the West Rim ($369).

Scenic Airlines ☏638-3200. South Rim by air, with ground tour by bus ($199–239).

Sightseeing Tours Limited ☏471-7155. Air tour without landing ($75); South Rim by bus ($45), airplane with ground tour ($90), or helicopter ($99–225).

view, you'll have to pay $2 to get into the huge parking lot on the Nevada side of the river, and then walk down to the

Hoover Dam Visitor Center (daily: April–Sept 8.30am–5.45pm, Oct–March 9.15am–4.15pm; ☎293-1824). Displays here explain the history and construction of the dam, and informative guided **tours** set off regularly. For $8, you get a 35-minute overview that includes a ride down to the bottom; hour-long "hard-hat" tours in a smaller group cost $25. Over a million visitors per year take one or other, so you may have to wait for a while.

Bus tours to the dam from Las Vegas, with Gray Line (☎384-1234) or other operators, cost around $20 for a five-hour trip; see p.11.

The Valley of Fire

While Red Rock Canyon certainly makes a tasty appetizer, to experience the true scale and splendor of the Southwestern deserts you need to make the hundred-mile round-trip drive to the **Valley of Fire**, northeast of Las Vegas. Its multicolored, strangely eroded rocks are the solidified remains of sand dunes laid down at the time of the dinosaurs, 150 million years ago. If they seem familiar, you may have seen them in any number of movies from *One Million Years BC* to *Star Trek – The Next Generation*.

The road into the valley, state Hwy-169, cuts away east from I-15 thirty long, empty miles up its course toward Salt Lake City. Passing briefly through a corner of the desolate Moapa River Indian Reservation, it then starts to undulate and climb the aptly named Muddy Mountains, whose grayochre wall forms the eastern boundary of the Dry Lake Valley.

THE VALLEY OF FIRE

VALLEY OF FIRE STATE PARK

Twelve miles from the interstate, Hwy-169 crests the Muddy Mountains and enters **Valley of Fire State Park**. A huge panorama opens up ahead, stretching down toward Lake Mead, but the road has to pick its way gingerly down, threading between abrupt, jagged outcrops. Having paid the $5-per-vehicle fee at the entrance station, you soon come to the first of the big red rocks, the ridged, bulbous **Beehives**.

A little further on, the park's **visitor center** is to the left, at the start of the spur road that holds its most spectacular formations (daily 8.30am–4.30pm; ©397-2088). Besides displays on the geology and history of the region, the center provides an introduction to local wildlife, including cases of live snakes.

The broad, paved road beyond the visitor center leads through a wonderland of misshapen stone monstrosities, worn smooth by millennia of wind and rain and striped in every conceivable color. Cream, yellow, gold, pink, and purple strata are interspersed among the lurid omnipresent red. Many hikers set off walking when the road dead-ends 5.5 miles along at the White Domes, but that entails plowing through thick sand drifts, and there are better trails earlier on.

Mouse's Tank

Less than a mile north of the Valley of Fire visitor center, an easy and interesting half-mile hike follows a sandy wash through **Petroglyph Canyon**. The rock walls at the base of certain sandstone monoliths here are thought to have been decorated by prehistoric Anasazi farmers (see opposite). Some symbols have been recognized as being similar to those used by the modern Hopi people of Arizona, but not all is necessarily what it seems. The depictions of bighorn sheep, for example, probably represent shamen rather than actual sheep.

The trail is forced to stop when the ground suddenly drops away at the far end of the canyon, where run-off after occasional desert storms has cut deep channels into the rock. Scrambling up the slopes adjacent to the edge enables you to peer down into a natural "tank" that can hold collected rainwater for months at a time. Known as **Mouse's Tank**, this remote reservoir was the hideout of Mouse, a fugitive Paiute Indian, during the 1890s.

Elephant Rock

One of the most photographed features of the Valley of Fire is located alongside Hwy-169 three miles east of the visitor center. Reached via a short but steep trail from the parking lot at the park's east entrance, **Elephant Rock** does indeed bear an amazing resemblance to a petrified pachyderm, dipping its trunk into the hillside.

THE LOST CITY MUSEUM

A mile outside the park, Hwy-169 meets Hwy-167, Northshore Drive, which circles back south toward Las Vegas. Staying on Hwy-169 as it heads north from this intersection is a much less attractive option – maps that suggest this is a scenic route are pretty wide of the mark – but it brings you in nine miles to Overton's intriguing **Lost City Museum** (daily 8.30am–4.30pm; $2).

Between around 300 BC and 1150 AD, a people known as the **Anasazi** are thought to have farmed in the Moapa Valley, immediately north of the Valley of Fire. This was the western extremity of their domain, which extended across the entire Colorado Plateau, from modern Utah and

Arizona into New Mexico and Colorado. The first to build the characteristic adobe villages that the Spaniards later called "pueblos," they were the ancestors of today's Pueblo Indians.

The "**Lost City**," by far the largest Anasazi settlement in Nevada, was really more of an elongated village. Stretching for around thirty miles along the Moapa Valley, and originally known to archeologists as the Pueblo Grande de Nevada, its ruins were partly submerged by the creation of Lake Mead. At that time, in the 1930s, the finest artifacts from the site were gathered into this museum, which was given a catchy name in the hope of making it easier to raise funds.

Displays at the museum are still very much rooted in the 1930s – techniques like painting over a slab of genuine petroglyphs would appall modern archeologists – but there's still plenty to fascinate casual visitors. The whole structure is designed in a mock-Pueblo style, with a replica of a dig on a genuine site inside, and reconstructions of Pueblo buildings, also on their original sites, in the garden outside.

NORTHSHORE DRIVE

The fifty-mile drive back to Las Vegas from the Valley of Fire along Hwy-167, **Northshore Drive**, takes you through some utterly stunning wilderness. Desolate and forbidding sandstone mountains soar in your path, the road dwindling to a thin gray streak dwarfed beneath stark serrated cliffs. Its name, however, referring to its position by Lake Mead, is misleading – you almost never see the lake itself, which remains on the far side of a high ridge. Here and there, side roads lead down to marinas on the lake, but unless you're going boating they're dismal spots.

LISTINGS

Accommodation

Las Vegas is the hotel capital of the planet, holding nineteen of its twenty largest hotels. There are well over 100,000 rooms in the city, almost all of them attached to casinos. The *MGM Grand* alone holds five thousand, while another thirteen casinos boast more than three thousand rooms apiece. All those giants line up **along the Strip**, Las Vegas Boulevard South, while there's another concentration of only slightly smaller properties downtown.

Whatever you may have heard, Las Vegas hotels no longer offer incredibly cheap deals at the drop of a hat. With occupancy rates averaging ninety percent year-round, they don't need to. It is true that serious gamblers can get their accommodation free, but to count as "serious" you'd have to commit yourself to gambling several thousand dollars, which is a pretty strange definition of "free." For ordinary tourists, all that can be said is that Vegas prices are consistently good value compared to similar properties elsewhere; at a rough estimate, they're around thirty percent lower than in typical US cities.

Be warned that **where you stay** does make a difference. The casinos are not only colossal, but they're deliberately designed to make it as hard as possible to leave the hotel without having to walk through the whole gaming area. As it can take half an hour to reach the Strip itself from a room

Accommodation reservations

The **Las Vegas Convention & Visitors Authority** offers an availability and reservations service on ✆1-800/332-5333. In addition, reservations across the full range of Las Vegas hotels are handled by the following agencies and organizations:

Las Vegas Holidays ✆702/697-8800 or 1-800/805-9528.

Las Vegas Reservation Systems ✆702/792-3811 or 1-800/233-5594.

National Reservation Bureau ✆702/794-4490 or 1-800/732-1194.

Reservations Plus ✆702/795-3999 or 1-800/805-9528.

Web sites:

lasvegashotel.com   lasvegasreservations.com

lasvegasrooms.com   lvholidays.com

lvrs.com   nrbinc.com

vegashotel.com

in the *MGM Grand* or *Caesars Palace*, it's worth choosing a hotel where you'll be happy to spend most of your time. Obvious factors to consider include the on-site restaurants and entertainment, the themed attractions, the provisions for children, the pool, and so on. Our list of "Strip favorites" on p.135 may help you decide.

For the most part, the **rooms** themselves are what you'd expect in any reasonable standard American hotel chain. On the Strip, most casinos make only token efforts to match their rooms to their overall "themes," as with the fake stonework wallpaper in *Excalibur* or the wannabe Arabian bedspreads in the *Sahara*. If you want to know you're in Las Vegas from the moment you open your eyes, *Luxor, New York-New York* and *Caesars Palace* offer the most enjoyably **themed accommodations**.

Precise **room rates** are entirely dictated by supply and demand. Even if you stay in the same room for several consecutive days, you'll be charged a different rate for each day, depending not only on the day of the week but also which conventions or events may be happening in town, and the hotel's general level of business. Whatever rate you're quoted for a particular day, it's always worth trying a little negotiation; you may get a discount if you're attending a convention, or simply for belonging to a motoring organization such as the AAA or the British AA. However, the only surefire way to get a cut-price room is to **visit during the week** rather than the weekend. Rates everywhere rise enormously on Friday or Saturday; expect to pay perhaps $30 extra per night in a lower-end property, more like $50 to $100 extra in the big-name casinos. On top of that, many hotels won't accept Saturday arrivals.

Broadly speaking, if you want to stay on the Strip, you should be able to find a room in a lesser casino for around $50 during the week and $80 on the weekend. Those figures rise to something like $80 and $130 for one of the more glamorous places like *Caesars Palace* or *New York–New York*, while you probably won't get to experience the luxury of *Bellagio* or the *Venetian* for less than $150. Downtown, it would be unusual to have to pay over $50 for a decent room – although a few places, like the *Golden Nugget*, will charge more than that on weekends – and budget hotels like *El Cortez* come much cheaper than that.

Very few conventional motels now survive either on the Strip or downtown, though plenty are scattered elsewhere in the city. Their rates are no lower than the typical casinos, however, so it's hard to see why anyone would choose to stay in them. For that reason, the reviews below concentrate on accommodation at all of the major Strip and downtown casinos – each of which you'll find described in

Price codes

All the accommodation prices quoted in this chapter are for the "rack rates" for a standard double room, and do not include **taxes** – levied at nine percent on the Strip and ten percent downtown. These rates can only serve as a general indication; in practice, the precise rate charged fluctuates daily, according to demand, and it's often possible to negotiate a discount.

① up to $30	② $30–45	③ $45–60
④ $60–80	⑤ $80–100	⑥ $100–130
⑦ $130–175	⑧ $175–250	⑨ $250+

more detail in the "Guide" chapters of this book – with just a few exceptional properties elsewhere.

Finally, it's worth mentioning that there *are* still large casinos in Nevada that offer $20 room bargains, they're just not in Las Vegas. Instead they're located close to the state line on each of the major approaches to the city – at **Primm** forty miles southwest, just in from California; at **Mesquite**, eighty miles northeast near Utah; and at **Laughlin**, a hundred miles southeast, across the Colorado River from Arizona.

THE STRIP

Bally's Las Vegas

Map 2, C3. 3645 Las Vegas Blvd S, Las Vegas NV 89109. ℂ702/739-4111 or 1-800/634-3434, fax 739-4405. *ballyslv.com*. *Bally's* is the rebuilt, renamed version of the old *MGM Grand*, formerly the world's largest hotel. Now overshadowed by *Bellagio*, across the Strip, and by *Paris* next door – which, like *Caesars Palace* and the *Flamingo* is owned by Park Place, who also own *Bally's* – it makes a very central place to stay, but not a particularly glamorous or exciting one. The rooms are large – each has a sofa – but they're not cheap, and most of the guests are conventioneers rather than tourists. Sun–Thurs ⑤, Fri & Sat ⑥.

The Barbary Coast Hotel & Casino

Map 2, C2. 3595 Las Vegas Blvd S, Las Vegas NV 89109. ✆702/737-7111 or 1-800/634-6755, fax 737-6304. *barbarycoastcasino.com*. The smallest of the Strip casinos is a real throwback, offering a mere two hundred chintzy guest rooms decked out to recall the San Francisco of a century ago. It's all quite cozy, and heavily oversubscribed, but not especially good value. Sun–Thurs ③, Fri & Sat ⑤.

Bellagio Resort & Casino

Map 2, B3. 3600 Las Vegas Blvd S, Las Vegas NV 89109. ✆702/791-7111 or 1-888/987-6667, fax 792-7646. *bellagiolasvegas.com*. *Bellagio* represents the very top end of the Vegas spectrum. Rooms are extremely luxurious, with plush European furnishings and marble bathrooms; the pool complex is amazing; and the restaurants are the best in town. By world standards, it's excellent value, but you can live the high life in other Vegas casinos – less tasteful perhaps, but much more fun – for half the price. Sun–Thurs ⑦, Fri & Sat ⑧.

Caesars Palace

Map 2, B2. 3570 Las Vegas Blvd S, Las Vegas NV 89109. ✆702/731-7222 or 1-800/634-6661, fax 731-6636. *caesars.com*. Despite being the epitome of Las Vegas luxury since the 1960s, in terms of room numbers *Caesars Palace* has only recently begun to match its neighbors. The older rooms still burst with pseudo-Roman splendor, while those in the newer Tower are more conventionally elegant. Standard rates aren't low, but they're very reasonable, and paying as little as $10 extra can get you a suite with a four-poster bed and mirrored ceiling. With

THE STRIP

its top-class shops, attractions and restaurants, *Caesars* ranks among the best bets in town. Sun–Thurs ⑤, Fri & Sat ⑥.

Circus Circus Hotel/Casino

Map 3, E6. 2880 Las Vegas Blvd S, Las Vegas NV 89109. ©702/734-0410 or 1-800/444-2472, fax 734-5987. *circuscircus-lasvegas.com*.

Only *Excalibur* – run by the same owners – matches *Circus Circus* for its family appeal and ambience, and both are similarly popular with budget tour groups. Kids love the theme park and (almost) nonstop circus acts, adults love the low room rates. Being able to park outside your door in the motel-like Manor section at the back is a real plus, but the rooms themselves are pretty grim; it's worth paying a little more to stay in the Tower section. Sun–Thurs ③, Fri & Sat ④.

> **Remember that the Strip hotel rates shown here are subject to an additional room tax of nine percent.**

The Desert Inn Resort

Map 3, E8. 3145 Las Vegas Blvd S, Las Vegas NV 89109. ©702/733-4444 or 1-800/634-6906, fax 733-4676.

This long-standing and very classy resort boasts the Strip's most impressive lobby, plus its own golf course, tennis courts and spa. Despite stunning renovations, however, it's had difficulties competing with the high-profile newcomers. The rooms are superb, and the bathrooms ultra-grand, but Sun International, who acquired the property in May 1999, may well make drastic changes in the near future. ⑧.

Excalibur Hotel & Casino

Map 2, B6. 3850 Las Vegas Blvd S, Las Vegas NV 89109. ©702/597-7700 or 1-800/937-7777, fax 597-7040. *excalibur-casino.com*.

This fantastically garish fake castle offers plenty to amuse the

Strip favorites

The top three Strip casinos in each category below are ranked in a completely subjective order of preference.

Best for Families
1. Treasure Island
2. Circus Circus
3. Excalibur

Best for Business Travelers
1. The Venetian
2. Desert Inn
3. Monte Carlo

Best for Gamblers
1. The Mirage
2. Imperial Palace
3. Monte Carlo

Best Pool
1. Mandalay Bay
2. Monte Carlo
3. Tropicana

Best Restaurants
1. Bellagio
2. Caesars Palace
3. MGM Grand

Best Themed Attractions
1. Caesars Palace
2. New York–New York
3. Luxor

Most Luxurious Rooms
1. Bellagio
2. The Venetian
3. Desert Inn

Best Shopping
1. Caesars Palace
2. The Venetian
3. Luxor

Best Overall Choice
1. New York–New York
2. Luxor
3. Caesars Palace

kids while the adults gamble away their college funds, but its four thousand rooms are pretty poor in quality, and only minimally themed. Few have views to speak of – many face in rather than out – and they have showers not baths. Thanks to an endless stream of tour groups and families, the whole place tends to be uncomfortably crowded; expect long lines at the restaurants. Sun–Thurs ③, Fri & Sat ④.

The Flamingo Hilton

Map 2, C2. 3555 Las Vegas Blvd S, Las Vegas NV 89109. ©702/733-3111 or 1-800/732-2111, fax 733-3353. *www.hilton.com*. The latest round of renovations has put Bugsy Siegel's *Flamingo* back in the premier league of Vegas casinos, with over 3600 well-appointed rooms and a great tropical-themed pool. Sun–Thurs ④, Fri & Sat ⑥.

Four Seasons Hotel Las Vegas

Map 2, B8. 3960 Las Vegas Blvd S, Las Vegas NV 89119. ©702/632-5000 or 1-877/632-5200, fax 632-5222. *fourseasons.com*. This first Las Vegas venture of the very upmarket *Four Seasons* hotel chain exists in a strange symbiotic relationship with the *Mandalay Bay*. Although it seems like an entirely separate building, entered via its own driveway from the Strip, that section only houses its lobby and its one formal restaurant; the five hundred extravagantly opulent guest rooms are in fact on the 35th to 39th floors of the *Mandalay Bay*. Its unique selling point is as a luxurious refuge from the noise and pace of the Strip; you can come and go without ever seeing a slot machine, let alone having to contend with the usual crowds. There's also a gorgeous pool. Sun–Thurs ⑧, Fri & Sat ⑨.

Harrah's Las Vegas

Map 2, C1. 3475 Las Vegas Blvd S, Las Vegas NV 89109. ©702/369-5000 or 1-800/427-7247, fax 369-6014. *harrahs.lv.com*. The addition of a new 35-story tower to this former *Holiday Inn*, facing *Caesars Palace*, means that it now offers a total of 2700 bright, big but somewhat anonymous and not notably cheap rooms. Sun–Thurs ④, Fri & Sat ⑤.

The Imperial Palace Hotel & Casino

Map 2, C2. 3535 Las Vegas Blvd S, Las Vegas NV 89109. ✆702/731-3311 or 1-800/634-6441, fax 735-8578. *imperial-palace.com*.
Behind its hideous facade, the *Imperial Palace* is one of the best-value options in the heart of the Strip. Its standard rooms are adequate if not exciting – all have balconies – while the irresistibly bizarre "luv tub" suites, at about $30 extra, offer huge beds, even bigger sunken baths, and mirrors absolutely everywhere you can imagine. Sun–Thurs ②, Fri & Sat ④.

La Concha

Map 3, E7. 2955 Las Vegas Blvd S, Las Vegas NV 89109. ✆702/735-1255, fax 369-0862.
One of the very few characterful old motels left on the Strip, this quintessential space-age edifice forms part of a little mall opposite the *Stardust*. Behind its vaguely Moorish arched entrance, it holds more than three hundred very ordinary rooms and a couple of swimming pools. What you lose in glamour and comfort you gain in convenience. Sun–Thurs ②, Fri & Sat ③.

Luxor Las Vegas

Map 2, B7. 3900 Las Vegas Blvd S, Las Vegas NV 89119. ✆702/262-4000 or 1-800/288-1000, fax 262-4406.
Spending a night or two in this vast smoked-glass pyramid is one of the great Las Vegas experiences; any longer than that, and you may well be sick of the endless trek to reach your room from the "inclinators." All the two thousand rooms in the pyramid itself face outwards, with tremendous views, and they're much larger than usual – partly to minimize the effect of the slanting windows, partly because there's space for them to stretch into the hollow interior. Unlike the additional two thousand rooms in the new tower next door, however – some of which have Jacuzzis next to the windows – most pyramid rooms have showers not baths. All are enjoyably Egyptian-themed. Sun–Thurs ③, Fri & Sat ⑥.

THE STRIP

Mandalay Bay Resort & Casino

Map 2, B8. 3950 Las Vegas Blvd S, Las Vegas NV 89119. ©702/632-7777 or 1-877/632-7000, fax 632-7190. *mandalaybay.com*.
Mandalay Resort Group's most upscale property, a kind of young-adult playground that takes on and beats the *Hard Rock Cafe* at its own game, but can feel a little far removed from the bustle of the central Strip. Each of its luxurious rooms has both bath and walk-in shower; the theming varies, and the floor plans can be a bit odd, but some have great Strip views. Guests have exclusive access to the spectacular wave pool. Sun–Thurs ⑥, Fri & Sat ⑦.

The MGM Grand Hotel/Casino

Map 2, C5. 3799 Las Vegas Blvd S, Las Vegas NV 89109. ©702/891-7777 or 1-800/929-1112, fax 891-1000. *mgmgrand.com*.
The downsides of staying at the world's largest hotel, with 5005 rooms and more on the way, are that waiting for any kind of service, especially check-in, can be horrendous, and that walking from one end of the place to the other can take half an hour. There are plenty of positives, however, including the standard of accommodation you get for the price, and the presence of several of Las Vegas's finest restaurants. Guest rooms come in four themes – *Oz*, *Gone With The Wind*, *Casablanca*, or generic Hollywood – and all have marble bathrooms. Sun–Thurs ④, Fri & Sat ⑤.

The Mirage

Map 2, B1. 3400 Las Vegas Blvd S, Las Vegas NV 89109. ©702/791-7111 or 1-800/627-6667, fax 791-7446. *themirage.com*.
The very glitzy *Mirage* is not the market leader it was ten years ago, and its generally smallish rooms seem less distinctive than ever now they've lost their tropical theming. Even so, the public areas downstairs remain impressive, and the weekday rates for staying in one of Las Vegas's most prestigious addresses aren't at all bad – plus, of course, you get to watch

the volcano from your bedroom window. Sun–Thurs ⑤, Fri & Sat ⑦.

The Monte Carlo Resort & Casino

Map 2, B5. 3770 Las Vegas Blvd S, Las Vegas NV 89109. ℂ702/730-7000 or 1-800/311-8999, fax 730-7250. *monte-carlo.com*.
With over three thousand rooms, the *Monte Carlo* is one of the Strip's largest properties, but it maintains a low profile, cultivating a sedate, sophisticated image that attracts affluent older visitors rather than families. The location is great, with a tram connection to *Bellagio* to the north and *New York–New York* all but next door to the south, while the huge pool area, complete with wave pool, is a boon in summer. Sun–Thurs ④, Fri & Sat ⑥.

The New Frontier Hotel & Gambling Hall

Map 3, D8. 3120 Las Vegas Blvd S, Las Vegas NV 89109. ℂ702/794-8200 or 1-800/421-7806, fax 794-8401. *frontierlv.com*.
The Strip's oldest resort has been refurbished many times, and behind its rather tacky casino the hotel itself is spiffier than you might expect. The two-room suites in the new Atrium Tower could even be called tasteful. Sun–Thurs ④, Fri & Sat ⑤.

New York–New York Hotel & Casino

Map 2, B5. 3790 Las Vegas Blvd S, Las Vegas NV 89109. ℂ702/740-6969 or 1-800/NYFORME, fax 740-6920. *nynyhotelcasino.com*.
Sheer attention to detail makes *New York–New York* the most exuberantly enjoyable casino on the Strip. It's also small enough that guests don't have to spend half their visit shuffling down endless corridors. Although the elevators leave from lobbies designed to resemble specific Manhattan skyscrapers, sadly these don't correspond with the external facade, and all the rooms are substantially similar; however, they're very nice, if a bit small, and filled with Art Deco furnishings and flourishes. Sun–Thurs ⑤, Fri & Sat ⑦.

THE STRIP

Paris–Las Vegas Casino-Resort

Map 2, C3. 3645 Las Vegas Blvd S, Las Vegas NV 89109.
℡702/967-4611 or 1-888/BONJOUR, fax 967-4288.
The rooms and services at the flamboyant *Paris* casino, which
opened in the fall of 1999, don't attempt to match every luxury
of Las Vegas's most upscale joints, but for location, views and
ambience, *Paris* more than holds its own. Sun–Thurs ⑦, Fri &
Sat ⑧.

The Riviera Hotel & Casino

Map 3, F6. 2901 Las Vegas Blvd S, Las Vegas NV 89109. ℡702/734-
5110 or 1-800/634-6753, fax 794-9663. *www.theriviera.com*.
Nothing about the longstanding *Riviera* casino makes it worth
paying the comparatively inflated rates to stay in one of its two
thousand-plus very ordinary rooms. If you do, the newer
Monaco Tower is marginally preferable to the older main
building. Sun–Thurs ④, Fri & Sat ⑤.

The Sahara Hotel & Casino

Map 3, G5. 2535 Las Vegas Blvd S, Las Vegas NV 89109.
℡702/737-2111 or 1-888/696-2121, fax 735-5921.
The *Sahara*'s garish Moroccan-themed rooms are in the finest
Vegas tradition, and are quite reasonably priced, though the
property itself is a bit of a trek from the best parts of the Strip.
Although it's right next to the Wet'n'Wild water park (see
p.72) – don't mistake that for its own small and rather exposed
pool – it caters more for older or business travelers rather than
for families with children. Sun–Thurs ③, Fri & Sat ④.

The Stardust Hotel & Casino

Map 3, D7. 3000 Las Vegas Blvd S, Las Vegas NV 89119.
℡702/732-6111 or 1-800/634-6757, fax 732-6296. *stardustlv.com*.
This Vegas veteran has seen better days, but the rooms in its
new purple-tinted tower are attractive enough, though they do
loom intimidatingly close to its tiny pool. Its older Motor Inn

section offers cheaper rates for a much lower standard of accommodation, but was scheduled for closure as this book went to press. Sun–Thurs ②, Fri & Sat ③.

The Stratosphere Hotel & Casino

Map 3, G3. 2000 Las Vegas Blvd S, Las Vegas NV 89104; ©702/380-7777 or 1-800/99-TOWER, fax 383-4755.

The *Stratosphere* has confounded the skeptics by surviving at all, despite its very unfashionable location at the far north end of the Strip, thanks largely to low room rates and a steady flow of budget tour groups. Its rooms are large but not fancy in any way, and only have small windows. None of the accommodation is in the hundred-story tower, so don't expect amazing views, but otherwise it's not a bad deal, and more likely than most to have last-minute availability. Sun–Thurs ②, Fri & Sat ④.

Tam O Shanter Motel

Map 3, D9. 3317 Las Vegas Blvd S, Las Vegas NV 89109. ©702/735-7331 or 1-800/727-3423, fax 735-2372.

Small motel, next door to the *Venetian*, which completely lacks the glamour and facilities of its mighty neighbors, but has a friendly staff and tolerable rooms. Sun–Thurs ②, Fri & Sat ④.

Treasure Island

Map 3, C9. 3300 Las Vegas Blvd S, Las Vegas NV 89109. ©702/894-7111 or 1-800/944-7444, fax 894-7414. *treasureisland.com*.

This sister hotel to the neighboring *Mirage* is geared toward young, affluent parents with their kids in tow; the theming of the building as a whole is quite fun, but the (smallish) rooms are quite subdued in a pastel-toned sort of way. Stay on the Strip side for a great view of the pirate battle, even though the balconies are just for show. Sun–Thurs ④, Fri & Sat ⑦.

THE STRIP

....

Remember that the Strip hotel rates shown here are subject to an additional room tax of nine percent.

....

The Tropicana Resort & Casino

Map 2, C6. 3801 Las Vegas Blvd S, Las Vegas NV 89109.
℃702/739-2222 or 1-800/634-4000, fax 739-2469.
Spruced up to match its giant neighbors, the *Tropicana* is an appealingly colorful flower-filled oasis, with a choice of three types of room decor: French in the Paradise Tower, tropical in the Island Tower, or cramped but cheap in the old motel section at the back. It still boasts the world's largest indoor-outdoor swimming pool, complete with swim-up gaming tables. Sun–Thurs ④, Fri & Sat ⑥.

Vagabond Inn

Map 3, E9. 3265 Las Vegas Blvd S, Las Vegas NV 89109.
℃702/735-5102 or 1-800/522-0155, fax 735-0168.
Presentable, neat little motel, surprisingly well geared for business travelers, across from *Treasure Island* and next door to the similar *Tam O Shanter* (see p.141), which offers an outdoor pool, an airport shuttle service, and no slot machines. ③.

The Venetian

Map 2, C1. 3355 Las Vegas Blvd S, Las Vegas NV 89109.
℃702/414-1000 or 1-888/283-6423, fax 733-5560. *venetian.com*.
Even the standard rooms at this upscale behemoth are split-level suites, offering gorgeously comfortable antique-style canopied beds on a raised platform, plus roomy living rooms equipped with fax machines-cum-printers. Each also has a marble bath and walk-in shower, and is located within reasonable walking distance of the hotel shops and restaurants. Sun–Thurs ⑦, Fri & Sat ⑧.

DOWNTOWN

Binion's Horseshoe Hotel & Casino

Map 4, F2. 128 E Fremont St, Las Vegas NV 89101. ℂ702/382-1600 or 1-800/237-6537, fax 382-5750.
The hard-bitten gambler's hangout of choice offers a handful of no-frills rooms in the main building, and a couple of hundred marginally more appealing ones in what used to be the *Mint* next door. Sun–Thurs ③, Fri & Sat ④.

California Hotel & Casino

Map 4, F2. 12 Ogden Ave at First St, Las Vegas NV 89101. ℂ702/385-1222 or 1-800/634-6255, fax 388-4463. Shared booking line with *Main Street Station* and *Fremont Hotel*: ℂ1-800/465-0711. *thecal.com*.
Most of the guests in this mid-range downtown casino are Hawaiian, and Hawaiian food and drink dominate the bars and restaurants. The actual rooms are plain but adequate. Sun–Thurs ③, Fri & Sat ④.

El Cortez Hotel & Casino

Map 4, G3. 600 E Fremont St, Las Vegas NV 89102. ℂ702/385-5200 or 1-800/634-6703, fax 385-1554.
Veteran downtown casino, a couple of blocks east of the Fremont Street Experience, where the cut-price rooms in the main building are a little better than the rather dismal gaming area downstairs might suggest, the mini-suites in the new tower are really good value at $40, and the bargain-basement accommodation in *Ogden House* across the street costs just $18. ①.

Fitzgeralds Holiday Inn Casino

Map 4, F3. 301 E Fremont St, Las Vegas NV 89101. ℂ702/388-2400 or 1-800/274-5825, fax 388-2230. *fitzgeralds.com/lasvegas*.
Very central downtown hotel where the guest rooms, thankful-

ly, feature standard-issue *Holiday Inn* decor rather than the endless cod-Irish codswallop of the casino downstairs. Most offer good views of either the Fremont Street Experience or the surrounding desert. Sun–Thurs ②, Fri & Sat ④.

Four Queens Hotel & Casino

Map 4, F3. 202 E Fremont St, Las Vegas NV 89101. ℂ702/385-4011 or 1-800/634-6045, fax 387-5123. *savenet.com/4queen.htm*.
Glittery old-style casino, popular with Vegas veterans, which offers two towers of reasonably tasteful rooms but little by way of diversions. Sun–Thurs ②, Fri & Sat ③.

Golden Gate Hotel and Casino

Map 4, E2. 1 E Fremont St, Las Vegas NV 89101. ℂ702/385-1906 or 1-800/426-1906.
Founded in 1906, when Las Vegas itself was just a year old, the *Golden Gate* is the oldest joint in town. With a hundred retro-furnished rooms, it's tiny by Vegas standards, and if nothing else slightly lower-key than its Fremont Street neighbors. Sun–Thurs ②, Fri & Sat ③.

> **The downtown hotel rates shown here are subject to an additional room tax of ten percent.**

The Golden Nugget Hotel & Casino

Map 4, F3. 129 E Fremont St, Las Vegas NV 89101. ℂ702/385-7111 or 1-800/634-3454, fax 386-8362. *goldennugget.com*.
The *Golden Nugget* was Steve Wynn's first major Vegas venture, and despite having gone on to better things with the *Mirage* and *Bellagio* he's still at the helm. The first downtown casino to go for the luxury end of the market is undeniably glittery, and the rooms are certainly opulent, but there are no attractions to speak of, the restaurants are nothing special, and it all feels a bit pointless. Sun–Thurs ③, Fri & Sat ⑥.

Jackie Gaughan's Plaza Hotel & Casino

Map 4, E2. 1 Main St, Las Vegas NV 89101. ℂ702/386-2110 or 1-800/634-6575, fax 382-8281.

The *Plaza* occupies one of Las Vegas's most historic locations, incorporating not only the spot where the first city lots were auctioned in 1905 but also the site of the former Amtrak station, but in itself it's a depressingly rundown low-rent kind of a place, even if the thousand-plus guest rooms have been refurbished to a surprisingly high standard. Sun–Thurs ②, Fri & Sat ③.

Las Vegas Backpackers Hostel

1322 E Fremont St, Las Vegas NV 89101. ℂ702/385-1150 or 1-800/550-8958, fax 385-4940. *hostels.com/lvbackpackers*.
Well-kept private hostel in a grim neighborhood ten blocks east of downtown, offering dorm beds for $15 and private double rooms for $45, plus use of a good pool. ①/③.

Las Vegas International Hostel

1208 Las Vegas Blvd S, Las Vegas NV 89104. ℂ702/385-9955.
This bare-bones AAIH hostel is located in a small, dilapidated former motel, in an insalubrious area on the fringes of downtown not far north of the *Stratosphere*. Dorm beds cost $14, rooms with shared bath under $30, which for two or more visitors is little cheaper than some Strip and several downtown hotels. Nonetheless, demand is heavy, especially in summer. Non-drivers won't enjoy walking in the immediate neighborhood, but the staff also arranges tours to state and national parks. ①.

Main Street Station

Map 4, E1. 200 N Main St at Ogden, Las Vegas NV 89101. ℂ702/387-1896 or 1-800/713-8933. Shared booking line with *Fremont Hotel* and *California Hotel*: ℂ1-800/465-0711. *mainstreetcasino.com*.
Downtown's best-value option, two short blocks from Fremont

DOWNTOWN

Street, holds four hundred large guest rooms plus a brew pub and an assortment of good restaurants. ③.

Sam Boyd's Fremont Hotel & Casino

Map 4, F2. 200 E Fremont St, Las Vegas NV 89101. ✆702/385-3232 or 1-800/634-6182, fax 386-4463. Shared booking line with *Main Street Station* and *California Hotel*: ✆1-800/465-0711. *fremontcasino.com*.

Medium-sized casino in the heart of the Fremont Street Experience, where the spacious rooms have been refurbished to a high if characterless level of comfort, and downtown's finest restaurant, the *Second Street Grill* (see p.174), is just downstairs. Sun–Thurs ②, Fri & Sat ④.

WEST OF THE STRIP

Gold Coast Hotel & Casino

Map 1, C5. 4000 W Flamingo Rd, Las Vegas NV 89103. ✆702/367-7111 or 1-888/402-6278, fax 367-8575. *goldcoastcasino.com*.
Old-fashioned, run-of-the-mill casino whose Western theme appeals most to older American travelers. The main selling point – unstated, of course – is that the much more upscale *Rio*, with all its restaurants and other facilities, is right next door. Free shuttle buses connect the *Gold Coast* to its sister property on the Strip, the *Barbary Coast*. Sun–Thurs ③, Fri & Sat ④.

The Orleans Hotel & Casino

Map 1, C5. 4500 W Tropicana Ave, Las Vegas NV 89103. ✆702/365-7111 or 1-800/675-3267, fax 365-7499. *orleanscasino.com*.
The *Orleans* is not a particularly exciting property, and it's almost a mile off the Strip (too far to walk, but free buses run to the *Barbary Coast*). However, the rates are not bad for such well-equipped rooms – many are L-shaped, with inglenook

seating by the windows – and the on-site bowling lanes and movie theaters are pluses. Sun–Thurs ③, Fri & Sat ⑤.

Rio Suite Hotel & Casino

Map 2, A2. 3700 W Flamingo Rd, Las Vegas NV 89103. ℂ702/252-7777 or 1-800/PLAY-RIO, fax 253-6090. *playrio.com*.

Rated as the world's top-value hotel by *Travel and Leisure* magazine in 1998, the *Rio* is the only Vegas casino not on the Strip or downtown that seriously attempts to rival the Strip giants, and it does a good job of it. The restaurants, bars and buffets are all excellent, the general theming isn't bad, and the rooms are large and luxurious, with floor-to-ceiling windows and great views – though most are not really suites, they just have sofas in one corner. However, the prices are not cheap, and whatever the *Rio* likes to pretend, the Strip stands half a mile away, along a highway no one would ever dream of walking. Sun–Thurs ⑤, Fri & Sat ⑦.

Texas Station

Map 1, C3. 2101 Texas Star Lane, Las Vegas NV 89030. ℂ702/631-1000 or 1-800/654-8888, fax 631-8120. *stationcasinos.com*.

Texas Station, a couple of miles northwest of downtown where North Rancho meets Lake Mead Blvd, is primarily a gambling joint for locals, but it's all very bright and friendly, with good restaurants and a movie theater, so staying in one of its two hundred guest rooms is not a bad idea. Mon–Thurs ③, Fri & Sat ⑤, Sun ④.

EAST OF THE STRIP

Hard Rock Hotel & Casino

Map 2, G4. 4475 Paradise Rd, Las Vegas NV 89109. ℂ702/693-5000 or 1-800/693-ROCK, fax 693-5010. *hardrockhotel.com*.

The *Hard Rock* name has such a high profile worldwide that if you didn't know Las Vegas you might assume that "the world's only rock'n'roll casino" is the best in town; it isn't. Over a mile east of the Strip, it is on the whole a pale and overpriced imitation of Las Vegas's showcase giants. That said, the guest rooms are well above average, with French windows that actually open, and the pool is great. Sun–Thurs ⑤, Fri & Sat ⑦.

Las Vegas Hilton Hotel & Casino

Map 3, G7. 3000 Paradise Rd, Las Vegas NV 89109. ℂ702/732-5111 or 1-800/732-7117, fax 794-3611. lv-hilton.com.

The *Hilton* is only a short way off the Strip, and its three-thousand-plus rooms and suites are as plush as all but the most expensive of its rivals, but it's a rather sedate property that's monopolized by conventioneers, where fun-seeking visitors are likely to feel that they're missing out on the party. Sun–Thurs ⑤, Fri & Sat ⑥.

Motel 6 – Tropicana

Map 2, F5. 195 E Tropicana Ave, Las Vegas NV 89109. ℂ702/798-0728, fax 798-5657.

Despite its 880 rooms, the largest *Motel 6* in the country is much the same as the rest – a low-rise straggle of very routine lodgings. The location is good, just ten minutes' walk off the Strip from the *MGM Grand*, and may well mean that it gets re-developed shortly. Sun–Thurs ②, Fri & Sat ③.

Sam's Town Hotel & Gambling Hall

Map 1, F5. 5111 Boulder Hwy, Las Vegas NV 89122. ℂ702/456-7777 or 1-800/634-6371, fax 454-8014.

This Wild West casino, over six miles east of the Strip, has made a determined and largely successful effort to upgrade its image, but remains primarily popular with older visitors. The registration desk is in its large central atrium, overlooked on all sides by 650 "Western themed" guest rooms that aren't nearly as garish as that might sound. Sun–Thurs ③, Fri & Sat ④.

Sunset Station

Map 1, F6. 1301 W Sunset Rd, Henderson NV 89014. ©702/547-7777 or 1-800/6STATIONS, fax 547-7606. *stationcasinos.com*.
From its Spanish-mission facade to its spacious, well-designed interior, *Sunset Station*, opposite Henderson's huge Galleria Mall, is the best of the Stations chain. The rooms and pool are good, and you're well poised for an early-morning getaway to Arizona, but really it's too far southeast of the Strip to recommend whole-heartedly. Mon–Thurs ③, Fri & Sat ⑤, Sun ④.

Super 8

Map 3, E3. 4250 Koval Lane, Las Vegas NV 89109. ©702/794-0888 or 1-800/800-8000, fax 794-3504.
The closest of Vegas's three *Super 8*s to the Strip offers three hundred rooms, a pool, its own little casino and a reasonable restaurant. Sun–Thurs ②, Fri & Sat ③.

EAST OF THE STRIP

Eating

Barely ten years ago, the **restaurant** scene in Las Vegas was governed by the notion that visitors were not prepared to pay for gourmet food. All the casinos laid on both pile-'em-high buffets at knock-down prices, and 24-hour coffeeshops offering bargain steak-and-egg deals, but virtually the only quality restaurants in town were upscale Italian places well away from the Strip. The theory was that the longer tourists spent lingering over their meals, the less time they had left to play the tables.

Now, however, the situation has reversed, as the major casinos compete to attract culinary superstars from all over the country to open Vegas outlets. The first such venture was Wolfgang Puck's *Spago* in *Caesars Palace*, back in 1992; these days, as each new casino opens, it's taken for granted that it will have as many as ten world-class restaurants. Asked what had persuaded him to relocate to Las Vegas, one leading chef replied "three million dollars." Many tourists now visit the city specifically to eat at several of the best restaurants in the United States, without having to reserve a table months in advance or pay sky-high prices. Which is not to say that fine dining comes cheap in Las Vegas, just that most of the big-name restaurants are less expensive, and less snooty, than they are in their home cities.

Another break with tradition is that these days the accountants require each sector of a casino-resort to be financially solvent. Where once it was considered worth running the restaurants and showrooms at a loss because they lured in gamblers, they now have to be self-supporting. Thus prices are not quite what they were, but on the whole Las Vegas is still great value. Buffets may be $6 rather than $3, or a breakfast special $3 not $1.99 – which still beats anywhere else in the country.

The restaurants reviewed in this chapter form only a small proportion of the total. If you're staying on the Strip in particular, the choice is overwhelming, and you'll almost certainly find a good restaurant to suit your tastes and budget in your own hotel. In terms of price or quality, let alone convenience, there are few reasons to venture off into the rest of the city; good places do exist away from the Strip and downtown, but the best are right where the tourists are. The one exception to that rule is that certain cuisines have as yet been unable to get a foothold on the Strip; if you want Indian, Thai, or healthy Greek food, for example, you'll have to drive out and find it.

BUFFETS

Almost every casino in Las Vegas has an all-you-can-eat **buffet**, open to guests and non-guests alike for every meal of the week. Even at the worst you're bound to find something you can keep down, and the cost is low enough that in any case you won't feel ripped off. At its best, the traditional buffet experience is in terms of both decor and flavor like being granted unrestricted access to the food court in an upmarket mall; you'll get top-quality fast food, but not a gourmet feast.

It's no coincidence that the better buffets tend to be in casinos that are **neither on the Strip nor downtown**, and depend on locals as well as tourists. At places like the *Rio* and casinos in the Stations chain, the buffet still serves the fundamental purpose of enticing in customers from elsewhere. Thus they've been at the forefront of innovations like having separate named areas serving different cuisines, or offering "action cooking," where your stir-fry, omelet, *fajita* or whatever is cooked to your specific order. By contrast, the buffets at the very largest casinos only have to be good enough to ensure that the crowds already in the building don't leave, while also coping with a daily deluge of customers. That explains the poor quality of the buffets at *Excalibur* and the *MGM Grand*, for example.

As for which is the **best of all**, there's no longer any question. *The Buffet* at *Bellagio* represents a quantum leap in standards, in serving food that would be considered excellent in any conventional restaurant. With dinner priced at $20, however, it has also dispensed with the idea that buffets are supposed to be cheap. *Paris* soon followed in its wake, unveiling a less varied but equally delectable and expensive spread. The best old-style bargains are the *Feast Around The World* buffets at *Sunset Station* and *Texas Station*.

As a rule, buffet prices include unlimited refills on beverages and sodas, but you have to pay extra for any alcoholic drinks. You'll also have to pay tax, plus a conventional $1 tip per person. If possible, try to avoid eating between 6pm and 9pm, when the lines at the larger casinos can be endless. Arriving early for breakfast (before 8am) and late for lunch (around 2pm or so) can also save some time otherwise spent on line.

BUFFETS ON THE STRIP

Bally's Big Kitchen Buffet
Map 2, C3. *Bally's*, 3645 Las Vegas Blvd S ☏702/739-4111.
Daily 7–11am $9, 11am–2.30pm $10, 4–10pm $14.

Among the best of the old-style buffets, reached by making a sharp right as soon as you enter *Bally's* from the Strip. A classy spread of fresh meats and seafood – including shrimp at lunchtime – plus a wide-ranging salad bar. Other than a few Chinese dinner entrees, however, it's all rather homogeneous. The *Big Kitchen* is not to be confused with *Bally's Champagne Sterling Brunch*, served in a separate room on Sundays (9.30am–2.30pm), where the roast meats, and fish from baked salmon to sashimi, are magnificent – as indeed they should be, for $50.

Bayside Buffet
Map 2, B8. *Mandalay Bay*, 3950 Las Vegas Blvd S ℃702/632-7777. Mon–Sat 7–10.45am $8.50, 11am–2.45pm $9.50, 3–10pm $13.50; Sun 7am–10pm $14.50.

Mandalay Bay's buffet has a much nicer setting than most of its rivals, overlooking the resort's pool and open when weather permits to the breezes. The food choice is not all that amazing, though, with none of the usual "stations" devoted to specific cuisines. If you're happy with one or two good roast meats from the carvery, like turkey or beef, plus a few specialty items such as crab legs or paella, you'll be fine; the pre-cut deli sandwiches at lunchtime make a welcome change.

The Buffet
Map 2, B3. *Bellagio*, 3600 Las Vegas Blvd S ℃702/791-7111. Mon–Thurs 7–10.30am $10, 11am–3.30pm $12.50, 4–10pm $20; Fri 7–10.30am $10, 11am–3.30pm $12.50, 4–11pm $20; Sat 8am–4pm $18.50, 4.30–11pm $20; Sun 8am–4pm $18.50, 4.30–10pm $20.

Far and away Las Vegas's best buffet. With other buffets, you may rave about what good value they are; with this one, you'll rave about what good food it is. The high prices keep the crowds relatively thin and the lines are never too long. While the large dining area is not especially attractive, it offers spacious seating; there are even restrooms inside, an astounding innovation. At 800 items, all prepared fresh in small quantities, the sheer range of food is extraordinary. For breakfast, as well as bagels, pastries, and eggs, you can have salmon smoked or baked, fruit fresh or in salads, and omelettes cooked to order, with fillings such as crabmeat. Lunch offerings include sushi and sashimi, cold cuts, dim sum, roasted game hen and seared quail, plus fresh-baked focaccia, tasty fruit tarts, figs and grapes, and fancy desserts. Dinner is similar, but the stakes are raised again with the addition of entrees like lobster claws, fresh oysters, and venison.

Le Village Buffet

Map 2, C3. *Paris*, 3655 Las Vegas Blvd S ©967-7000. Mon–Thurs 7.30–11.30am $10, noon–5.30pm $13, 5.30–10.30pm $20; Fri & Sat 7.30–11.30am $10, noon–5.30pm $13, 5.30–11pm $20; Sun 7.30am–4pm $20, 4.30–10.30pm $20.

Eschewing the current vogue for incorporating every conceivable cuisine, *Paris*'s buffet opts instead for showcasing only French dishes, and does so extremely well. The seafood is superb, ranging from Dover sole and mussels to rich *bouillabaisse* stews; roast chicken comes fricasseed, as *coq au vin*, or with mustard; vegetables such as baby squash and pinto beans are super-fresh; and there's even a full French cheese board. The setting is a little cramped, with the tables squeezed almost like an afterthought into the central square – a very Disney-esque French village – but the food is *magnifique*.

The Mirage Buffet

Map 2, B1. *The Mirage*, 3400 Las Vegas Blvd S ©791-7111. Mon–Sat 7–10.45am $8.50, 11am–2.45pm $9.50, 3–9.30pm $14.50; Sun 8am–9.30pm $14.50.

You have to pick your way quite carefully through the buffet in this bright, pleasant dining room, decked out with mirrors and artificial flowers. The salads are very good, with lots of New-

York-style deli trimmings like gefilte fish, pickled herrings, and pastrami, and the freshly prepared meats at the carveries and stir-fry stations are also recommended. The precooked dishes, however, are generally dull and tasteless; the cheesy toppings and sauces smothered over the meat or fish to stop it drying out tend to congeal a bit too rapidly.

Roundtable Buffet

Map 2, B6. *Excalibur*, 3850 Las Vegas Blvd S ℗597-7777. Mon–Thurs 6.30–11am $6, 11am–4pm $7, 4–10pm $9; Fri & Sat 6.30–11am $6, 11am–11pm $9; Sun 6.30–11am $5, 11am–10pm $9.

Reviewed here because it's the city's largest and most popular option, capable of seating up to 1300 people at a time, the *Roundtable Buffet* is truly atrocious. It's the only one where the long lines outside shuffle straight to the serving counters, so you can't survey the field to see what's on offer. You're not seated until after you've filled your plate, and, crucially, you have to be seriously assertive to go back for second helpings. Not that you're likely to want to; the room is filled by the stench of overcooked synthetic meats stored in lukewarm water, and the very first item you come to is a basin of lurid green jello. With the exception of tamales and Kung Pao chicken, the food is very American. Watch out for the breakfast bagels, each of which is perhaps a quarter of the size of the smallest bagel you've ever seen in your life.

Stratosphere Buffet

Map 3, G3. *The Stratosphere*, 2000 Las Vegas Blvd S ℗380-7777. Mon–Thurs & Sat 7–11am $5.50, 11am–3pm $6.50, 4–10pm $9; Fri 7–11am $5.50, 11am–3pm $6.50, 4–10pm $11.25; Sun 11am–4pm $9, 4–10pm $11.25.

Like much else in the *Stratosphere*, the *Buffet* is rather half-hearted in its theming – half a dozen little hot air balloons – and its ambience – it's basically a passageway on the north side of the building – but it does offer pretty good value. The food is reasonable without being exceptional, and with Mexican, Chinese, and Italian sections as well as the predictable American, it should satisfy most appetites. Note that visiting the top of the Tower (see p.76) entitles you to a discount here.

DOWNTOWN BUFFETS

Garden Court Buffet
Map 4, E1. *Main Street Station*, 200 N Main St ℂ387-1896.
Mon & Wed 7–10.30am $5, 11am–3pm $7, 4–10pm $10; Tues & Thurs 7–10.30am $5, 11am–3pm $7, 4–10pm $11; Fri 7–10.30am $5, 11am–3pm $7, 4–10pm $14; Sat & Sun 7am–3pm $8, 4–10pm $10.
This spacious dining room features attractive brickwork and cast iron, and plenty of natural light by day. Everything is clean and spruce, but not all that exciting, despite dishes ranging from fried chicken and corn at "South to Southwest," to tortillas at "Olé," and pork chow mein and oyster tofu at "Pacific Rim." The salad selection is very weak, there's little fish except on specialty nights – Tuesday is T-bone, Thursday is steak and scampi, and Friday is seafood – and no fruit.

Golden Nugget Buffet
Map 4, F3. *The Golden Nugget*, 129 E Fremont St ℂ385-7111.
Mon–Sat 7–10.30am $5.75, 10.30am–3pm $7.50, 4–10pm $10.25; Sun 8am–10pm $11.
With its gold chandeliers and low mirrored ceiling, the *Golden Nugget's* buffet is presumably meant to look elegant; in fact it's small and claustrophobic. There's not much room for a kitchen either, so while the salad bar is excellent the choice of cooked food is limited. What there is, however – especially the carvery – isn't bad, and the casino-front location is a definite advantage.

Sam Boyd's Fremont Paradise Buffet
Map 3, F2. *Sam Boyd's Fremont Hotel*, 200 Fremont St ℂ385-3232.

Mon, Wed & Thurs 7–10.30am $5, 11am–3pm $6.50, 4–10pm $10;
Tues 7–10.30am $5, 11am–3pm $6.50, 4–10pm $15; Fri 7–10.30am
$5, 11am–3pm $6.50, 4–11pm $15; Sat 7–10.30am $5, 11am–3pm
$6.50, 4–11pm $10; Sun 7am–3pm $9, 4–10pm $15.

This tropical-themed buffet is a classic slice of old-style downtown Vegas glamour, all splashing water, glitter, and artificial
plants. As a rule, the food is dependably good, but much the
best time to come is for the pricier "Seafood Fantasy" on Tues,
Fri & Sun evenings, when the plates are piled high with crabs,
lobsters and raw oysters, plus scampi and steamed mussels.

BUFFETS ELSEWHERE IN THE CITY

Carnival World Buffet
Map 2, A2. *Rio*, 3700 W Flamingo Rd ©252-7777.
Mon–Fri 8–10.30am $8, 11am–3.30pm $10, 3.30–11pm $13; Sat
8.30am–11.30pm $13; Sun 8.30am–10.30pm $13.

Thanks to its location, the *Rio* is the only major casino that still uses
its buffet as a loss-leader, setting out to lure bargain-hunting tourists
away from the Strip. Even here the prices are not what they were,
but the value is excellent. The variety is immense, including Thai,
Chinese, Mexican and Japanese stations – the latter does good sushi
– as well as the usual pasta and barbecue options, and even a
fish'n'chip stand. Desserts too are great, with plenty of sugar-free
ones for all the good they'll do you. You can also buy a 46-oz margarita for $13, or two normal ones for $5. The only real drawback
is that the lines are invariably long. Note that the *Rio* also holds the
more expensive *Village Seafood Buffet*, offering self-explanatory and
highly recommended lunches and dinners for $25.

Feast Around The World
Map 1, F6. *Sunset Station*, 1301 W Sunset Rd ©547-7777.
Mon–Sat 8–11am $5, 11am–3.30pm $7, 3.30–10pm $10; Sun
8am–3.30pm $9, 3.30–10pm $10.

All four casinos in the Stations chain – *Sunset*, *Texas*, *Boulder*, and *Palace* – offer similarly appealing, good-value buffets, and attract large crowds of loyal locals. At the large, colorfully themed, *Feast Around The World*, in the very center of *Sunset Station* (and also in *Texas Station*), a wide range of international cuisines are dispensed by sections like "Mama Mia's" pizzas, "Chinatown," "Country Bar B Que," and "Viva Mexico."

French Market Buffet

Map 1, C5. *Orleans*, 4500 W Tropicana Ave ©365-7111.
Mon 7–10am $4, 11am–3pm $6.50, 4–10pm $14; Tues–Sat 7–10am $4, 11am–3pm $6.50, 4–10pm $9; Sun 8am–3pm $9, 4–10pm $9.
While not as strongly New Orleans-themed as you might expect, this pleasantly decorated buffet is among the best for old-fashioned Southern barbecued chicken and ribs, with a few spicier Cajun and Mexican specialties for variety. Monday night is seafood night.

The Great Buffet – Sam's Town

Map 1, F5. *Sam's Town*, 5111 Boulder Hwy ©456-7777.
Mon, Wed, Thurs & Sat 8–11am $4, 11am–3pm $7, 4–9pm $9; Tues & Fri 8–11am $4, 11am–3pm $7, 4–9pm $13; Sun 8am–3pm $8, 4–9pm $9.
Unassuming, inexpensive buffet, a few miles east of the Strip, where the food is consistently good if not exactly adventurous. Prices only exceed $9 for the $13 seafood extravaganza on Tuesdays and Fridays, when selections include steamed crab, raw and cooked oysters, shrimp, and Cajun fish dishes.

RESTAURANTS

RESTAURANTS ON THE STRIP

America

Map 2, B5. *New York–New York*, 3790 Las Vegas Blvd S ©740-6451.

Daily 24 hours.

Cavernous diner, tucked in behind the registration desk, which derives its knowing retro-chic feel from a vast 3-D "map" of the United States, measuring 30ft by 90ft, that curls down from the ceiling. The menu is staggeringly eclectic, but each item supposedly comes from some specific part of the country. Thus appetizers include California sushi rolls for $7, Cajun mini sticks for $4, and super nachos at $6, while the entrees range from Maryland crabcakes for $17, via New York pizzas ($7–9), down to peanut butter sandwiches from Plains, Georgia (home to Jimmy Carter), for $4. At any hour of day or night, there really is something for everyone, and it's all surprisingly good.

Aqua

Map 2, B3. *Bellagio*, 3600 Las Vegas Blvd S ℗693-7223.
Daily 5.30–11pm.

This offshoot of San Francisco's celebrated seafood restaurant has quickly established itself in Las Vegas's very highest echelon. Its tasteful, understated decor matches the exquisite delicacy of the cuisine. The standout appetizer is the $12 black mussel soufflé, while the miso-glazed Chilean sea bass with shellfish consommé, at $29, is typical of the entrees. Rather strangely, the only alternative to seafood is foie gras, ranging from a $20 appetizer up to an entire roast one for $80. If you can't bear to decide, there's a $70 tasting menu, with a vegetarian alternative at $55.

China Grill

Map 2, B8. *Mandalay Bay*, 3950 Las Vegas Blvd S ℗632-7404.
Mon–Thurs & Sun 5.30–11pm, Fri & Sat 5.30pm–midnight.

This very large, ultra-fashionable Asian restaurant claims to derive its concept from Marco Polo's thirteenth-century return to Europe from the Orient, though nowhere is it recorded that he brought back wasabi mashed potatoes or lobster pancakes. The main dining room is cone-shaped, with a $750,000 psy-

RESTAURANTS ON THE STRIP

159

chedelic light show projected on the ceiling. If you enjoy Eastern flavors, the food is delicious, with appetizers like a crackling calamari salad for $10 and tempura sashimi for $16, and entrees such as dry aged Szechuan beef with sake and soy for $27.50, or pan-seared tuna for $26. However, under a bizarre serving policy, the dishes arrive as they are made; your appetizers may appear before, after or simultaneously with your entrees, and your "accompaniments" can turn up long after you've finished both. If that doesn't suit you, you're made to feel very uncool indeed. In the much more minimal *Zen Sum*, behind a bead curtain and sharing a futuristic restroom area of stand-alone white booths, diners sit at a counter and pick plates of tasty dim sum from a conveyor belt.

Chinois

Map 2, B2. Forum Shops, *Caesars Palace*, 3570 Las Vegas Blvd S ℂ737-9700.

Cafe daily 11.30am–midnight, restaurant daily 6–10.30pm.

Wolfgang Puck's quintessentially postmodern Asian-fusion restaurant offers cafe-style terrace seating at the mall level, and a more formal dining room upstairs; whichever you choose, FAO Schwarz's Trojan horse watches your every move. The ambience is self-consciously minimal; there are no tablecloths, ornaments, or even condiments, and the young black-clad staff is too busy posing glamorously to provide attentive service. The food itself is upmarket, nouvelle-tinged Chinese. Appetizers at $7–10 include moo shu duck – a healthier version of Peking duck – while the best of the entrees, all priced under $20, is a delicious pepper-crusted red snapper in a mushroom-soy broth.

Coyote Cafe

Map 2, C5. The *MGM Grand*, 3799 Las Vegas Blvd S ℂ891-7349.

Cafe daily 7.30am–11pm, Grill Room daily 5.30–10pm.

When it opened in 1993, this outpost of Mark Miller's definitive "Modern Southwestern" restaurant, originally based in Santa Fe, helped to blaze the trail for gourmet cuisine in Las Vegas, and it remains among the city's best options. It's divided into two sections; the cheaper *Cafe*, open to the main casino walkway, offers good-value breakfasts and light lunches as well as much the same dinner menu as the quieter, more formal, *Mark Miller Grill Room* behind. Decked out in tasteful terracotta colors, the latter can be relied on for signature appetizers like plantain-crusted sea bass ($11), and slightly less adventurous entrees at $25–30, such as steak and beans or grilled ahi, adorned with corn and chili salsas.

Delmonico's Steakhouse

Map 2, C1. *The Venetian*, 3355 Las Vegas Blvd S ©414-3737. Daily 5.30–10.30pm.

Although Emeril Lagasse has given Las Vegas a classic New Orleans steakhouse, *Delmonico's* decor is "modern Tuscan," in deference to the *Venetian's* Italian roots. Only one of its many dining rooms, equipped with arched ceilings and a fireplace, is at all intimate or appealing; the rest are austere and minimal. The whole place reeks of money; a humble baked potato costs $6, while several wines hit the $3000 mark. Even the least likely items come swimming in butter – Emeril's not one to stint – but the meat at the core of the experience is excellent, with each large and very tender steak priced at $25–30. Other entrees include stuffed shrimp for $28, and whole chickens at an absurd $46 (designed to feed two), while among the predictable Cajun appetizers, there's a "*Venetian*-style" beef carpaccio for $10.

Dive!

Map 3, C9. Fashion Show Mall, 3200 Las Vegas Blvd S ©369-DIVE. Mon–Thurs & Sun 11am–10pm, Fri & Sat 11am–11pm.

Stephen Spielberg's *Dive!* is undeniably eye-catching; its exterior consists of a giant yellow submarine crashing through the wall of the Fashion Show Mall. Inside, the concept is that the whole restaurant is forced repeatedly to dive to the bottom of the ocean, but the "windows" of the diner-style booths, and the scattered TV-screen portholes elsewhere, are too small for the illusion to be convincing, and the endless mechanical rumblings and strobe-light effects are downright irritating. On top of that, the food itself – sandwiches or subs for $10, chicken or ribs in gloopy barbecue sauce for closer to $15 – is overpriced and tasteless. Closet voyeurs will love the periscope beside the bar, which enables you to spy not only on the Strip but also neighboring hotels.

Emeril's New Orleans Fish House

Map 2, C5. *The MGM Grand*, 3799 Las Vegas Blvd S ℅891-7374. Daily 11am–2.30pm & 5.30–10.30pm, seafood bar 11am–10.30pm.

TV chef Emeril Lagasse has carved an authentic slice of New Orleans into the heart of the vast *MGM Grand*; complete with aged red brickwork and black cast-iron railings, his French-Quarter-style restaurant features "terrace," "indoor," and counter dining. While Cajun seafood with a modern (but never low-cal) twist is the specialty, with barbecue shrimp for $18 at lunchtime and redfish in red bean sauce for $25 at dinner, the menu also includes meat options such as three-way chicken ($21) and steak ($24). Oysters are available all day at $18 per dozen. If you find the entrees gut-bustingly rich, wait until you see the desserts; but it's all so fabulous you can't help throwing caution to the winds.

Fat Burger

Map 2, C5. 3765 Las Vegas Blvd S ℅736-4733. Dining room daily 10.30am–10pm, drive-thru window daily 24 hours.

There's no more to this gleaming, all-American burger joint, next door to the World of Coca-Cola and the *MGM Grand*, than meets the eye. Quite simply, you can walk or drive in

from the Strip at any time, and get a perfect burger, fries and
shake.

Hamada

Map 2, B7. *Luxor*, 3900 Las Vegas Blvd S ℂ262-4000.
Mon, Tues & Sun 11am–midnight, Wed–Sat 11am–2am.
Las Vegas's best sushi restaurant. In comparison to *Hamada*'s
other branch, at 598 E Flamingo Rd (ℂ733-3005), the one in
Luxor is somewhat small and unglamorous, but it's far more
convenient for tourists, and it's also open for both lunch and
dinner. Daily lunch specials cost around $7, while a full sashimi
meal costs $19.50 during the day or $21.50 in the evening.

Il Fornaio

Map 2, B5. *New York–New York*, 3790 Las Vegas Blvd S ℂ740-
6403.
Mon–Thurs & Sun 7am–10pm, Fri & Sat 7am–midnight.
Much the nicest place to enjoy the atmosphere of *New
York–New York*, with a high-ceilinged "indoor" dining room
plus terrace seating alongside Central Park, this rural-Italian
restaurant, staffed by very flirtatious waiters who speak Italian
among themselves, is a real joy. Grab a pizza for around $10, or
linger over a full meal of perhaps soft-shell crab ($9) or carpac-
cio of beef ($8) to start, followed by gnocchi with smoked
salmon ($14), baked sea bass with cherry tomatoes ($18.50), or
rotisserie chicken ($14.50). *Il Fornaio*'s delicious olive breads,
pastries and espresso coffees are also sold in the separate deli
alongside the front desk.

Isis

Map 2, B7. *Luxor*, 3900 Las Vegas Blvd S ℂ262-4773.
Daily 6–11pm.
A real only-in-Vegas experience, this very classy gourmet restaurant matches any in the city for cuisine, while nonetheless revel-
ing in its high-camp Egyptian trimmings. Guests have to wear

"appropriate" formal attire – ties are not compulsory – and run an Indiana-Jones gauntlet of gilded statues and columns to get in. You also have to spend at least $28 per person, which isn't too hard when vegetables are $6 per portion. Typical meat entrees like grilled veal scallopine with oysters cost $27, seafood or fowl alternatives a little less. Appetizers such as oysters Rockefeller "from the sacred lake at Karnak" – not a claim to appeal to anyone who's seen the lake in question – are more like $12.

La Rotisserie des Artistes

Map 2, C3. *Paris*, 3655 Las Vegas Blvd S ©946-7144.
Daily 11.30am–2.30pm & 5.30–11pm.

Stylish, elegantly modern European-style grand café, set on two levels in the heart of *Paris*, and serving high-quality French bistro cuisine. From the mosaics and Monet-inspired uphol-stery, to the graceful double staircase that swirls up toward the Belle Epoque ceiling, the atmosphere is just right, though *Bellagio*-owner Steve Wynn can at least console himself with the thought that the Van Goghs here are reproductions. The three-course *prix fixe* lunch, with prime rib, salmon or chicken, is a real bargain at $16; dinner entrees, such as the rack of lamb or the skewered scallops, are mostly in the $20–30 range; and the dessert pastries are out of this world.

Le Cirque

Map 2, B3. *Bellagio*, 3600 Las Vegas Blvd S ©693-8100.
Daily 5.30–11pm.

Surprisingly small showpiece restaurant, where if you manage to penetrate the dramatic vault-like portals – this is one of the very few restaurants in Las Vegas that requires male patrons to wear jacket and tie – you find yourself in a stunning Deco interior, overlooking the *Bellagio*'s lake. The Mediterranean-French menu closely follows the example of its New York parent, *Le Cirque 2000*, with an exquisite and expensive selection of $25–30 appetizers such as *tartare de thon* and "black tie" sea scallops with black truffles followed by $30–40 entrees like black sea bass and rabbit in Riesling. The full five-course *Menu de Degustation* costs $90.

Le Provencal

Map 2, C3. *Paris*, 3655 Las Vegas Blvd S ℂ946-6932.
Sun–Thurs 7–10.30am,11.30am–2.30pm & 5.30–11pm; Fri & Sat 7–10.30am,11.30am–2.30pm & 5.30–11.30pm.

Bright, cheerful restaurant specializing in regional French cooking, with earthy wooden tables and crockery, plus waitstaff dressed in jerkins and britches who cavort intermittently in a mercifully brief floor show of songs extolling the virtues of Provence. The prices of dinner entrees like lobster risotto or pepper-stuffed pork – typically $30–45 – may seem high, but they include a full meal in which you get four appetizers, two hot and two cold, such as escargots or mushrooms with beef, and also four delicious desserts. It's not that dissimilar to the buffet, in fact, except that you get a substantial and well-prepared main course. Breakfast and lunch are humbler affairs, with lunchtime pastas and salads costing under $10.

Margarita's Mexican Cantina

Map 3, D8. *The New Frontier*, 3120 Las Vegas Blvd S ℂ794-8433.
Daily 11am–10.30pm.

This appealingly old-fashioned bar-cum-restaurant on the main casino floor of the *New Frontier*, where the south-of-the border decor includes murals, fake vine trellises and high-backed wooden chairs, offers the best-value Mexican food on the Strip. Warm tortillas and dips are served as soon as you sit down, while the satisfyingly substantial tacos, burritos, or *fajitas* cost $8–12, and a 12oz margarita to wash it all down is a mere $3.25.

Motown Cafe

Map 2, B5. *New York–New York*, 3790 Las Vegas Blvd S ℂ740-6440.
Mon–Thurs & Sun 7.30am–11pm, Fri & Sat 7.30am–2am.

Coffee

Most of the upmarket casinos on the **Strip** have a specialty **coffee bar** somewhere on the premises. *Mandalay Bay* and the *Venetian* have coffee outlets in their food courts, *New York–New York* has the *Il Fornaio* deli next to the registration desk, *Caesars Palace* has *Cafe Caesars II* in the Forum, the *Sahara* has *Jitters*, *Harrah's* has *Club Cappuccino*, and *Treasure Island* has a *Starbucks* up by the tram station. If you can't find at least a cart in your hotel, head for the surprisingly pleasant and relaxed *Starbucks* at 3049 Las Vegas Blvd S, opposite the *Stardust*, which is unique on the Strip in offering sidewalk tables.

Downtown's only dedicated coffee outlet, on the other hand, is a cart on the pedestrian section of Fremont Street, though the *Enigma Garden Cafe* (see p.174) and *Cafe Neon* in *The Attic* (see p.219) are not far away.

Elsewhere, Las Vegas has plenty of the sort of coffee-houses you'd find in any major US city. As well as the *Coffee Pub* (see p.174) and the bookstore cafés in Borders and Barnes & Noble (see pp.236–37), there are several options in major shopping malls and also near the university on S Maryland Parkway, like *Cafe Espresso Roma* at 4440 and *Buzzy's Espresso* at 4755.

Very large, split-level, theme diner at the front of *New York–New York*, where you're assailed by a constant barrage of Motown music and videos. In this high-tech neon-trimmed Fifties diner, the chairs and benches are upholstered with glittery patent leather, the stairs and ceilings are inlaid with gold records, and the wallpaper bursts with shiny holograms. Memorabilia is everywhere, while the lower level, laid out like a nightclub with mannequins of the Temptations on stage, offers after-hours dancing nightly. After all that, the food itself is a bit of an anticlimax. Basically Southern soul food, with a dose of Cajun for the more adventurous and plenty of burgers and meatloaf for the less so, it's perfectly well prepared and edible, but you're supposed to be too excited to notice. Most entrees cost $10–12.

The Noodle Kitchen

Map 2, B1. *The Mirage*, 3400 Las Vegas Blvd S ℭ456-4564. Daily 11am–4am.

The inexpensive but top-quality dim sum, and the wide range of noodle dishes ($8–14), stand out on a largely Chinese menu that also extends to meaty plates of pork or duck, and more rarefied delights such as congee with 1000-year-old egg ($9). The odd location, tucked inside the larger *Caribe Cafe* diner – and sharing the same anonymous, over-bright buffet-style decor – means you can order a conventional American dessert to round it all off.

Olives

Map 2, B3. *Bellagio*, 3600 Las Vegas Blvd S ℭ693-8181. Daily 11am–3pm & 5–11.30pm.

Bellagio's best-value gourmet restaurant has a lovely terrace setting, facing the Eiffel Tower across the lake. Run by Todd English and Victor LaPlaca from Boston, it's kitted out with a playful yellow decor, featuring candy-striped columns and a mosaic floor – despite consisting largely of colored plastic spoons, the central chandelier-cum-mobile cost $1 million. Even if it is the kind of place that calls a $10 pizza an "individual oven-baked flatbread," and your food is more likely to be arranged vertically than horizontally, the largely Mediterranean menu is uniformly fresh and superb. It's a great spot for lunch, with $10–13 appetizers like tuna or beef carpaccio and crispy fried oysters on jumbo ham hocks, pasta dishes like Israeli couscous carbonara ($9.50), and specials such as barbecued yellow-fin tuna on roasted onion polenta with spicy avocado salad ($18.50). Dinner entrees are pricier, but at least you get their trademark platter of huge, delicious olives as soon as you sit down.

The Palm

Map 2, B2. Forum Shops, *Caesars Palace*, 3500 Las Vegas Blvd S ©732-7256.

Daily 11.30am–11pm.

Classy, upmarket steakhouse/diner near the Forum entrance, closely modeled on the New York power-dining original and festooned with caricatures of local celebrities. The food may not be all that exciting, cooked with a better-safe-than-sorry approach that can make it all pretty heavy, but it's somehow deeply reassuring, and the service is impeccable. Sizable salads and deli sandwiches priced well under $10 make it a good lunchtime option, while steak, veal or lobster dinner entrees can top $30.

Picasso

Map 2, B3. *Bellagio*, 3600 Las Vegas Blvd S ©693-7223.

Sun, Mon, Tues & Thurs 6–10pm, Fri & Sat 6–11pm.

Despite sky-high prices, *Bellagio*'s "lakeside" Mediterranean restaurant, run by chef Julian Serrano, is currently Las Vegas's hottest ticket. Its gimmick is that the walls are hung with original Picassos, while the dining room was in part designed by his son, Claude Picasso. To inspect the paintings, however, you have to crane over whoever happens to be sitting at the table below, and they're far from masterpieces in any case. That leaves the food – an unexceptional Californian-Mediterranean hybrid, heavy on seared lumps of fish or meat stranded on oversized plates – and the appallingly rude service to justify prices of $70 for the *prix fixe* menu, or $80 for the *Menu Degustation*. Both menus change nightly, and male diners are required to wear jackets.

Pinot Cafe

Map 2, C1. *The Venetian*, 3355 Las Vegas Blvd S ☏414-8888.
Daily 11am–11pm.

Friendly, informal European-style "sidewalk" café, complete
with wicker chairs and round marble tables, at the start of the
Venetian's Restaurant Row. Ideal for a light, zestful lunch, with
$5–7 appetizers like scallop tartare, French onion soup, or
braised whole artichoke followed by bistro favorites such as
mussels ($12) or steak ($17) with fries, or salmon or chicken
salads ($15). The more formal *Pinot Brasserie* inside, with its
brass fittings and red leather seats, is open for dinner only, serving the same items, generally at slightly higher prices, plus a
few fancier entrees and daily specials such as Monday's $20
suckling pig with sauerkraut. Both offer a shellfish platter for
two people for $39.

Rainforest Cafe

Map 2, C5. *The MGM Grand*, 3799 Las Vegas Blvd S ☏891-8580.
Mon–Thurs 8am–midnight, Fri & Sat 8am–1am, Sun 8am–11pm.

This exuberant theme restaurant at the *Grand*'s Strip entrance
boasts the most fabulously over-the-top decor in town, consisting of a dense jungle filled with huts and waterfalls, giant butterflies and animatronic animals. How all that running water
helps preserve scarce resources is anyone's guess, but it's a fun
place to bring the kids, and the food is pretty good too. At
breakfast, you can get a fruit plate or eggs benedict for around
$10; later on, entrees such as pot roast or meatloaf cost $12, a
"primal steak" is $19, and, for visitors with a new respect for
the animal kingdom, a vegetarian burger is $9. The central cof-
fee and juice bar makes a welcome way-station if you're just
passing through.

rumjungle

Map 2, B8. *Mandalay Bay*, 3950 Las Vegas Blvd S ☏632-7408.
Mon–Thurs & Sun 5.30–11pm, Fri & Sat 5.30pm–1am.

RESTAURANTS ON THE STRIP

Part restaurant, part nightclub, *rumjungle* is more about spectacle than food – but it's such a fabulous spectacle that eating here is an essential Vegas experience. Its entire facade is a "fire wall" of erupting gas jets, while semi-naked showgirls gyrate at the front door, and the staff at the huge double-sided bar regularly take time out to dance in the glass "cage" at its core. The menu consists mostly of pricey appetizers – such as jerk chicken wings ($7), Honolulu Caesar salad with rare ahi ($10), or Calypso salad with guava-grilled prawns ($12.50) – and rich, fruity desserts. There's also a colossal list of good-value cocktails and specialty rums. The very chic, well-dressed and beautiful crowd is mostly Latin, and stays up dancing to pounding Latin music until 2am on weekdays, 4am on weekends (see p.182).

Smith and Wollensky

Map 2, C5. 3767 Las Vegas Blvd S ©862-4100.
Daily 11.30am–4am.

The Strip's only stand-alone gourmet restaurant, this busy and very upmarket steak joint is located opposite the *Monte Carlo* in a smart 1998 facsimile of New York's 1977 original. Nominally it's divided into two sections, with steaks priced at around $30 in the more formal main dining room and more like $24 (for a 14-oz sirloin) in the adjoining, late-opening *Grill*; in fact, the two share a kitchen and are barely distinguishable. Prices at first seem reasonable, with a bowl of split pea soup costing just $5, but every side dish, even fries, costs extra, so a full dinner with tip costs at least $50. The service has a deliberately grouchy New York tinge – in fact, if it weren't for the succulent inch-thick chunks of charred steak, there'd be no point coming.

Spago's

Map 2, B2. Forum Shops, *Caesars Palace*, 3570 Las Vegas Blvd S ©369-6300.
Cafe daily 11am–midnight, Dining Room Sun–Thurs 6–10pm, Fri & Sat 5.30–10.30pm.

Surreal New Californian restaurant that remains Vegas's premier site for star-spotting, with a space-age decor to complement the weirdness of *Caesars*' blue-domed Forum. Watch the
world go by with a designer pizza or sandwich in the mall-
level, all-day sidewalk *Cafe*, priced at $10–20, or sneak the odd
peek at your elite co-diners in the exclusive (but extremely
noisy) interior *Dining Room*, while you swoon over the tuna
sashimi, steamed lobster, or Chinese duck (entrees $15–30).

Star Canyon

Map 2, C1. *The Venetian*, 3355 Las Vegas Blvd S ℂ414-3772.
Daily 11.30am–3pm & 5pm–midnight.

Stephan Pyles' *Star Canyon* is a runaway success in Dallas,
where tables are booked months in advance. It's slightly less at
home in the *Venetian*; with primary-colored Stetsons and cow-
boy boots in wall niches, longhorn-shaped iron light fittings,
and a yellow rose on every table, it can't decide whether to be
tasteful, minimal or postmodern, and ends up looking like a
pretentious brew pub. The "New Texas Cuisine," however, is
appetizing and exciting, if overwhelming in its sheer volume.
First courses for around $10 include grilled shrimp and jicama
soup with fresh goat's buttermilk and basil, and Shiner Bock
barbeque steamed mussels with goat cheese scallion toasts. Yet
for once the entrees are even more fanciful: coriander-cured
venison with sweet potato-creamed corn tostada and chipotle
barbeque for $30; and the house specialty, a bone-in cowboy
rib-eye steak served with pinto-wild mushroom ragout and red
chile onion rings for $32. There's no let-up with the desserts
either, the *pièce de resistance* being a stacked banana creme
brulee tostada.

Top of the World

Map 3, G3. *The Stratosphere*, 2000 Las Vegas Blvd S ℂ380-7711.
Mon–Thurs & Sun 11am–3.45pm & 4–11pm, Fri & Sat
11am–3.45pm & 4pm–midnight.

RESTAURANTS ON THE STRIP

So long as you're happy to settle for good rather than gourmet food, dining at this 106th-floor revolving restaurant is an utterly memorable experience; the view is simply phenomenal. The best time to come is after dark, when the menu – a catch-all mixture of Californian, quasi-Asian and routine American dishes – is more interesting than at lunch, and the lights of the Strip are at their most spectacular. Typical dinner entrees, such as Santa Fe rotisserie chicken or prime rib, cost $24–30; be sure to order the replica chocolate Stratosphere Tower for dessert ($10).

Wolfgang Puck Cafe

Map 2, C5. *The MGM Grand*, 3799 Las Vegas Blvd S ©895-9653.
Mon–Thurs & Sun 8am–11pm, Fri & Sat 8am–midnight.

Brightly tiled designer-diner-cum-café, facing the Sports Book at the *MGM Grand*, where they'll whisk you through your meal in the blink of an eyelid, but you won't be disappointed with the food. The large breakfast menu includes well-priced benedicts and omelets, and three eggs as you like for $6, but you have to pay for each item, including coffee or juice, so the check soon mounts up. Later on, $10 buys one of Puck's signature postmodern pizzas or a delicious salad, pad Thai noodles or meatloaf go for $13–15, and sesame-seared ahi with horseradish mashed potatoes costs $19. No reservations.

DOWNTOWN RESTAURANTS

Andre's

Map 4, F5. 401 S Sixth St at Lewis Ave ©385-5016.
Daily 6–10pm.

Of the few gourmet restaurants downtown, this is the only one not in a casino. Instead it's housed in a former private home, styled to resemble an antique-furnished French country inn. The ingredients are drawn from all over the world, from Australian lobsters to Maryland crabs, but the cuisine is classic European – and so are the prices, with the appetizers averaging over $10 and no entrees under $20. Don't expect a low-cal experience – whether you go for red meat in a thick fruity sauce, or fish swimming in butter, you've still got the impossibly rich desserts to contend with. *Andre's* has another branch in the *Monte Carlo* on the Strip (Map 2, B5).

Binion's Horseshoe Coffee Shop

Map 4, F2. *Binion's Horseshoe*, 128 E Fremont St ©382-1600. Daily 24 hours.

The round-the-clock Las Vegas coffeeshop of your dreams. The setting is exactly right, down in the basement of *Binion's Horseshoe* with no natural light but plenty of glittery and/or plush trimmings, and the food is American-diner-heaven. Prices for the changing timetable of specials are consistently excellent; the best bargain is the all-night steak dinner, which between 10pm and 5am costs just $3, but even at prime time, 4.45–11.45pm, a 16-oz T-bone is only $6.75. Breakfast is highly recommended too, and better value than any buffet; the $3 "Benny Binion's Natural," served 2am–2pm, consists of two eggs, bacon or ham, toast, tea or coffee, and magnificent home fries.

California Pizza Kitchen

Map 4, F3. *The Golden Nugget*, 129 E Fremont St ©385-7111. Mon–Fri 11am–3.30pm & 5.30–11pm, Sat & Sun 11am–11pm.

Very close to the *Nugget*'s main lobby, but hard to find thanks to its lack of displays or menus, this "designer pizza" joint is more stylish than you'd expect from a national chain, and it's infinitely better than the hotel's poor coffeeshop, the *Carson Street Café*. With its black-and-white checked tiles and rattan chairs, it makes a pleasant refuge from the casino floor. The actual menu is not all that radical, hoisin duck and Thai chicken pizzas notwithstanding, but all the pizza and pasta entrees cost around $10, and they taste a cut above fast-food alternatives. There's another, less distinctive *California Pizza Kitchen* on the Strip, in the *Mirage*.

Enigma Garden Cafe

Map 4, E7. 918 S Fourth St ℗386-0999.

Daily except Mon 8am–midnight.

Las Vegas's best-known "alternative" café spreads through the garden and two outbuildings of an ordinary little house in what its owners like to call the funky "Gateway District"; to more objective eyes, it's a pretty seedy area that's a little too far to walk to from Fremont Street. It serves all the coffees, teas, and sodas you'd expect, plus deli sandwiches (not all vegetarian), hummus wraps, tortillas and so on for $5–7. The service is shaky, but it's a good place to pick up on non-mainstream local happenings.

Second Street Grill

Map 4, F2. *Sam Boyd's Fremont Hotel*, 200 E Fremont St ℗385-3232.

Sun–Thurs 5–11pm, Fri & Sat 5pm–midnight.

Downtown's most original fine-dining option, an up-to-the-minute "Pacific Rim" restaurant that occupies a disappointingly dull wood-paneled room near the *Fremont*'s front door. The influence of Hawaiian master chef Jean Marie Josselin, credited as a consultant, is apparent throughout the pan-Asian menu, which draws heavily on Chinese, Thai and Japanese traditions. Appetizers, mostly costing $10–12, are largely seafood-oriented, including ahi (tuna) sashimi and crab cakes; there are more meat entrees, such as steaks for $22–24 or Chinese duck for $19, but the signature dish is a whole red snapper, prepared Thai style, for $28.

RESTAURANTS WEST OF THE STRIP

Coffee Pub

Map 3, B4. 2800 W Sahara Ave ℗367-1913.

Mon–Fri 7am–3pm, Sat & Sun 7.30am–3pm.

Large, bright and rather upmarket coffeehouse, tucked into a small modern mall. Few of its clientele, drawn from the surrounding banks and offices, have the time to linger, but it's a nice enough place to sit, and has some outdoor seating. As well as specialty coffees and baked goods, the breakfast menu includes huevos rancheros or eggs benedict for around $6; lunchtime salads, deli sandwiches, burgers, and pizzas cost slightly more.

Dragon Sushi

Map 1, C5. China Town Plaza, 4115 W Spring Mountain Rd ©368-4328.
Sun–Thurs 10.30am–10.30pm, Fri & Sat 10.30am–midnight.

Good if not exceptional sushi at $4–6 per piece, plus noodle entrees at more like $10, served in intimate, friendly mall restaurant where individual private Japanese-style dining rooms are also available.

Laredo del Mar

Map 1, C3. *Texas Station*, 2100 Texas Star Lane ©631-1000.
Mon–Thurs & Sun 5–10pm, Fri & Sat 5–11pm.

The Stations chain's team of designers has done a great job of turning this fake-adobe casino restaurant into an atmospheric Mexican seafood taverna, and the food does justice to the appealing setting. It's all well priced, with appetizers like oysters baked with salsa and cheese, stuffed clams, *queso fundido*, or ceviche costing $5 or less, and the huge entrees, such as *chimichangas*, *fajitas*, and the *caldo de marisco* fish stew, at little over $10. If margaritas don't do the job quick enough for you, try an oyster shot with tequila for $3.

Napa

Map 2, A2. *Rio*, 3700 W Flamingo Rd ©247-7961.
Wed–Sun 6–11pm.

Very classy, very expensive New Californian restaurant in the *Rio*'s Masquerade Village area, with an exceptional wine list: a hundred wines are sold by the glass, for $5–60, while bottles go for up to $20,000. You need to be very familiar with the latest buzzwords to make head or tail of the menu, but you can rest assured it's all delicious, from $16 appetizers like the cold tomato nage with lobster mirepoix to entrées such as sea scallop quenelles for $32.

Thai Spice
Map 1, C5. 4433 W Flamingo Rd at I-15 ℗362-5308.
Daily except Sun 11am–10pm.
Some of Las Vegas's finest Thai food, served in an anonymous but clean and cheerful modern setting opposite the *Rio*.
Noodle dishes such as pad Thai are reasonably priced and very tasty, and the soups are good too. Lunchtime specials are excellent value at $6 or so, while even a full dinner works out under $20.

RESTAURANTS EAST OF THE STRIP

Carluccio's
Map 1, E5. 1775 E Tropicana Ave ℗795-3236.
Daily except Mon 4.30–10.30pm.
Conventional upscale Italian restaurant with an irresistible angle – it was designed by Liberace himself, whose museum now stands next door (see p.104). Hence the mirrored lounge and piano-shaped bar, not to mention the entire English pub he shipped over. The menu is wide ranging and consistently rich, with pizzas at $9–15, chicken dishes at $9–11, and linguini with mussels for $13, but it's hard to resist Liberace's own personal favorite, the $8 baked lasagna.

Costa del Sol Oyster Bar
Map 1, F6. *Sunset Station*, 1301 W Sunset Rd ℗547-7777.
Mon–Thurs & Sun 11am–11pm, Fri & Sat 11am–midnight.
Pleasant, spacious casino restaurant, sadly a long way off the Strip, that serves consistently good seafood from around the

world. You can get your shellfish raw, with oysters or clams at $8 per half-dozen; steamed, with clams at $12 and New Zealand mussels at $13; in Mediterranean stews, like a French *bouillabaisse* or an Italian *cioppino*, for $16; or in a gumbo or roast, with crab, lobster, or shrimp again at around $16. For $12 you can also get six oyster shooters, each with a different liquor. The adjoining *Costa del Sol* restaurant serves an even longer menu for dinner, Wed–Sun only.

Green Shack
Map 1, E4. 2504 E Fremont St ✆383-0007.
Daily except Mon 4–10pm.
Characterful, old-fashioned and homey diner that's been run-ning since 1929 – longer than any other Las Vegas restaurant. Nostalgia is the most enjoyable dish on the menu, but the fried chicken isn't bad either. On weekends a one-man band pro-vides chintzy entertainment.

Lawry's The Prime Rib
Map 2, F2. 4043 E Howard Hughes Pkwy at Flamingo ✆893-2223.
Mon–Thurs & Sun 5–10pm, Fri & Sat 5–11pm.
Lawry's has been a Beverly Hills tradition since 1938, but the Las Vegas branch only opened in 1997. Even so, it's a lovely, stylish tribute to the Art Deco era, enhanced by flamboyant service. Prime rib is no longer (quite) the only thing on the menu, but it's the only reason you'd bother to come here, and *Lawry's*, at $20–30 per entree, may well be the best you've ever tasted.

Marrakech
Map 2, G2. Citibank Park, 3900 Paradise Rd ✆737-5611.
Daily 5.30–11pm.
All-you-can-eat banquets of rich Moroccan food, costing around $25 per person and eaten with your fingers from low-lying tables around which you sit on scattered cushions. The

RESTAURANTS EAST OF THE STRIP

tasty but very meaty couscous and pastry dishes are comple-
mented by some unexpected seafood alternatives, and followed
by heavy desserts. The main reason to come is to enjoy the
faux-Arabian Nights atmosphere, belly dancers and all, so it's
not a place for a quick meal on your own.

Mediterranean Cafe and Market

Map 1, D5. Tiffany Square, 4147 S Maryland Pkwy at Flamingo
©731-6030.
Daily except Sun 11am–9pm.

This simple but highly recommended Middle Eastern restaurant – much easier to reach if you're heading south rather than
north on Maryland – is Vegas's best vegetarian option. In most
US cities that might make it an "alternative" hangout; here it's
just a popular, good-value but not very atmospheric lunchtime
rendezvous. The Cretan murals are attractive, though, and the
food is tasty and substantial. Salads cost $5–8, pita sandwiches
mostly $6, and spinach pie $9, while dips such as hummus or
the eggplant-based baba ganosh are $6, with half portions at
$3.50. A mountainous best-of-everything combination plate is
just $10.

Mr Lucky's 24/7

Map 2, G4. *Hard Rock Hotel*, 4455 Paradise Rd ©693-5000.
Daily 24 hours.

Oddly enough, the *Hard Rock Cafe* itself is not in the casino
proper – see p.94 – so wannabes who want to soak up the
casino atmosphere but can't afford the room rates have to
hang out in *Mr Lucky's*, its 24-hour coffeeshop, instead. With
its open kitchen, faux-fur booths, and subdued tan-and-
cream paint-job, it's actually a very stylish place, and the food
is well above average too. As well as all the usual breakfast
items, it serves burgers, sandwiches, pizzas and pasta dishes for
$6–10, a 12-oz steak for $14, and milkshakes or microbrews
for $3.50.

Shalimar

Map 2, G2. Citibank Park, 3900 Paradise Rd ℂ796-0302.
Daily 11.30am–2.30pm & 5.30–10.30pm.

If you're an Indian food fanatic, you probably won't think that
Shalimar's rather conventional menu of lamb and chicken cur-
ries and tandooris is all that exciting, but it's the best you're
going to find in Las Vegas. Lunchtime buffets aren't worth the
trip, but the dinner menu includes a wide selection of vegetarian dishes, with the cheese-and-peas specialty *matar paneer*
priced at $9.50, and the *naan* and *roti* breads – not to mention
the brass fittings – are satisfyingly authentic. Meat entrees cost
around $13, a bit more for a biryani with rice, and the service
is very friendly.

Z'Tejas Grill

Map 2, G2. 3824 Paradise Rd ℂ732-1660.
Daily 11am–11pm.

Despite its tiresome name – taken, apparently, from a former
chef's mispronunciation of "The Texas Grill" – and its
overblown reputation for "daring," the food at *Z'Tejas Grill* is
good enough to merit venturing a mile off the Strip. The
vaguely Southwestern cuisine takes in everything from New
Orleans to the Pacific, and down to Mexico too, while the
outdoor patio is a little close to the road but at least offers a bit
of fresh air after all those casinos. The appetizers are the most
interesting part; in fact you could skip the chicken burritos,
catfish tacos and so on, for a meal of appetizers like the seared
and peppered sesame tuna, or the sushi-esque grilled and
chilled seafood roll. At $8, each costs roughly the same as the
entrees anyway, and is just as substantial.

RESTAURANTS EAST OF THE STRIP

Bars and clubs

As the perfect fuel to turn a dithering gawker into a diehard gambler, **alcohol** is very easy indeed to come by in Las Vegas. If you want a drink in a casino, there's no need to look for a bar; instead, a tray-toting waitress will come and find you. Beers and cocktails are delivered free of charge to anyone hovering near, let alone seated at, the tables and slot machines, and assuming you keep on tipping the waitress, the supply will keep on going around the clock.

All the casinos do have actual **bars** as well, ranging from open-sided **lounges** in the heart of the gaming area to **brewpubs** and themed nightspots tucked well away from the action. All are invariably equipped with cacophonous slot machines; even the lounges at *Bellagio* have video poker screens inlaid into their solid marble counters. Customers who are actively gambling can usually get their drinks free.

If you're staying at a major casino on the Strip or downtown, you should have no difficulty finding a suitable place to drink either in or very near your hotel. Neither area, however, holds any significant bars other than those attached to casinos. Elsewhere in the city, neighborhood bars do exist where you can drink and eat away from the frenzy of the casinos – the most popular local pub chain, *PT's*, has almost twenty locations. However, very few tourists bother to seek them out.

Until very recently, Las Vegas was almost completely devoid of cutting-edge **nightclubs**. One or two off-Strip places catered for local urban youth, but clubbers were considered a breed apart from tourists. As places like the *Hard Rock* and *Mandalay Bay* have started to attract younger and slightly hipper visitors, however, the big casinos have been opening their own on-site clubs. Not all have got it right, but a scene is beginning to emerge.

> **Bars and clubs that function primarily as venues for live music are reviewed in Chapter Nine, Entertainment.**

BARS

Crown and Anchor
Map 1, D5. 1350 E Tropicana Ave ℂ739-8676.
Daily 11am–5am.
Counterfeit English pub in the University District, with mock-Tudor decor and a raucous atmosphere. Lots of European beers on draft, plus a pool table, quiz nights, and English soccer games on the TV.

Double Down Saloon
Map 2, G4. 4640 Paradise Rd ℂ791-5775.
Daily 11am–5am.
Cool, dark, post-apocalyptic bar on the edge of the University District, furnished from thrift stores and daubed with psychedelic scrawlings. When obscure live bands aren't playing, the fabulously eclectic jukebox surely is.

Gaudi Bar
Map 1, F6. *Sunset Station*, 1301 W Sunset Rd, Henderson ℂ547-7777.
Daily 24 hrs.

BARS

181

By far the most weird and wonderful casino lounge in Las Vegas. *Sunset Station* claims to "have left no tile unbroken" to create this billowing mosaic-encrusted toadstool of a tribute to Spanish architect Gaudi, complete with faux-sky underbelly and best appreciated with the aid of a $3.50 specialty martini.

rumjungle

Map 2, B8. *Mandalay Bay*, 3950 Las Vegas Blvd S ℂ632-7408.
Mon–Thurs & Sun 5.30pm–2am, Fri & Sat 5.30pm–4am.
You have to run a gauntlet of go-go dancers and volcanic gas jets just to get into *rumjungle*, *Mandalay Bay*'s hybrid bar-restaurant-nightclub (for a review of the food, see p.169). Inside, the leopardskin-clad staff serves a wide array of well-priced cocktails, plus a vast menu of rums after 11pm nightly, and it's too loud to do anything more than watch, or join, the dance floor action.

....

To buy or consume alcohol in Nevada, you must be aged 21 or over, and have photo ID to prove it.

....

Sky Lounge

Map 2, C5. *Polo Towers*, 3745 Las Vegas Blvd S ℂ261-1000.
Mon–Thurs & Sun 11am–1am, Fri & Sat 11am–2am.
One of the Strip's better-kept secrets, partly because it's a little hard to find your way into *Polo Towers* at street level. This conventional 19th-floor lounge has panoramic windows that offer great views of the night-time light show.

VooDoo Lounge

Map 2, A2. *Rio*, 3700 W Flamingo Rd ℂ252-7777.
Daily noon–3am.
Vegas'a hottest bar, popular with tourists and locals alike for its amazing views and super-cool atmosphere. You'll have to wait a while, and pass a dress-code inspection (no T-shirts or sneakers)

BARS

Lounge life

In addition to the bars and brewpubs reviewed in this chapter, all of Las Vegas's casinos hold at least one **lounge**, usually adjacent to the gaming tables and open 24 hours daily. Some are lavishly themed, others are exactly the way you'd imagine from a million Vegas movies. Here's a list of ten favorites to look out for, all of which feature no-cover live music nightly.

The Bar at Times Square, *New York–New York*. Dueling pianos dominate this rowdy slice of the Big Apple.

Captain Morgan's, *Treasure Island*. A deliciously macabre haunt, lit by see-through human bones.

Coral Reef Bar, *Mandalay Bay*. Ocean-themed late-night hangout; dip your hands in the sushi bar or the fish tank, as you prefer.

Horse-Around Bar, *Circus Circus*. Pull up a saddle on this fairground carousel to unwind from a grueling day of family fun.

Lagoon Saloon, *The Mirage*. Gloriously over-the-top tropical hangout, complete with seashells and sand.

Nefertiti's Lounge, *Luxor*. Cheesy entertainment in classical Egyptian surroundings.

Quark's Bar, Star Trek Experience, *The Las Vegas Hilton*. No Trekkie will want to miss this fun, futuristic vision.

Starlight Lounge, *The Stardust*. A vintage throwback to the old-style Las Vegas, complete with plush armchairs.

Top of the World, *The Stratosphere*. Classy sky-high venue for sunset cocktails.

Tropics Lounge, *The Tropicana*. Half-zoo, half-jungle; where the wild things are.

LOUNGE LIFE

before they'll let you ride the elevator to the 51st floor. The
outdoor terrace boasts a fabulous prospect of the entire Strip,
half a mile east – come for sunset if possible. Inside, the purple-
tinted windows make it hard to see out, but most of the self-
consciously beautiful crowd prefer to admire their own reflec-
tions anyway. The ersatz New Orleans voodoo-themed decor,
and the "mixologists" diligently setting cocktails aflame, add to
the ambience, the food is pretty good, and there's live music
nightly except Mon.

BREWPUBS

Gordon Biersch Brewery
Map 2, G2. 3987 Paradise Rd ✆312-5247.
Mon & Sun 11.30am–midnight, Tues–Sat 11.30am–2am.
Cavernous and ultra-trendy chain microbrewery a mile off the
Strip, packed with local big spenders and featuring fine lagers
brewed on site, reasonable food, live music from swing to reg-
gae, and, best of all, no slot machines.

Holy Cow
Map 3, G4. 2423 Las Vegas Blvd S ✆732-2697.
Daily 24 hrs.
The Strip's first brewpub stands at the sign of the colossal cow,
across from the *Sahara*. Its frat-boy atmosphere can be off-
putting, the food should be left firmly alone, and the noise levels would be bad enough without the loads of clamoring slot
machines, but it's as close as the Strip comes to a stand-alone
pub serving distinctive beer.

Monte Carlo Pub & Brewery
Map 2, B5. *The Monte Carlo*, 3770 Las Vegas Blvd S ✆730-7000.
Sun–Thurs 11am–3am, Fri & Sat 11am–4am.
The *Monte Carlo*'s massive microbrewery isn't bad for an early-

A bar with no booze?

If you want proof of how much Las Vegas is changing, head for the city's most unusual bar, located opposite a Borders bookstore in a small open mall a couple of miles west of the Strip. Roll over Dean Martin, it doesn't even serve alcohol. Instead, **Breathe . . .**, 4750 W Sahara Ave, Suite 32 (Mon–Fri 10am–10pm, Sat & Sun 10am–midnight; ©258-4502), is an **oxygen bar**, where customers wait at the counter to be hooked up to canisters of pure oxygen.

Naturally, it comes in assorted flavors, filtered through aromatherapy oils suspended in colored water. Options range from *Clarity*, infused with eucalyptus, to *Totally Groovy*, thanks to spirulina and wheatgrass. The experience costs a dollar a minute, for a minimum of ten minutes, though the friendly staff (velvet shirts are *de rigueur*) will most likely give you a little extra. You also get to keep the tube that hooks the canister to your nostrils, for obvious reasons, and can buy "smart drinks" made with the latest offbeat herbs and algae. And what's the point of it all, other than being able to wear your new "It's OK To Inhale" T-shirt?

For a taste of the *Breathe . . .* experience nearer the Strip, you can drop by their small roadside stand outside the *Tropicana* casino.

evening drink – the beers produced in its gleaming copper vats taste pretty good – but from 9pm onwards it turns into a deafening retro dance club usually showcasing low-grade mock-Eighties rock bands.

Sunset Brewing Company

Map 1, F6. *Sunset Station*, 1301 W Sunset Rd, Henderson ©547-7777. Mon–Thurs 4–10pm, Fri 4pm–midnight, Sat noon–midnight, Sun noon–10pm.

High-quality casino brewpub, serving a good selection of
home-brewed beers (such as Red Bikini and Deep Dark Tan)
in an elegant Deco interior, plus a wide-ranging food menu –
and even featuring a separate cigar lounge. Live music events
include regular swing nights on Tues.

Triple Seven Brewpub
Map 4, E1. *Main Street Station*, 200 N Main St ℂ386-4442.
Daily 11am–7am.
The service at this roomy, high-ceilinged downtown brewpub
is slow and even rude, but the beers are great, the food tasty (as
well as pizzas, burgers and ribs, you can get six oysters for $6),
and there's often live entertainment as well. Tues is no-cover
blues night (6.30–10.30pm); Fri & Sat, the Divine Divas floor
show (8pm, 10pm & midnight) features tributes to soul singers
like Tina Turner, Diana Ross, Whitney Houston . . . and
Michael Jackson!

NIGHTCLUBS

The Beach
Map 3, G7. 365 Convention Center Dr ℂ731-1925.
Daily 24 hrs. Cover charge (for men only) usually $10.
This round-the-clock multiroom dance club, opposite the
Convention Center, is at heart a permanent Spring Break,
attracting a very young crowd to the massive dance floor
downstairs, decked out with palm trees and coconuts, and
sports bar upstairs. Monday night is "Studs'n'Suds," Tuesday
brings "Build Your Own Bikini"; less congruous is the gospel
brunch on Sunday mornings.

Cleopatra's Barge
Map 2, B2. *Caesars Palace*, 3570 Las Vegas Blvd S ℂ731-7110.
Daily except Mon 9pm–4am. No cover.

A replica Egyptian ship, genuinely afloat and fronted by a golden in-your-face figurehead, which holds a small, very busy dance floor as well as a lively bar, and hosts live bands and DJs nightly.

Club Rio

Map 2, A2. *Rio*, 3700 W Flamingo Rd ©252-7777.
Wed–Sat 10.30pm–4am. Men $10, women $5.
Upmarket, relatively staid dance club that takes over the *Rio*'s main showroom after hours to play mainly Eighties music to a predominantly thirty-plus throng.

Club Utopia

Map 2, C5. 3765 Las Vegas Blvd S ©390-4650.
Wed–Sat 10pm–10am. $10.
The Strip's one purpose-built stand-alone modern dance club, where the three dance rooms delight young locals with an emphasis on rave and techno, plus a Latin showcase on Thursdays.

Orbit Lounge

Map 2, G4. *Hard Rock Hotel*, 4455 Paradise Rd ©693-5000.
Fri & Sat 12.30–6am. Men $10.
When whoever's topping the weekend bill at the *Joint* (see p.199) is finally through, the *Orbit Lounge* steps in, to keep the usual crew of *Hard Rock* habitues dancing until dawn.

Ra

Map 2, B7. *Luxor*, 3900 Las Vegas Blvd S ©262-4400.
Wed–Sat 10pm–6am. Men $10, women $5.
Despite the gloriously camp Egyptian motifs, including bare-breasted Nile maidens at both entrances, *Ra* feels like a real city nightclub, catering to a ferociously hip and very glamorous crowd that includes a surprisingly high proportion of locals. Cage dancers watch over a changing schedule of special nights,

NIGHTCLUBS

usually with playful quasi-erotic tinges, such as the House-oriented Pleasuredome on Wednesdays and Decadence on Thursdays.

Studio 54

Map 2, C5. *The MGM Grand*, 3799 Las Vegas Blvd S ©891-1111. Mon–Sat 10pm–5am. Men Mon–Thurs $10, Fri & Sat $20.

There's more to running a nightclub than owning the rights to a famous name. No expense has been spared on this three-story, four-dancefloor recreation of New York's legendary *Studio 54*, so naturally it boasts state-of-the-art lighting and sound, but a pointlessly off-putting door policy and a clientele of one-off tourists don't make for a great atmosphere. The music is mostly house and electronic rather than 1970s disco.

Ententainment

There was a time when performing in Las Vegas represented the absolute pinnacle of any show-business career. In the early 1960s, when Frank Sinatra's Rat Pack were shooting hit movies like *Ocean's 11* during the day then singing the night away at the *Sands*, the city could claim to be the capital of the international entertainment industry. It was even hip.

The money is still there in Las Vegas, as was shown by the *MGM Grand* paying Barbra Streisand a reported $20 million to perform on Millennium Eve 1999, but the world has moved on. As the great names of the past fade from view, few of the individual performers popular with traditional Vegas visitors are now considered capable of carrying an extended-run show. Today's stars, on the other hand, don't want to spend their lives playing Vegas; top-selling musicians make quite enough money from recordings and occasional tours not to need to spend months at a time in the desert.

Nonetheless, **live entertainment** remains a crucial component of the Las Vegas package, and the days of the big-budget "spectacular" are far from over. The tendency nowadays is to rely on lavish stunts and special effects rather than global megastars, with the illusionist-magicians **Siegfried and Roy** now into their second decade at the *Mirage*. A fair number of old-style Vegas revues are still soldiering on, but there are more stimulating contemporary productions than you might imagine. In particular, the arty Canadian-based circus/theater troupe, **Cirque du Soleil**, has revolutionized attitudes toward what Las Vegas audiences might be able to handle. Its two stunning shows, *Mystère* at *Treasure Island* and the magnificent *O* at *Bellagio*, are currently the biggest tickets of all.

It also looks as though Las Vegas might finally be getting more into tune with the **musical** tastes of the baby-boom generation. You can still see Tom Jones, Englebert Humperdinck, even Wayne Newton if you're in town at the right time, and lots of unfashionable names from the Seventies and Eighties linger on, but both the *Joint* at the *Hard Rock* and the *House of Blues* at *Mandalay Bay* are now showcasing the biggest names in contemporary rock, reggae, blues, and soul.

A representative cross-section of Las Vegas shows is reviewed below, including some of the worst as well as the best. Note that all take place on **the Strip**; a few of the downtown casinos have showrooms, but none currently features anything of interest. The only potential rival is the *Rio*, on the verge of opening a huge new showroom as this book went to press, with the first show scheduled to be a star vehicle for David Cassidy.

SHOWS AND SPECTACULARS

Caesars Magical Empire
Caesars Palace, 3570 Las Vegas Blvd S (731-7333,
Tues–Sat 4.30pm onwards. $75, ages 5–10 $37.50. Also free tours,

Fri–Tues 11am–3.30pm.

The *Magical Empire* is a peculiar, hard-to-define cross between a dinner theater, a theme park, and a nightclub, to which guests are admitted in groups of up to twenty a time. Each group is shepherded to one of ten dining rooms hidden amid a labyrinth of caves, performance spaces, and simulator rides, all linked by tunnels and secret passageways and set in various parts of the "ancient world." Magicians, warlocks, and sorcerers entertain you at every stage, including as you eat an adequate but not exceptional four-course meal. A fun evening out for (affluent) families, it's a bit patchy and expensive for adults without kids.

Very few casinos offer dinner shows these days; you can only eat at those shows where the review explicitly says so.

Chicago

Mandalay Bay, 3950 Las Vegas Blvd S ℗632-7580.

Tues–Fri & Sun 7.30pm, Sat 7.30pm & 10.30pm. $55, $65, $80.

The musical *Chicago* was a good choice to open the *Mandalay Bay*'s plush, jet-black theater; already a worldwide hit, it requires minimal staging, with a set almost entirely styled in black and white. That said, it's also taking a chance. Some Las Vegas shows bend over backwards to accommodate all tastes, some seek to overwhelm with sheer spectacle; this one aims uncompromisingly for aficionados. Previous Vegas productions of Broadway shows have trimmed the originals to fit into 1hr 30min; *Chicago* is better value in sticking to 2hr 30min. If you like a choreographed Broadway show, you'll love this tale of scandalous goings-on in Jazz Age Chicago, as murderer Roxie Hart copes with her fleeting moment of fame. Big-name stars (Ben Vereen and Chita Rivera initially, though the cast is liable to change regularly) are backed up by a high-energy troupe of singers and dancers, with some show-stopping numbers and set pieces, and a seventeen-piece orchestra on stage throughout. If show tunes aren't your thing, however, the story is too banal to sustain interest.

Crazy Girls

Riviera, 2901 Las Vegas Blvd S ℭ794-9433.
Daily except Mon 8.30pm & 10.30pm. $19 & $26.50, including two drinks.

The crowd at the Strip's best-known "adult revue" consists largely of overweight college boys interspersed with a few swinging middle-aged couples, crammed in at little tables and emitting the occasional frightened squeal when the dancers come too close. Urged on by a lackluster (female) comedian, eight world-weary showgirls, not only topless but also sexless for good measure, dance their desultory way through a set of hackneyed chestnuts, wearing cheerleader costumes for *Rock Around The Clock*, biker gear for *Leader of the Pack*, and so on.

The Dream King

Holiday Inn-Casino Boardwalk, 3750 Las Vegas Blvd S ℭ730-3194.
Tues–Sat 8.30pm. $25.

It's possible that the *Holiday Inn-Casino Boardwalk*, next door to the *Monte Carlo*, will have vanished by the time you read this, but the King himself, in the form of Trent Carlini, will probably go on forever; this review is included in the hope that he finds a better home. Las Vegas's foremost "Elvis stylist," Trent skillfully emulates Elvis at every stage of his career. Unfortunately, however, when they said the show was high class, that was just a lie. Trent is left to flounder through the low-budget show on his own, singing to backing tapes and dashing off periodically to change his costumes, leaving you to endure embarrassingly long interludes of watching his home videos before he returns with his shirt hanging out of his pants. Sadly, though you'd expect there to be a huge audience for this sort of kitsch in Las Vegas, it only seems to attract a small crowd of obsessives.

EFX

The MGM Grand, 3799 Las Vegas Blvd S ℂ891-7777.
Tues–Sat 7.30pm & 10pm. $51.50 & $72; ages 5–12 $37.

In its efforts to please, the *Grand*'s major production show throws so much into the pot that it can't help but be incredibly uneven. It has always been a strange hybrid of special-effects spectacular (hence the title) and star vehicle. Both Michael Crawford and David Cassidy served two years as ringmaster, before six-foot-six sexagenarian sexpot Tommy Tune took over in 1999; each time, the show has been rejigged to suit the new marquee name. Grafted-on elements of whatever's currently hip have all but obscured its original theme, of a young boy who discovers that dreams do come true; thus it now incorporates chunks of *Riverdance* and *Stomp* alongside scenes of Harry Houdini cheating death. In Tommy Tune's case, his "dream" was to star in a traditional Vegas show, so he got to sing a few Broadway-style showtunes. Tommy will probably have moved on in turn by the time you read this, with Gregory Hines among his rumored replacements. To be fair, however, so long as you enjoy showpieces like King Arthur and Merlin fighting two huge mechanical dragons without worrying about their relevance to anything, it's not a bad night out.

Forever Plaid

The Flamingo Hilton, 3555 Las Vegas Blvd S ℂ733-3333.
Daily except Mon 7.30pm & 10pm. $22.

This lightweight but enjoyable off-Broadway comedy is a surprise for the Strip. It focuses on the return to Earth of the Plaids, a doo-wopping quartet who despite being wiped out in 1964 by a busload of Beatle-mad teenagers manage to come back from the dead for one final gig. Close-harmony versions of hits from the 1950s and even earlier go down well with older members of the audience, and there's enough self-knowing humor to keep even young-ish kids in their seats.

Imagine

Luxor, 3900 Las Vegas Blvd S ☏262-4400.
Mon, Wed, Fri & Sat 7.30pm & 10pm, Sun & Tues 7.30pm. $40.

Completely un-Egyptian, despite playing in *Luxor*'s wonderful Egyptian theater, *Imagine* is a prime example of post-Cirque du Soleil entertainment, artfully tailored to offer plenty of the same thrills as *Mystère* at half the price. None of the cast speaks a word, as the show opts for style over content, sweeping happily along on the energy of its young performers. Costs have been cut by concentrating on sets and costumes rather than special effects, and keeping the overall length down to 1hr 15min. In that time, it crams in a stunning array of tumblers, acrobats, and contortionists, some sexy traditional showgirls and showboys, and lots of magical illusions, all accompanied by a barrage of thunderous semi-orchestral rock. It's so fast-moving, there's no time to get bored, let alone worry whether you're missing the point – there is no point. It's certainly not better than the Cirque du Soleil, but it's one of the best-value shows around.

Almost all Las Vegas showrooms now have pre-assigned seating; the days are gone when you had to tip the maître d' $20 or more to get a good seat.

King Arthur's Tournament

Excalibur, 0050 Las Vegas Blvd S ☏597-7600.
Daily 6pm & 8.30pm. $35.

Excalibur can always be relied upon to know which side its bread is buttered; if the kids are happy, then everyone's happy. The *Tournament* is a twice-nightly piece of mock-medieval slapstick and schlockery, centering on a jousting match between a bad black knight and a good white knight that's accompanied by a great deal of tumbling, acrobatics, and hell-raising audience participation, plus the chance to devour a Cornish game hen without the benefit of silverware. It's top-notch family fun, though clearly more directed at the younger set.

Lance Burton

The Monte Carlo, 3770 Las Vegas Blvd S ✆730-7160.
Tues–Sat 7.30pm & 10.30pm. $40 & $45.

In 1996, the *Monte Carlo* lured master magician Lance Burton, who had featured in the *Folies Bergères* for nine years then starred at the *Hacienda* for five years, with a thirteen-year contract to direct and star in his own purpose-built 1200-seat theater. It was money well spent; Burton is a superb and very charming performer, who accompanies stunning sleight of hand with self-knowing patter in a gentle Kentucky drawl. Though no longer quite as young as his publicity photos, he's far more energetic and likable than rivals Siegfried and Roy, who form the butt of many an onstage joke. Most of the show consists of traditional but very impressive stunts with playing cards, handkerchiefs, and doves, but he also takes on the Teutons at their own game, with large-scale illusions like the disappearance of an entire airplane and a narrow escape from hanging. With plenty of kids' participation too, it's the best family show in Vegas.

Legends in Concert

The Imperial Palace, 3535 Las Vegas Blvd S ✆794-3261.
Daily except Sun 7.30pm & 10.30pm. $34.50, ages 12 and under $19.50, including two drinks.

The older of the Strip's two celebrity-tribute shows – the other is at the *Stratosphere* – is also the better, with a changing roster of stars that ranges from the Righteous Brothers to Shania Twain. It's a quick-fire revue in which each member of the cast performs as just one star, with no lip-synching and no doubling up, but plenty of showgirls in flamboyant costumes. For musical prowess, the slick Four Tops are unbeatable, but the surreal recreation of Michael Jackson's *Thriller*, with decaying corpses and dancing skeletons, is a joy to behold, and a tongue-in-cheek Elvis clowning through *Viva Las Vegas* makes a fitting finale. Even full-price tickets are good value, but before you buy, check whether they're giving them away on the sidewalk outside.

Mystère

Treasure Island, 3300 Las Vegas Blvd S ©894-7722.
Wed–Sun 7.30pm & 10.30pm. $70, ages 12 and under $35.

When they first signed a ten-year contract with *Treasure Island* in 1993, Canada's Cirque du Soleil were widely seen as being too "way-out" for Las Vegas. In fact, *Mystère* proved to be the perfect postmodern product for the Strip, and its success has re-defined the city's approach to entertainment. Almost wordless, *Mystère* is all things to all people. At base it's a showcase of fabulous circus skills, with tumblers, acrobats, trapeze artists, pole climbers, clowns, and strong men – two amazing Portuguese brothers. Unless you read the program, you might not realize there's a plot – something about two hungry babies of different species at opposite ends of the universe – but whether you see its dreamscape symbolism as profound and meaningful or labored and empty, it's such a visual feast, and there's so much more going on than you could ever hope to follow, that it barely matters.

O

Bellagio, 3600 Las Vegas Blvd S ©693-7722.

Mon, Tues & Fri–Sun 7.30 & 10.30pm. $90 & $100.

Las Vegas's most expensive show, both in terms of ticket prices
and production costs, is an extraordinary spectacle. For anyone
with an interest in theater, the Cirque du Soleil's latest extravaganza is an absolute must-see, a remarkable testament to just
how much is possible when the budget is barely an issue.
Bellagio built its theater specifically to house *O*, whose name is
a pun on the French for "water." Any part of the stage at any
time may be submerged to any depth. One moment a performer can walk across a particular spot, the next someone may
dive headfirst into that spot from the high wire. With even less
of a plot than *Mystère*, *O* is never portentous; from its beaming
synchronized swimmers onwards, the cast simply revel in the
opportunity to display their magnificent skills to maximum
advantage. Highlights include a colossal trapeze frame draped
like a pirate ship and crewed by a fearless assortment of acrobats
and divers, and footmen flying through the air in swirls of velvet drapery.

Siegfried and Roy

The Mirage, 3400 Las Vegas Blvd S ©792-7777.
Mon, Tues & Fri–Sun 7.30pm & 11pm. $89, including drinks.

Austrian magicians Siegfried and Roy have appeared well
over four thousand times at the *Mirage*, and it shows, not
just in their sheer professionalism but in their air of going
through the motions. The highest-paid entertainers in Vegas
history put on an impressive display of illusions, causing elephants and even dragons to vanish, and teleporting themselves across the arena, but even though you can't tell how
it's done, you know they're basically technicians operating
industrial machinery. When the stage fills up with their
beloved white lions and tigers, Siegfried and Roy finally
perk up enough to take a cloying, self-congratulatory bow
for their dedication to wildlife, and even seem lively by
comparison with the dozy cats. The narcissism of the whole

SHOWS AND SPECTACULARS

thing is as breathtaking as the magic; you'll probably remember Roy's penchant for riding large wild animals bareback, wearing nothing but a black leather codpiece, longer than you'll remember his perfunctory conjuring. The show does feature a large cast of dancers, and some spectacular special effects, but for the price you're entitled to expect more from its stars.

Splash!

The Riviera, 2901 Las Vegas Blvd S ℗794-9433.
Daily 7.30pm & 10.30pm. $39.50 & $49.50.

Despite billboards all over town boasting that *Splash!* was voted the best show in Vegas (not that they say when, exactly), it's hard to imagine anything could offer worse value for money than this cheesy, low-budget, variety show. It's almost worth seeing just to appreciate how far things have progressed since this kind of rubbish was acceptable, with its homophobic comedians pretending to confuse "the Bay area" with "the Gay area" and reciting inane anti-Japanese routines to bemused Asian tour groups, and a chorus line of dispirited showgirls (who go topless in the late-evening shows). The staggeringly inept musical sequences re-tread tired songs from tired movies, with such delights as dancers dressed as the Bay City Rollers cavorting to the theme from *Shaft*, a "John Travolta" who looks as though he's escaped from the Planet of the Apes, and a "Madonna" performing endless songs from *Evita* as she dangles from a cardboard train. There's one incongruous highlight, when four motorcyclists race head-over-heels inside a giant spherical cage, before the whole thing peters out, without even a big finale.

LIVE MUSIC

There's very little point reviewing most of Las Vegas's

venues for **live music**. Other than those stadium acts who appear at the University of Nevada's huge, dreary Thomas & Mack Center (©895-3801), all the biggest gigs in town take place in the casino theaters, almost none of which has a particularly consistent booking policy or is worth visiting in its own right. Thus the *MGM Grand* is home to the 650-seat *Hollywood Theatre*, which plays host to a succession of typically one- or two-week engagements by the likes of Engelbert Humperdinck (tickets usually cost in the region of $50), but can also open up the 16,000-seat *Grand Garden* for stars like the Rolling Stones (tickets $100–400).

For full details of who's playing when you're in town, check newspapers like *City Life* and the *Las Vegas Review Journal*, or call casinos like the *Grand* or *Caesars Palace*. In general, it'll help if your tastes are rooted in the 1960s or earlier, but some of the newer casinos are now orienting themselves toward younger audiences. *Mandalay Bay* and the *Hard Rock* are the current trendsetters, but the re-built *Aladdin* is also expected to be a strong contender, when it finally unveils its mysterious "Music Project."

House of Blues

Map 2, B8. *Mandalay Bay*, 3950 Las Vegas Blvd S ©632-7600.
Happy to play host to this outpost of the burgeoning national live-music chain, *Mandalay Bay* leaves the *House of Blues* to chart its own voodoo-tinged, folk-art-decorated course, with definite but not exclusive emphasis in its programming toward blues, r'n'b, and the like. Typical prices range from around $25 for medium names up to $65 for stars like BB King.

The Joint

Map 2, G4. *Hard Rock Hotel*, 4455 Paradise Rd ©693-5066.
The *Hard Rock*'s 1400-person showroom remains the venue of

Movie theaters

Las Vegas **movie theaters** typically charge around $4 for matinee performances, starting before 6pm, and $7 for evening shows. The only option on the Strip is the *Showcase*, next door to the *MGM Grand*; elsewhere, the Stations casino chain is a good bet. All theaters listed below show first-run films.

Boulder Station 11, *Boulder Station*, 4111 Boulder Hwy ©221-2283.

Century Orleans 12, *Orleans*, 4500 W Tropicana Ave ©227-3456.

Gold Coast Twin, *Gold Coast*, 4000 W Flamingo Rd ©367-7111.

Las Vegas Drive In, 4150 W Carey Ave ©647-1379.

Rainbow Promenade, 2321 N Rainbow Blvd ©225-4828.

Redrock, 5201 W Charleston Blvd ©870-1423.

Regal Village Square 18, 9400 W Sahara Ave ©221-2283.

Showcase 8, 3769 Las Vegas Blvd S ©225-4828.

Sunset 13, *Sunset Station*, 1301 W Sunset Rd, Henderson ©221-2283.

Texas 18, *Texas Station*, 2101 Texas Star Lane, ©221-2283.

choice for big-name touring rock acts, not least because its affluent baby-boomer profile enables someone like Ringo Starr to charge $125 for a ticket. Differing levels of admission for performers such as Elvis Costello or Neil Young range between around $40 and $80; the cheaper rates are for the much less atmospheric balcony.

The Railhead

Map 1, E5. *Boulder Station*, 4111 Boulder Hwy ©432-7777.

In most respects, *Boulder Station* is an ordinary "locals" casino, but the *Railhead* is a sizable and appealing lounge, where the big stage welcomes not only country names like Merle Haggard and Jerry Lee Lewis, but also soul, r'n'b, and reggae acts, with the cover charge generally around $20 on weekends.

COMEDY CLUBS

Catch a Rising Star
Map 2, C5. *The MGM Grand*, 3799 Las Vegas Blvd S ℂ891-7777. Daily 7.30pm & 10pm. $17.50.
Cozy showroom featuring two to four up-and-coming acts nightly, many of which have already had TV exposure.

Comedy Stop
Map 2, C6. *The Tropicana*, 3801 Las Vegas Blvd S ℂ739-2411. Daily 8pm & 10.30pm. $14, includes two drinks.
The atmosphere at the *Tropicana*'s large, long-standing upstairs venue tends to be more sedate than at its rivals, with four hundred customers seated at round tables to enjoy mostly mainstream comedians.

The Improv
Map 2, C1. *Harrah's*, 3475 Las Vegas Blvd S ℂ369-5111. Daily except Mon 8pm & 10.30pm. $20.
Chicago's famous *Improv* found a new home at *Harrah's* in 1996, just up the stairs inside the main entrance. The formula remains the same, of three or four polished stand-ups per show rather than free-for-all improvisation.

Riviera Comedy Club
Map 3, E6. *The Riviera*, 2901 Las Vegas Blvd S ℂ794-9433.

Mon–Thurs & Sun 8pm & 10pm, Fri & Sat 8pm, 10pm & 11.45pm. $15, including two drinks.

Vegas's most adventurous and stimulating comedy venue; pro-gramming for the late-night shows includes all-gay and "XXXtreme" nights.

Gambling

Gambling remains the bedrock of the Las Vegas experience. At most recent count, 29 other US states had joined Nevada in offering some form of casino gambling, but thanks to its colossal volume of business, Las Vegas still does it better than the rest. Ninety percent of visitors to the city gamble, with an average budget of $500, and in the end, everything else is just frippery; it's the gambling that makes every flourish possible. The shows and restaurants, volcanoes and theme parks – no matter how profitable any might be – are all just designed to make you stick around longer and spend more money on the slots and tables.

While the casinos these days prefer to talk about "gaming" rather than gambling, no one plays for fun alone. It's the gut-wrenching excitement of staking your own hard cash in pursuit of a fortune that keeps the atmosphere at fever pitch. Most visitors have their own preferred form of gambling, with the three main choices being **table games** such as blackjack or craps, played in the public gaze and surrounded by glamorous trimmings; **slot machines**, a more private pleasure in which the potential winnings are enormous, and you're spared the fear of not seeming *au fait* with the rules; and **sports betting**, with its hyped-up atmosphere and scope for proving that you know more than the bookies.

The fact that the gambling industry is still booming is a credit to the casinos' ability to change with the times. During the first few decades of Las Vegas's supremacy, the typical gambler was male and likely to be familiar with a wide range of card games thanks to years spent in military service. Since 1983, however, slots and other machines have overtaken the tables, and they now generate around sixty percent of Nevada's gaming revenue. In the face of the large proportion of modern visitors who see casino games as complicated and intimidating, the casinos are desperate to make gambling as easy, user-friendly and innocuous as possible. All offer free lessons, instructional videos on their in-room TVs, and the like. On the surface, those well-dressed and welcoming dealers make things seem democratic and casual, but all that deference serves in fact to make anyone who sits down at the tables feel like part of an exclusive and sophisticated elite.

Despite Las Vegas's reputation as a stronghold of **crime**, there's no suggestion that gamblers themselves are being cheated. The casinos don't need to cheat; they know they're certain to make money. Yes, the occasional high-roller can seriously damage the corporate balance sheet – thus Australian TV magnate Kerry Packer once won twenty consecutive hands of baccarat in twenty minutes at the *Mirage*, at $250,000 per hand. Overall, however, the odds are stacked in the casinos' favor. In the case of table games, as explained in more detail below, each has some combination of a quantifiable "house edge" incorporated into its rules, or a set way of skimming the top off players' winnings. With slots, it's even more straightforward – they're simply programmed to pay out less than they take in, though only the casinos themselves know just how much less.

Gambling is of course supremely addictive, and Las Vegas not surprisingly has a higher percentage of problem gamblers than any other city in the world. The generally accepted advice for visitors who want to experience the thrill while minimizing the risk is never to gamble more than you're prepared to lose. In addition, if you want to play for any length of time, don't bet more than around one-fiftieth of your total budget at any one moment. Thus if you've set aside $250 with which to gamble, it makes sense to play $5 slot machines, or bet with $5 roulette chips; if you've got $50, play with $1 stakes. Remember that even if the house edge on your chosen game is as low as two percent, that doesn't mean you'll lose two percent of your money and walk away with the remaining 98 percent. It means that if you play long enough, you'll almost certainly lose it all.

As for **where to gamble**, that really depends on how you see gambling. If you think it's all about fun and glamour, then the **Strip** is the place to be, though the high minimum stakes at the largest casinos can mean you'll lose your money uncomfortably fast. If you feel that an authentic gambling hall should be a bit gritty and grimy and peopled by hard-bitten "characters," you may be happier **downtown**. If you see betting as a business, and want as much bang for your buck as possible, head instead for a **locals casino** (see p.93), and especially the members of the Stations chain, which tend to offer more generous odds at video poker and the like.

The average slot machine on the Strip generates $107 profit per day; each table game makes an average of $1777.

TABLE GAMES

Casino "games" are not really games in the same sense as the games you might enjoy at home, where each player has the same chance of winning. They're carefully structured business propositions, in which the casinos know that over time they are certain to end up ahead.

Most casino games have a built-in "**house edge**." Imagine taking turns tossing a coin with a friend. If you call it correctly, he gives you $1, while if he calls it correctly you give him $1. Now imagine that he suggests a change in the rules; you still have to give him $1 when he's right, but from now on he'll only pay you 95¢. It's still possible that if you play for a few minutes, you may have a run of luck and win lots of 95¢ pay-outs. If you play all day, however, you're going to lose; if he can persuade millions of others to join in and play all day, every day, he's going to get very rich, very quickly. Thus, for example, the roulette table in most Las Vegas casinos holds 38 squares, numbered 1 to 36 plus "0" and "00." If you bet $1 on the correct number, the casino should in theory recognize that you had a 1-in-38 chance of being right, and pay you $38 (including your original $1 stake). Instead, they pay $36, or 94.74 percent; the $2 they hold back works out at 5.26 percent of the total, and that's the "house edge."

In addition to the edge, the casino also knows that most people don't bet at the best odds. It's too boring only to bet on one number for each spin of the roulette wheel, so you may well place a $1 chip on each of three numbers. Only one can possibly be correct, however, so even if you do win the casino grabs back another $2 in the process. According to casino insiders, the rate at which gamblers actually lose their money playing roulette amounts to **thirty percent** per spin of the wheel.

In any case, different people gamble for different reasons. Devotees of blackjack argue that the house edge is much lower than on other games, and that with enough cool calculation it's possible to even come out ahead. Others are far more drawn to the possibility of a quick big win playing craps and roulette, and say that it's about luck, not arithmetic.

BACCARAT

Despite its sophisticated image – lavishly cultivated by most casinos (not to mention numerous James Bond films) – the card game **baccarat** is at root a simple game of chance, which requires no skill or judgment from its players. Its name, pronounced *bah-kah-rah* not *back-a-rat*, comes from the Italian for "zero," in that all the cards that are worth ten points in other games – 10s, jacks, queens, and kings – are here worth nothing at all. Aces count as one, and other cards are worth their face value.

Even though up to fifteen gamblers can sit around the table, no more than two hands are ever dealt. One is called the "**player**," and the other the "**bank**," but you're free to bet on whichever you choose. Each round starts with a different gambler being invited to deal two cards to each hand. According to a complicated but fixed set of criteria, a third card may then be dealt to either hand or both, starting with the "player." The aim for each hand is to add up to as close to nine as possible; with totals of ten or more, the first digit is always discarded. Thus a 4 and a 3 total seven; a jack and a 3 total three; and a queen, a 9 and a 4 also total three.

To bet on baccarat, you don't need to understand the precise circumstances in which the third card is dealt; the spectacle simply unfolds before you, as often as not in complete silence. All you need to know is that only three bets are possible – "player," "bank," and "tie" – and that although successful "tie" bets pay off at 8 to 1, the house has a 14.4 percent advantage on these, so they're never worth making. "Player" and "bank" both pay back even money, but as "bank" is marginally more likely to win, the casino levies a five percent commission on successful "bank" bets. Even taking that into account, the house advantage is 1.06 percent on "bank" bets, and 1.24 percent on "player" bets. Betting "bank" is thus always slightly the better option.

BACCARAT

The very narrow house "edge" on baccarat explains why the game is traditionally reserved for high-rollers; only the top echelon of casinos offer it, usually in roped-off enclaves where the minimum stake is at least $100. These days, however, you may encounter the all-but-identical, if faster-paced, game of "**mini-baccarat**" being played out on the main casino floor, for lower minimum stakes.

BINGO

It's not easy to find the good old-fashioned game of **bingo** in Las Vegas, but what games there are tend to rank among the city's best deals. That's because, like a cheap buffet restaurant, bingo is seen by lesser casinos as a great way to lure in local customers. The game itself may not even run at a profit; the idea is that with intervals of up to two hours between sessions, bingo buffs will end up playing the slots and other games. Only the *Monte Carlo* and the *New Frontier* on the Strip, and *Binion's Horseshoe* downtown, bother to offer bingo at all; the best places to play elsewhere are *Sam's Town* and the *Gold Coast*.

BLACKJACK

Blackjack is the most popular table game in Las Vegas. The main reason is probably that many people are used to playing similar card games at home, whether that be "21" in North America or "pontoon" in Europe. In any case, it's easy to learn, and although you do have to play against the casino, the dealer is forbidden to exercise any skill or judgment, so there's no danger of being outwitted or cheated. Most tempting of all, not only are the odds relatively good to start with, but there is also a mathematically "correct" way to play blackjack, which may not guarantee success but can cut the house advantage even lower.

Although blackjack is played with a conventional pack of 52 cards, divided into four suits, the suits play no part in the game. All that matters is the **point value** of each card. The numbered cards, from 2 to 10, are counted at their face value; jacks, queens, and kings are worth ten points; and players can choose to count aces as worth either one or eleven. Each player attempts to assemble a hand whose total value adds up as close as possible to, but not more than, **21**; that value must also be higher than, or equal to, the dealer's own hand. Thus a jack, a 3, and an 8 add up to 21, which is good; a 9, a 4, and a 6 add up to 19, which is pretty good; and a king and two 7s add up to 24, which is more than 21 and therefore bad. An ace and a 4 counts as either 5 (the "soft" total) or 15 (the "hard" total). Best of all is an ace and any card worth ten, which adds up to 21, and is known as either a "**natural**" or a "blackjack." (In early versions of blackjack, an ace plus a black jack was considered especially good – hence the name – but now a blackjack is any two-card combination that totals 21.)

In the most usual form of blackjack, each round begins with each player placing the chips they wish to stake in their own designated betting area. All are then dealt two cards, face down, while the dealer receives one card face down, and one face up. Look at your cards by raising the edge, but don't pick them up. Starting with the player on the dealer's left, each player then plays his or her own hand in its entirety. On your turn, you repeatedly choose whether to "hit," and be dealt another card face up – which you signal by either scratching your fingers toward you on the table or just saying "hit." When you don't want to hit any more, which may well be immediately, signal that you've decided to "**stand**" by pushing your cards, unexposed, beneath your stake money. If, after you "hit," your total exceeds 21, you're "**bust**," and you must say so by turning all your cards face up; the dealer will respond by taking your cards and your stake.

Only once all the players have finished does the dealer turn both his or her cards face up and play out his or her own hand. The dealer, however, has no discretion as to how to proceed – the instructions are written on the table for all to see. The dealer must hit if the total is 16 or lower, and stand as soon it reaches 17 or higher, so he or she has to keep on hitting even when his total of 16 would in theory beat all the players. When the dealer's final total is settled, all the players' hands are revealed and the bets are paid off; you'll either get your original stake back, plus the same amount again, if you've beaten the dealer; lose your stake if you've been beaten; or simply keep it if you've tied. If the dealer has a "natural," that beats any total of 21 that uses three or more cards. If on the other hand you're dealt a "natural," you can immediately turn them over to announce this fact. The dealer will then check his or her cards for a natural; if the dealer also has one, it's a tie (and the hand is over for everyone else); otherwise you're paid off at three-to-two odds.

There are three further possibilities. If you're dealt a "pair" – two 3s, two aces, whatever – you can **"split"** them and play two separate hands, doubling your original stake so that you have the same bet on each. You can also **"double down,"** which means that if your original two cards are such that being dealt one, and only one, more card is likely to give you a winning total, you can double your stake and take that chance. Both those strategies are sound in some circumstances (see opposite for examples); the third, however, an option called **"insurance"** which is too complicated to be worth explaining here, is said by experts never to be a good bet.

The casinos' built-in advantage at blackjack stems from the fact that you have to play your own hand before the dealer plays, and you forfeit your stake for going "bust" whether or not the dealer subsequently also goes bust. However, the lure of the game for serious gamblers stems from the work of computer expert Edward Thorp, whose 1962 book *Beat The Dealer* proved that by memorizing the cards as they are dealt, skilled players can consistently beat the house. At first, Las

Vegas casinos panicked, banning all "card counters"; then they made things harder, by using several packs of cards at once, and shuffling at random intervals. It soon transpired that in any case hardly anyone can count cards accurately in the noisy, stressful conditions of a modern casino, and most gamblers went on losing at the same rate as ever.

Computer analysis has also shown that if you compare your own cards with the dealer's face-up card, there's a "correct" response to every permutation. Charts displaying this "basic strategy," which reduces the house advantage to a mere one percent, are widely available in specialist gambling books; some casinos even distribute them. In essence, if your total is between 12 and 16, you should stand if the dealer's face-up card is between 2 and 6 (with a few exceptions, like if you have 12 and the dealer is showing a 2), and hit if it isn't; if your total is 17, stand (unless you're dealt an ace and a 6); and always stand if your total is 18 or over. On top of that, if you're total is 10 or 11, and the dealer has from 2 to 9, you should "double down"; while if you're dealt a pair of 8s, or a pair of aces, you should "split."

The usual minimum stake for blackjack games on the Strip is $5, although it tends to rise in the evening at the larger casinos to $25. The *Sahara*, however, guarantees $1 tables 24 hours per day. Many casinos also offer gimmicky blackjack variations such as "double exposure," in which the dealer's hand is dealt face up, and **Spanish 21**, in which all the 10s are removed from the pack. These feature a host of other minor rule changes, detailed either on the table itself or on leaflets. The odds aren't necessarily any better or worse than usual, but the optimum strategy will differ.

If you want to play single- or double-deck blackjack for low minimum stakes you may be better off heading downtown rather than to the Strip.

CASINO WAR

Casino War is the easiest, fastest, and most banal card game imaginable, introduced to suit an era when fewer and fewer people know any card games at all. Each player, including the dealer, is dealt one card face up. If your card is higher than the dealer's, you win your bet; if it's lower, you lose. If they're the same, you can either "surrender," and lose half your stake, or go to "war," by doubling your stake. You both then get another card; this time if you beat, or tie with, the dealer, you win your original stake only, whereas if you lose the dealer takes both your bets. Assuming you always go to war – the better option – the house advantage is 2.9 percent.

CRAPS

The dice game known as **craps** is the most exciting, frenzied, and noisy game on any casino floor, but it's also the most intimidating for novices. It all happens too fast to learn by observation, so prospective players should take a lesson or two first. That said, it's not as hard as it looks, and you don't need to know all the rules to enjoy playing – in fact the easier bets on the table pay much better odds than the more complicated "sucker" ones.

Craps is played on a baize table with high, padded, and slightly rounded walls. Each game is operated by four casino employees; the "boxman," who's in overall charge; two dealers, to handle the bets at either end of the table; and the "stickman," who uses a stick to recover and distribute the dice. However, it's the players who actually throw the dice, so craps is much more of a participatory experience than other casino games, and a player on a hot streak can take the credit for a table-full of winners.

At the start of each game, the stickman invites a different player to be "shooter"; you can decline if you prefer. The shooter then lays a bet, on "**PASS**," and makes the "come-out roll" by throwing two dice hard enough to bounce against the end of the table. Meanwhile, the other players have laid any bets they want to make, mainly on either PASS or "**DON'T PASS**." In effect, they're betting with or against the shooter, although it's the casino that actually pays the bets.

If the come-out roll is 7 or 11, then the shooter, and everyone else who has bet on PASS, wins immediately, while everyone who bet on DON'T PASS loses. If, on the other hand, the come-out roll is "craps," meaning 2, 3, or 12, the shooter and all PASS bettors lose; DON'T PASS bettors win on 2 or 3, or retain their stake on 12.

Any other come-out roll – the possibilities are 4, 5, 6, 8, 9, and 10 – becomes the "point," and a marker is placed in the corresponding position on the table. The shooter's sole aim is now to throw the point again before throwing a 7, or "sevening out." If the shooter succeeds, PASS wins and DON'T PASS loses; if not, DON'T PASS wins, PASS loses.

"Craps" is a noun, the name of the game; "crap" is the matching adjective, as in "crap table."

At any point after the come-out roll, anyone – even players who have not bet so far – can also bet on either **COME** or **DON'T COME**. These are the same as PASS and DON'T PASS, in that the next throw becomes your "come number," and a COME bet wins if the shooter throws that number again before throwing a 7. If the shooter throws the point before either a 7 or the "come number," then COME bets stay on the table.

In addition, after a come-out roll that's neither 7, 11, nor craps, anyone who has bet PASS/DON'T PASS or COME/DON'T COME can make an extra **ODDS** bet on that same bet. This time, you're betting according to the

CRAPS

actual odds that the relevant point or come number will or will not be thrown before a 7. To place an ODDS bet, say "odds" to the dealer and either put your chips behind the PASS line if you've already bet PASS, or give them to the dealer to go with your original COME, DON'T COME, or DON'T PASS bet. ODDS bets are the best-value bets in the casino, in that they pay according to the precise likelihood of throwing that particular dice combination compared to a 7. Some casinos only allow ODDS bets up to double the original stake; others allow them to be as much as a hundred times higher. For serious gamblers, the ODDS bets are the prime reason to play craps at all.

Note, however, that the actual odds for ODDS bets are not marked on the table. All those bets that *are* marked, such as the dice pictured in the middle, are not only harder to understand, but they're also much worse propositions – which is why they're not worth explaining here. If you see "crapless craps" advertised, that's a simpler version in which every number other than 7 can be the point after the come-out roll.

Though the usual minimum stake for craps on the Strip is $5 or $10, *Silver City* has 25¢ tables, the *Sahara* always offers $1 tables, the *Stardust* goes for $2, and *Circus Circus* and *Excalibur* start at $3. At *Bellagio* and *Caesars*, it can be hard to find a table that accepts stakes of less than $100. *Binion's*, downtown, is one of the more boisterous and atmospheric spots to play, and tables can be as low as 25¢, too.

KENO

By contrast with the superficially similar game of bingo (see p.208), **keno** is renowned in Las Vegas for offering abysmal odds. The crucial difference is that bingo is played out until someone has circled all the numbers on their score sheet, so there's always a winner. With keno, on the other hand, each player chooses up to twenty numbers between 1 and 80, and their choice is then compared with the twenty drawn by the casino. Even if you select twenty numbers, the probability of five being correct is less than one in 300; of picking eight, is one in 250,000; and of picking ten is one in ten million. Compare those odds with the returns actually paid by the casinos, and you'll see why they're on to such a good deal.

POKER

In its traditional form, **poker** is unique among Las Vegas card games in that gamblers play against each other, not the house. The casinos simply provide a room and a dealer, in return either for a percentage on every hand, which varies from one to ten percent, or, less usually, charging by the hour. Playing poker against a bunch of total strangers is undeniably exciting, but it's not a risk to take lightly. It might be melodramatic to imagine that your opponents are cheats or crooks, but they may well be professionals, and it's downright crazy to assume they're worse at the game than you are. The two most widely played variations, both of which offer scope for endless rounds of betting, are **Seven Card Stud**, in which each player is dealt two cards face down, four more face up, and then a final one face down, and **Texas Hold 'Em**, in which each player gets two face-down cards, and then five communal cards are dealt face up on the table. The object in both games is to make the highest hand possible using five of the seven cards, though often how you bet is more crucial than the cards on on which you're betting.

Casinos generally see traditional poker as a service for guests who will also gamble on other games, though several have begun to stage poker tournaments, along the lines of the wildly successful **World Series of Poker** held in late April each year at *Binion's Horseshoe* downtown (see p.84 for more information).

In addition, most casinos offer what are essentially hybrids of poker and blackjack. These new games, played

on blackjack-like tables, are designed to pit gamblers directly against the house – and thus seem less intimidating –
while also maximizing the house advantage. The usual minimum bet on the Strip is $5, though you might find a $3
table.

In **Caribbean Stud Poker**, originally developed for
cruise ships, each player makes an ante bet, and is dealt five
cards face down, while the dealer gets four cards face down
and one face up. You can now either "fold" – surrender
both hand and bet – or "call," by adding another bet that's
double your original ante. Each hand is compared individu-
ally with the dealer's. If you beat the dealer, you win your
ante bet at even odds, while your call bet might win a
bonus of as much as a hundred to one, depending on how
high a hand you have. There's an outrageous twist, however; if the dealer has an especially bad hand, of anything less
than an ace and a king, it's said not to "qualify," and call
bets are returned rather than paid off. Betting an additional
$1 per hand enters you for a progressive jackpot, payable on
royal flushes, that can reach over $100,000.

Let It Ride is an unorthodox variation in which you
make three separate but equal bets on the three cards you're
dealt, but can then withdraw one bet at a time as two further communal cards are revealed. You're not competing
against anyone else here, not even the dealer; bets are paid
off according to a chart that shows each winning hand and
the (severely under-valued) odds against it.

Pai Gow Poker – as distinct from the Chinese domino
game Pai Gow, which you may also encounter – is played
with an ordinary pack of cards plus a single joker, which
can count as either an ace or a "wild" card to complete a
flush or straight. Each player, including the dealer, receives
seven cards and has to divide them into one five-card hand
and one two-card hand. Although the two-card hand must
be worth less than the five-card one, *both* have to defeat *both*

the dealer's hands for you to win. If only one beats the dealer, it's a "push," and bets are returned. The house levies a five percent commission on winning bets.

For an account of video poker, see p.222.

ROULETTE

Roulette, a game of pure chance, revolves around guessing which of the numbered compartments of a rotating wheel will be the eventual resting place of a ball released by the dealer. Players use the adjoining baize table to bet not only on the precise number, but also on whether it is odd or even, or "black" or "red," or falls within various specified ranges.

The oldest of the regular casino games, roulette was introduced to the casinos of Paris in 1765 with official police blessing, on the grounds that it was impossible to cheat. That doesn't mean, however, that your chances of winning are especially good.

All roulette wheels hold the numbers 1 to 36, of which half are colored red and half black, plus a green 0; almost all the wheels in Las Vegas also feature a green 00. On this "double-zero" layout, the wheel has 38 compartments, so gamblers have a 1 in 38 chance of choosing the right number (it's possible to bet on 0 or 00, although neither counts as red or black, or odd or even). When there's only one zero, the true odds are 1 in 37. However, the odds for successful bets are always the same, set as if there were no zeroes at all. A correct number is paid off at 35 to 1, guessing the correct pair of numbers pays 17 to 1, the correct block of three pays 11 to 1, and so on.

Roulette means "little wheel" in French.

Thus it's the zeroes that give the house its advantage, and the addition of the double zero doubles that advantage from the standard 2.7 percent in Europe to 5.26 percent in Las Vegas. That may sound like a small difference, but it means that you'll lose your money twice as fast on a double-zero table as on a single-zero one, and it explains why only one in fifty of Las Vegas gamblers bothers to play roulette at all.

Three strategies can improve your chances. The first is to play only single-zero tables. On the Strip, the *Monte Carlo* and the *Stratosphere* always offer at least one single-zero game, while the *MGM Grand*, *Caesars Palace*, and a few others occasionally provide single-zero roulette for high rollers. The second is to avoid the bet that covers 0, 00, 1, 2, and 3, which pays at 5 to 1 – a house advantage of 7.89 percent – and therefore offers the worst odds on the table. The third is the most boring of all; the fewer spins you take part in, the better, so you should stake all you can afford to risk just once, on one of the (almost) even-money bets – such as red/black, or odd/even – and then walk away, win or lose.

Nonetheless, roulette ranks second only to blackjack for the number of elaborate "systems" devised by hopeful gamblers. Most are variants of the "martingale," which requires you to keep doubling (or trebling, or whatever) your stake on red or black until your first win, and then stop. The trouble is, you need to have a large reserve of cash to cover even a short sequence of losses, so your initial stake can only be a small proportion of your total cash – and yet all you can ever hope to win is that initial stake. On top of that, each game has a maximum bet, so you can't keep doubling your stake anyway. Other systems, which predict which numbers are "due" to fall, are so sure to fail that most casinos provide electronic boards listing the last twenty or so successful numbers. In a nutshell, in the words of blackjack guru Edward Thorp, "there is no 'mathematical' winning system for roulette and it is impossible ever to discover one."

For an account of how some physicists tried to build a
computer system to predict the roulette wheel, read
The Newtonian Casino (review on p.277).

As for the etiquette of the game, only players seated at the table are supposed to play, although in practice dealers usually allow passers-by to stake a bill or two on a straightforward bet. Each player starts by buying a pile of uniquely colored chips, valid only for roulette, so the dealer can keep track of who owns which chips. After each spin, all losing chips are swept from the table; winning stakes, however, remain in place, so unless you remove successful chips yourself you're betting them again on the next spin.

The value of the chips used at each table varies, and is always displayed together with the size of the minimum bet accepted. These aren't necessarily the same; a table using $1 chips may well require gamblers to bet at least $5 in total on each spin. The typical chip value on the Strip is $1; *Silver City* offers 25¢ chips, and *Circus Circus* and *O'Sheas* 50¢ chips, while places like the *Mirage* and *Caesars* tend to start at $5.

Finally, don't be tempted by roulette tables that offer "Back to Back" betting. With rewards of 1000 to 1 for naming two consecutive winners, and 10,000 to 1 for three, these give the house an advantage of an abysmal 27 percent and an outrageous eighty percent respectively.

WHEEL OF FORTUNE

The game variously known as **Wheel of Fortune**, or Big Six, or Money Wheel, is a traditional carnival sideshow that offers some of the worst odds in any casino. Few gamblers play more than once only, on a passing whim; the main appeal is that you can stake cash, not chips.

The dealer spins a rotating pointer on a dartboard-like wheel marked with 54 different dollar amounts, while players place bets on those same dollar amounts on a glass-topped table. If your number matches the pointer, you win that many dollars per dollar staked. As a rule, the house edge is lowest on the 24 or so segments marked with $1, and highest on the two that show a joker or some other house symbol, which pay off at forty to one.

SLOT MACHINES

It's now over a century since the first "one-armed bandits" appeared in the saloons of San Francisco, but **slot machines** are more popular than ever. Thanks to glitzy new technology and highly competitive odds – not to mention some truly huge jackpots – the casinos have largely dispelled the old image of slot arcades as joyless places where tight-lipped seniors pump bucketfuls of small change into unresponsive machines. These days, even casinos like the *Mirage* make twice as much money on slots as they do on the tables, and slot-players are no longer second-class citizens.

Traditionally, the house advantage on slot machines used to be around twenty percent, which is to say that for every dollar you gambled, you might win back eighty cents, while the operator kept the other twenty. Those would now be regarded as "tight" odds, as casinos vie to offer "looser" machines – promoted with slogans such as "99% SLOTS GUARANTEED!" – where the house advantage is as little as five or even one percent. The main reason they can do that is that gamblers these days are prepared to invest much higher stakes, staking $1 or $5 a time rather than the old standard of 25¢. So long as each time you spin the reels, the casino can expect to win 5¢, they're equally happy to achieve that with quarter slots that pay 80 percent, dollar slots that pay 95 percent, or $5 slots set at 99 percent.

Modern, computerized slot machines are far more sophisticated than their mechanical forebears. Most still contain giant wheels decorated with different symbols – customers have proved suspicious of machines that just show pictures of those symbols on video screens – but, contrary to appearances, the reels don't simply spin until they stop. Instead, a micro-chip inside each machine generates an unending stream of random numbers. Whenever you set the reels spinning, the current number determines where they will stop. Just because you hit a combination that looks close to a jackpot doesn't mean that you nearly hit the jackpot, and no sequence of combinations, or lack of winners, can ever indicate that a machine is "ready" to hit.

Beneath all the surface glitter, there are basically two different types of slot machine. "**Non-progressive**" machines have fixed paybacks for every winning combination, and in principle pay lower prizes, more frequently. "**Progressive**" ones, such as *Megabucks* or *Quartermania*, are linked into networks of several similar machines, potentially covering the entire state of Nevada. The longer it takes before someone, somewhere hits the jackpot, the higher that jackpot will be – digital displays show mounting totals that can run into millions of dollars.

All the major casinos operate **slot clubs**, which keep track of how much you gamble and reward you with points redeemable for discounts and upgrades, show tickets, or even cash. The value is never that high – at the *MGM Grand*, for example, inserting $2000 into the slots entitles you to $12.50 cash back – but it costs nothing to join, so if you plan to gamble for any length of time you might as well.

As for **where to play**, the slots are "loosest" (which is good) downtown, and anywhere locals play regularly, and notoriously "tight" at places such as the airport or supermarkets, where most customers are just passing through. Strip options range from the *Riviera*, "where the nickel is king" and you can play for days on end, to the $500 machines in the marble-walled High Limits room at *Bellagio*.

To play the slots, you must be over 21 and have the ID to prove it; underage winners are not paid off. US citizens must pay tax on wins of $1200 or more.

VIDEO POKER

The only video game to win widespread acceptance in Las Vegas casinos is **video poker**, a cross between "five-card draw" poker and a conventional slot machine. Each time you play, five cards are "dealt" onto the screen. You can then, once only, be dealt replacements for as many of those five as you choose not to "hold." While it is a game of skill, you're not required to know the rules of poker; the odds paid for all possible winning hands are listed on the body of the machine.

Apart from sparing you the embarrassment of having to cope with a real dealer or other players, the appeal of video poker is that the odds can be very good indeed. You can assess just how good a machine is by what it pays for a full house and a flush. There are "progressive" and "non-progressive" video poker machines, just like ordinary slot machines (see p.220); "loose" progressive machines generally offer eight coins for a full house and five for a flush, while loose non-progressives tend to pay nine and six respectively. On a "nine/six" machine the house edge is a mere half percent or so, but several casinos now offer "ten/six" or "nine/seven" machines on which the advantage is technically slightly in the gambler's favor. The snag is that to have that edge, and win consistently, you have to play perfectly.

Entire books have been written on what constitutes perfect strategy in video poker. It's not the same as in ordinary poker, and it depends on whether the machine you're playing features "wild" cards or not. In brief, because the highest rewards are paid for **royal flushes**, you should almost always play for that at the expense of any other possible – or even certain – win.

SPORTS BETTING

Although Nevada is the only state in the country where it's legal to place bets on the outcome of sporting events, large-scale **sports betting** is a relatively recent addition to the Las Vegas scene. The first casino to open what's called a "**Sports Book**" was the *Plaza* in 1975, and they've only become widespread since changes in federal taxation in the mid-1980s. Now, almost every casino has one, and in most instances it's a "Race and Sports Book," where you can bet on horse-racing as well.

You might imagine that where you do your sports betting would depend on which casino offered the best odds. In fact, although odds do change minute by minute, almost all are set centrally, and there's little variation between individual casinos. On top of that, mobile phones and recording devices are banned by Nevada law from all Sports Books, so the only way to compare odds is to trudge from one casino to the next.

The choice instead centers on what sort of atmosphere you prefer. There, the range is enormous. Some Sports Books are high-tech extravaganzas, their walls taken up by vast electronic scoreboards interspersed with massive TV screens; during major sporting occasions, they're basically sports bars, filled by shrieking crowds. Prime examples include those at *Caesars Palace*, the *Stardust* (which you can enter via a doorway direct from the Strip), *Mandalay Bay* (which boasts the biggest screen in town), the *Rio*, and the *Las Vegas Hilton*.

Others opt instead for a hushed, reverential ambience, giving each gambler a personal TV monitor to watch their event of choice, and hand-writing the odds with marker pens on white boards. The Race Book at the *Imperial Palace* is an especially irresistible example, rising in tiers above the Strip entrance. There are also those that resemble elegant gentlemen's clubs, like the one at *Bellagio* with its massive padded leatherette armchairs.

Still others, especially at the locals casinos in outlying neighborhoods, seem like throwbacks to the Victorian era, modeled perhaps on schoolrooms or offices. Rows of gamblers sit at long workbenches, studying poorly printed tip sheets and form books as they await the news from far-off racetracks with names like Gulfstream, Laurel, and Aqueduct.

As for what you can bet on, the options are nearly limitless; not only can you wager on who will win pretty much any conceivable game, fight, or race, you can make more specialized bets, like predicting the combined points total in a game (referred to as the "over-under").

One thing all the Sports Books have in common is the provision of **free alcohol** to gamblers; there's usually a snack bar close to hand as well.

Shopping

The last ten years have seen a dramatic turnaround in the profile of **shopping** in Las Vegas. Before the unveiling of the mind-boggling Forum at *Caesars Palace* in 1992, none of the casinos had its own shopping mall, and the city's stores catered almost exclusively to locals. Since then, malls and arcades have been opening everywhere, and the shopping craze has reached the point where an amazing two thirds of visitors to Las Vegas in one survey cited the shops as the main reason to come.

Not that Las Vegas is a great destination for bargain hunters; apart from the odd souvenir store, it's not tacky, and it's not cheap. Instead, tourists can expect to encounter jazzed-up outlets of all the usual chains to be found in any US suburban mall, plus a leavening of high-end international names. What's really generating all the excitement is that the big casinos have started to bring Las Vegas's traditional flair for display and presentation to these shopping malls, turning them into must-see attractions. As for what makes the malls the **most profitable** in the nation, it would be nice to imagine that the city is full of successful gamblers who can't wait to flaunt their new-found wealth. However, the truth is more likely that visitors find themselves losing so much on the tables and slots, with nothing to show for it, that getting something in return for their money – however expensive – suddenly seems a miraculous alternative.

Along the Strip in particular, the shopping boom shows no signs of faltering. *Bellagio* positioned itself at the top of the spectrum in 1998 with the small but exquisite Via Bellagio, while 1999 saw the *Venetian* open the Grand Canal Shoppes as a fully fledged large-scale rival to the Forum. As this book went to press, the similarly sized Desert Passage at the revamped *Aladdin* was approaching completion, while Mandalay Resort Group had announced the construction of a huge new mall between *Luxor* and *Mandalay Bay*, to be anchored by a *Nordstrom's* department store.

Not every casino has succumbed to the mall-building craze, however. Both the *MGM Grand* and the *Mirage* devote a tiny proportion of their space to shopping, while others among their neighbors stick to the traditional formula of offering only souvenir-type stores, such as *Luxor's* enjoyable selection of Egyptian-themed outlets.

Neither is there all that much variety between one major Strip mall and the next, in terms of actual stores. Thus Ann Taylor, Banana Republic, bebe and Caché have three outlets each within a quarter of a mile, at the Forum, the Grand Canal Shoppes, and the Fashion Show Mall. *Bellagio* may have won a much-publicized tussle to secure the Armani store that the *Venetian* wanted, but there was already one at the *Mirage*, and an Armani Exchange in the Forum.

As a city of over a million inhabitants, Las Vegas has of course its fair share of busy shopping districts – most notably along **South Decatur Boulevard** and **South Maryland Parkway**, a couple of miles west and east of the Strip respectively – as well as the kind of malls you'd find anywhere in the United States. Once again, however, few visitors bother to stray far from the Strip.

Until the Neonopolis development opens – see p.88 –
there are no significant shopping opportunities in
downtown Las Vegas.

MALLS ON THE STRIP

Fashion Show Mall
Map 3, C9. 3200 Las Vegas Blvd S ℂ369-0704.
Mon–Fri 10am–9pm, Sat 10am–7pm, Sun noon–6pm.
The Fashion Show Mall caused a sensation when it opened in
1981, as the first significant shopping mall to appear on the
Strip. Back then, its range of department stores, high-end
designer emporia, and even its run-of-the-mill mall outlets
were a welcome novelty for Las Vegas. These days, however,
the stakes on the Strip are much higher, and while in fairness
the Fashion Show Mall would in most parts of the US represent a very classy place to shop, it offers none of the excitement
of the major casino malls. Where it does score over its newer
neighbors is in boasting large department stores such as
Neiman Marcus, Sak's Fifth Avenue, Macy's, Dillard's, and
Robinsons-May, but in a city where shopping has become an
eye-grabbing experience, the Fashion Show Mall, for all its
recent expansion, is something of a seen-it-all-before snooze.

Forum Shops
Map 2, B2. *Caesars Palace*, 3500 Las Vegas Blvd S ℂ893-4800.
Mon–Thurs & Sun 10am–11pm, Fri & Sat 10am–midnight.
The mall that kick-started Las Vegas's shopping boom in 1992
continues to be the most successful in the United States, generating four times the national average revenue per square
foot. That's largely because it's a great tourist destination in its
own right. The basic concept is gloriously over the top, with

faux-Roman columns and fountains everywhere, "statues" that come alive, and an artificial sky that wheels each hour between dawn and dusk. Many of the larger stores join in the fun, so Mickey Mouse rides a chariot in the Disney Store, Elmer Fudd sports a toga at Warner Brothers, and Barbie strikes classical poses at FAO Schwarz. Others take themselves more seriously, resulting in the Forum boasting the city's most eclectic mixture of stores. At more than a hundred, there are far too many to list here, but clothing outlets range from Gap and Banana Republic, through Diesel and DKNY, to Emporio Armani; there are eight jewelers and eight shoe stores, including the karaoke-happy Just for Feet (reviewed on p.234) and a showpiece Nike Town; specialty stores include the excellent Virgin Megastore (see p.237). The Forum doesn't have a food court as such – there's one not far away in the casino proper – but it does hold some of Las Vegas's finest restaurants, like *Chinois* (see p.160), *Spago's* (p.170), and *The Palm* (p.168).

> While exploring the Forum, don't neglect the *other* mall at Caesars Palace – the Appian Way Shops, home to a replica of Michelangelo's *David* and a small but intriguing assortment of expensive stores.

Grand Canal Shoppes

Map 2, C1. *The Venetian*, 3355 Las Vegas Blvd S ©414-1000.
Sun–Thurs 10am–11pm, Fri & Sat 10am–midnight.

Naturally enough, the shopping mall at the *Venetian* claims to draw its inspiration from Venice itself, but its true model is rather closer to hand. From its false Italian sky (here set permanently to early evening) down to many of the actual stores, the Grand Canal Shoppes slavishly imitates the most effective elements of the Forum across the street. In some respects it surpasses the original – the Grand Canal itself is breathtaking, not least for the sheer *chutzpah* of locating a full-blown canal, complete with working gondolas, on the second story of the building – but as a mall pure and simple, it's not (yet) large or varied enough to outdo *Caesars*. It is, however, easier to reach, being accessible via double escalators immediately inside the main casino entrance, or a moving walkway from the Campanile on the Strip. Both lead to an impressive anteroom decorated with dramatic frescoes, though the toy shops to either side strike a banal note. Beyond that, you'll find a number of conventional mall outlets, like Banana Republic and New Balance, but the general emphasis is more consistently upscale than at the Forum, with designer clothing stores like Oliver & Co (see p.232) and Pal Zileri, and jewelry specialists such as Ca'D'Oro (gold), Erwin Pearl (pearls), and Simayof (diamonds). Less familiar "shoppes" include some making their first appearance outside Venice, like Il Prato, selling carnival masks and paper goods, and Ripa de Monti, specializing in exquisite glassware.

Sales tax in Nevada is set at 7.25 percent.

Via Bellagio

Map 2, B2. *Bellagio*, 3600 Las Vegas Blvd S ℂ693-7111. Daily 10am–midnight.

While Via Bellagio isn't on anything like the scale of the malls at *Caesars Palace* and the *Venetian*, its single-minded focus on the very top end of the spectrum has made it the chicest place to shop in Las Vegas. Even so, its stores epitomize the city's democratic approach to shopping: when even the scruffiest of dressers may turn out to be a big spender, anyone is welcome to browse. Just ten stores are ranged on either side of the plushly carpeted Via Bellagio, the walkway connecting the north end of *Bellagio* (facing *Caesars*) with the Strip. As well as Gucci, Georgio Armani, Chanel, Tiffany &

Co, and the self-styled "enfant terrible," Moschino (see p.232), the catch-all Bellagio Collections stocks clothing and footwear by more than a dozen other internationally known designers.

MALLS ELSEWHERE

The Boulevard

Map 1, D5. 3528 S Maryland Pkwy at *The Desert Inn* ℂ732-8949. Mon–Fri 10am–9pm, Sat 10am–8pm, Sun 11am–6pm.

Nevada's largest shopping mall has stood a couple of miles east of the Strip for over thirty years, but thanks to a recent overhaul it looks as good as new. Consisting of a single story centered on a bright glass-covered atrium, and anchored by department stores like Sears, JC Penney, Dillard's, and Macy's, it's the locals' favorite for day-to-day shopping. As well as over 150 outlets, including such mall regulars as Gap, Victoria's Secret, Body Shop, Radio Shack, and the entire gamut of Footlockers, it has a good-quality food court.

CAT bus #203 connects the Boulevard Mall with the Strip, running along Twain Avenue from the Fashion Show Mall.

Galleria at Sunset

Map 1, D7. 1300 W Sunset Rd, Henderson ℂ434-0202. Mon–Sat 10am–9pm, Sun 11am–6pm.

Las Vegas's latest mega-mall is eight miles southeast of the Strip, opposite *Sunset Station* in suburban Henderson, a location convenient only if you're heading to or from the Hoover Dam or Arizona. In terms of stores, it's much the same as the Boulevard, with a Macy's and a JC Penney, plus another 130 conventional mall outlets.

FACTORY OUTLETS

Belz Factory World

Map 1, D7. 7400 Las Vegas Blvd S ©896-5599.
Mon–Sat 10am–9pm, Sun 10am–6pm.

Roughly two miles south of *Mandalay Bay*, on the east side of
Las Vegas Boulevard (which by this point is no longer called the
Strip), Belz Factory World is a large, aesthetically challenged
mall that offers the city's best bargain shopping. Among almost
150 manufacturer's outlets, boasting discounts of up to 75 percent, you'll find clothing and footwear retailers such as Levi's,
Dress Barn, Calvin Klein, Osh'kosh B'gosh, Nike, and Reebok,
plus the odd specialist store like Wolf Cameras (see p.238).

Fashion Outlet Las Vegas

32100 Las Vegas Blvd S, Primm ©874-1400.
Mon–Sat 10am–9pm, Sun 10am–8pm.

Despite the street address and the deliberately misleading name,
the Fashion Outlet is not in Las Vegas at all, but forty miles
southwest, just short of the California state line in Primm. It
carefully defines itself as a factory outlet center on the basis that
more than half its stores offer discounts of between twenty and
seventy percent on usual retail prices. The reason you may find
it worthwhile to venture out this far is that it features much
bigger names than Belz, including Donna Karan, Polo Ralph
Lauren, Gap, Banana Republic, BCBG, Timberland, Tommy
Hilfiger, Benetton, Just For Feet, Last Call from Neiman
Marcus, and Versace, with outlets loosely divided between a
glitzy "New York" area and a less formal "South Beach" area.

**For details of shuttle buses from the Strip to
Fashion Outlet Las Vegas, priced at $10 for the
round trip, call ©874-1400.**

FACTORY OUTLETS

FASHION AND ACCESSORIES

Moschino

Map 2, B2. Via Bellagio, *Bellagio*, 3600 Las Vegas Blvd S ✆693-7926.

Daily 10am–midnight.

Ideally suited to its postmodern setting, Moschino revels in displaying its playful, ultra-pricey women's wear and accessories on mock-reverential plinths and pedestals.

Oliver & Co

Map 2, B2. Grand Canal Shoppes, *The Venetian*, 3355 Las Vegas Blvd S ✆733-1623.

Sun–Thurs 10am–11pm, Fri & Sat 10am–midnight.

Traditional, very upscale men's clothiers at the St Mark's Square end of the Grand Canal, stocking special collections put together by designers like Giorgio Armani and Calvin Klein.

Ross Dress For Less

Map 1, E5. 2420 E Desert Inn Rd ✆733-9001.

Mon–Sat 9am–9pm, Sun 11am–7pm.

The men's, women's, and children's clothing and shoes on offer at this east-of-the-Strip outlet are considerably more attractive than the name might suggest, with the women's wear department in particular boasting a high local reputation.

Structure

Map 2, B2. Forum Shops, *Caesars Palace*, 3500 Las Vegas Blvd S ✆892-0421.

Mon–Thurs & Sun 10am–11pm, Fri & Sat 10am–midnight.

Fashionable but affordable men's clothing. Also in the Galleria at Sunset, the Fashion Show Mall, and the Boulevard Mall.

Western Emporium
Map 1, F5. *Sam's Town*, 5111 Boulder Hwy ℂ454-8017.
Daily 10am–10pm.

The Western-themed *Sam's Town* casino, six miles east of the
Strip, makes an appropriate setting for the city's finest array
of Western wear. As you'd expect, there's a vast assortment of
jeans and Stetsons, but the boots are the real stunners, with a
green python-skin pair at $145, and an ostrich-skin pair
more like $500.

VINTAGE CLOTHING

The Attic
Map 4, C6. 1018 S Main St ℂ388-4088.
Mon–Sat 10am–7pm, Sun 11am–5pm.

Located in an insalubrious area south of downtown (just a little too far away to walk), this shrine to vintage Americana
both chic and kitsch charges customers a dollar simply to
cross its portals. Once inside, there's some amazing stuff,
though it's all a bit too cannily priced to expect to leave with
your arms full. Clothes and costumes of all kinds range from
old Levi's and bell-bottoms to flamboyant 1960s creations,
and there's a great assortment of shoes, hats, and accessories.
The furniture too is a delight, with turquoise vinyl armchairs
and the like.

Buffalo Exchange
Map 1, D5. 4110 S Maryland Pkwy ℂ791-3960.
Mon–Sat 11am–7pm, Sun noon–6pm.

Buffalo Exchange, a chain of vintage-clothing
stores familiar to Western bargain-hunters, is a bit less
characterful than the Attic, but the atmosphere is just as
cool, and it's a more dependable source of inexpensive
retro items.

VINTAGE CLOTHING

SHOES

Jimmy Choo
Map 2, C1. Grand Canal Shoppes, *The Venetian*, 3355 Las Vegas Blvd S ✆733-1802.
Sun–Thurs 10am–11pm, Fri & Sat 10am–midnight.
The last word in elegant female footwear, brought to you by the aptly named Malaysian designer who was a personal favorite of Princess Diana.

Just For Feet
Map 2, B2. Forum Shops, *Caesars Palace*, 3500 Las Vegas Blvd S ✆791-3482.
Mon–Thurs & Sun 10am–11pm, Fri & Sat 10am–midnight.
What's said to be the world's largest athletic shoe store, with four thousand big-name styles, faces the living statues just inside the Forum as you come in off the Strip. The prices generally aren't bad, but you can get a reduction of twenty percent or more merely for singing one song and gyrating like a loon on top of the counter during one of their regular karaoke sessions.

Nike Town
Map 2, B2. Forum Shops, *Caesars Palace*, 3500 Las Vegas Blvd S ✆650-8888.
Mon–Thurs & Sun 10am–11pm, Fri & Sat 10am–midnight.
This gleaming, high-tech, two-story superstore, behind Atlantis at the far end of the Forum, is as much museum as shoe store, but if there's even a hint of foot fetishism in your make up you won't be able to resist its adoration of the sports shoe. Each section is devoted to a specific sport.

GIFTS AND SOUVENIRS

Ancient Creations
Map 2, C1. Grand Canal Shoppes, *The Venetian*, 3355 Las Vegas Blvd S ©414-3701.
Sun–Thurs 10am–11pm, Fri & Sat 10am–midnight.

An antiques store with a fascinating difference; these are real antiques, dating back in some cases thousands of years. The exact stock varies of course, but can include Roman water jars priced at $18,500, Greek statuettes for $2400, or a 1611 edition of the King James Bible at $99,000. Individual coins from the Classical world can cost as little as $25. Ancient Creations has another branch in the Appian Way Shops in *Caesars Palace.*

Bonanza Gift Shop
Map 3, F4. 2460 Las Vegas Blvd S ©385-7359.
Daily 8am–midnight.

Located at a busy intersection, across from the *Sahara* and a few blocks south of the *Stratosphere*, the self-proclaimed "World's Largest Gift Store" is not all that big really, but it's the best single outlet for all those tacky souvenirs you'd hope to find in Las Vegas. Beyond the predictable array of used playing cards from all the casinos (costing $1), gaming boards, fuzzy dice, whoopee cushions, fart candy, postcards, and male and female nudie ballpoint pens, you'll find a more surreal world of Las Vegas snowstorms, Elvis clocks, and inflatable aliens, plus every permutation thereof – like alien Elvises trapped in snowstorms.

Gamblers General Store
Map 4, D5. 800 S Main St ©382-9903 or 1-800/322-2447.
Daily 9am–5pm.

For a truly authentic Las Vegas souvenir, you can't do better than the Gamblers General Store a few blocks south of downtown. As well as selling old slot machines for $999 – be sure to check the list of states where it's illegal to possess one even in your own home – and full-sized craps table for $4000, they have felt mats with roulette, blackjack, and craps layouts for $40, and packs of cards from all the casinos for 99¢. There's also a large library of books on gambling, detailing techniques for blackjack, craps, horses, and even slots, though paying $20 for a photocopied pamphlet explaining why you'll never win has to be a waste of money even by Las Vegas standards.

BOOKS

Albion Book Company
Map 1, E5. 2466 E Desert Inn Rd ✆792-9554.
Daily 10am–6pm.
The valley's best stock of secondhand books, including large sections on Las Vegas and the West, plus a big collection of used audio books at bargain prices – handy if you're setting off on a road trip.

Barnes & Noble
Map 1, B3. 2191 N Rainbow Blvd ✆631-2216.
Daily 9am–11pm.
This chain outlet is several miles west of downtown, just beyond the point where US-95 veers north, but has a copious selection of new books on every subject, plus a roomy café that's ideal for a light lunch. Also, and equally inconveniently, at 567 Stephanie St in Henderson.

Bookstar
Map 1, D5. 3910 S Maryland Pkwy ✆732-7882.
Daily 9am–11pm.
The largest bookstore serving the University District, a couple of miles east of the Strip.

Borders

Map 1, C4. 2323 S Decatur Blvd ℂ258-0999.
Mon–Sat 9am–11pm, Sun 9am–9pm.

An excellent range of new books and magazines, a couple of miles west of the Strip along Sahara Ave. Other branches at 2190 N Rainbow Blvd (across from Barnes & Noble) and 1445 W Sunset Rd in Henderson (near Sunset Station).

MUSIC

Tower Records at WOW

Map 1, C4. 4580 W Sahara Ave ℂ364-2500.
Daily 10am–midnight.

Two miles west of the Strip and a couple of blocks east of Borders, Tower boasts a good collection of new CDs – with a better chance of finding a bargain than at Virgin – and forms part of a larger complex that also sells videos and musical equipment.

Virgin Megastore

Map 2, B2. Forum Shops, *Caesars Palace*, 3500 Las Vegas Blvd S ℂ696-7100.
Mon–Thurs & Sun 10am–11pm, Fri & Sat 10am–midnight.

One of the Forum's few multistory stores, the only music store on the Strip stocks the broadest selection of new CDs in town, and also has a small but very hip book section.

ELECTRONIC EQUIPMENT AND CAMERAS

The Good Guys

Map 1, C4. 4580 W Sahara Ave at Decatur ℂ364-2500.
Daily 9am–midnight.

The best source in Las Vegas for electronic good of all kinds,

from computers to TVs and audio equipment. Also at
Boulevard Mall.

Wolf Cameras
Map 1, D7. Belz Factory World, 7400 Las Vegas Blvd S ©896-4271.
Mon–Sat 10am–9pm, Sun 10am–6pm.

All films, cameras, and accessories here are likely to be better
value than anything you'll find on the Strip, but British visitors
in particular will be pleased to note that they sell PAL-system
camcorders.

Sports and activities

L as Vegas is not exactly renowned for its healthy lifestyle, but if you start to feel the need for exercise, opportunities do exist. For visitors, the highest profile activity these days is **golf**. The city currently boasts around forty golf courses – though only one hotel, the *Desert Inn*, has its own public course – and is adding more at a ferocious rate. Most casinos do at least have a **swimming pool**, with the larger ones on the Strip offering full-service **spas** and tennis facilities as well. "Locals" casinos, on the other hand, usually out in more residential neighborhoods, specialize in offering popular year-round indoor pursuits such as **bowling** and **ice-skating**.

As for **spectator sports**, Las Vegas lacks high-profile professional teams. Although tourists flock from all over the nation to watch events like the Super Bowl on large-screen TVs – and of course, bet on them – the only sport to draw sizable crowds for live action is championship **boxing**.

INDOOR SPORTS AND ACTIVITIES

Gold Coast
Map 1, C5. 4000 W Flamingo Rd ℂ367-4700.
Daily 24 hrs.
The usual rate of $2.05 per game at the 72-lane Brunswick bowling center drops to $1.50 between midnight and 8am.

Orleans
Map 1, C5. 4500 W Tropicana Ave ℂ365-7111.
Daily 24 hrs.
Adult rates at the *Orleans'* large upstairs bowling arcade are $2.25 per game.

Sam's Town
Map 1, F5. 5111 Boulder Hwy ℂ456-7777.
Daily 24 hrs.
Rates at this bright 56-lane downstairs bowling center drop from $1.90 to $1.30 per game between midnight and 8am.

Santa Fe Hotel & Casino
Map 1, B2. 4949 N Rancho Drive ℂ658-4995.
Daily 24 hrs.
The *Santa Fe's* 60-lane bowling alley, back to back with the ice arena, charges $2.25 per game, and features Bowlervision, an electronic device that tracks the path of your ball.

Showboat
Map 1, E4. 2800 Fremont St ℂ385-9153.
Daily 24 hrs.
At 106 lanes, the *Showboat* boasts the largest bowling alley in the US, and plays host to the Showboat Invitational Bowling

Spas

Most of the major Strip casinos offer their own luxurious spa facilities. Typical rates start at around $20 per day, with a vast range of more expensive treatments available. Among the best are:

Bellagio; daily 6am–8pm; ✆693-7472.

Caesars Palace; daily 6am–8pm; ✆731-7776.

The Desert Inn; daily 6am–10pm; ✆733-4571.

The Mandalay Bay; daily 6am–10pm; ✆632-7777.

The MGM Grand; daily 6am–7pm; ✆891-3077.

The Monte Carlo; daily 6.30am–7.30pm; ✆730-7590.

Tournament, the oldest pro event in the country, each January. $2.65 per game.

GYMS AND HEALTH CLUBS

Las Vegas Athletic Club

Map 1, D4. 2655 S Maryland Pkwy ✆734-5822.

Daily 24 hrs.

The city's largest health-club chain, with five different valley locations (not all 24-hour) that feature indoor and outdoor pools, exercise equipment and classes, saunas and spas, and other sports facilities. Membership $10 per day, $25 per week.

Las Vegas Sporting House

Map 3, C7. 3025 Industrial Rd ✆733-8999.

Daily 24 hrs.

In addition to a full gymnasium and fitness center with all the latest equipment, the Sporting House offers tennis, squash, and handball courts plus an outdoor pool. Membership costs around $15 per day or $50 per week, but check to see if your hotel has special privileges.

SPAS

Santa Fe Ice Arena

Map 1, B2. *Santa Fe Hotel & Casino*, 4949 N Rancho Drive ℅658-4993.

Hours vary.

Las Vegas's only casino ice rink charges $5 admission, with skate rental for $1.50, and offers a varied schedule of pick-up hockey games, figure skating, and so on.

OUTDOOR SPORTS AND ACTIVITIES

BUNGEE JUMPING

A.J. Hackett Bungy

Map 3, E6. *Circus Circus*, 810 Circus Circus Drive ℅385-4321.

Hours vary.

Should you feel the urge to plummet approximately 200 feet toward but not into a swimming pool, attached to a rubberized rope, look no further. It's $61 for your first jump, $25 each for the second and third, and nothing at all for the fourth.

> **Hikes in the Las Vegas region are detailed in Chapter 5, Out of the city.**

GOLF

Desert Inn Golf Club

Map 3, E8. 3145 Las Vegas Blvd S ℅733-4290.

The only golf course left on the Strip, an extraordinary expanse of green stretching as far as the eye can see. Guests $160, non-guests $225.

Las Vegas Golf Club

Map 1, B4. 4300 W Washington Ave ℂ646-3003.
Busy city-owned course that offers exceptionally cheap rates
for locals. Non-residents can play eighteen holes for $59
Mon–Thurs, $79 Fri–Sun, or nine holes for $36 and $48
respectively.

Las Vegas National Golf Club

Map 1, E5. 1911 E Desert Inn Rd ℂ796-0013.
Originally the Sahara Country Club, and home to the Las
Vegas Invitational Tournament, this appealing course, a couple
of miles east of the Strip, charges the general public $75
Mon–Thurs, $105 Fri–Sun.

Painted Desert Golf Club

Map 1, B2. 5555 Painted Mirage Way ℂ382-4653.
The first Vegas golf course to embrace its desert setting rather
than attempt to grow lush fairways, located northwest of the
city en route toward Mount Charleston, charges green fees of
$100 on weekdays, $125 at weekends.

**For reservations at most of Las Vegas's forty or so golf
courses, call Golf Reservations of Nevada Inc ℂ732-
3119 or 1-800/597-2794, *www.golfvegas.com*.**

HORSE RIDING

Mount Charleston Horseback Riding

Mount Charleston Lodge, Kyle Canyon Rd. ℂ872-5408 or 1-
800/955-1314.
Hours vary.
Ninety-minute riding expeditions on the flanks of the Spring
Mountains, for $30.

HORSE RIDING

243

Black Canyon Raft Tours

1297 Nevada Hwy, Boulder City ©293-3776 or 1-800/696-RAFT, *www.rafts.com*.

By reservation, Feb–Nov only.

One-day rafting trips downriver from Hoover Dam as far as Willow Beach, for $80 per person including hotel pickup.

SKIING

Las Vegas Ski and Snowboard Resort

Hwy-156, Mt Charleston ©385-2754.

Late Nov to early April only. Lifts operate Mon–Fri & Sun 9am–4pm, Sat 9am–4pm & 4.30–10pm.

Las Vegas's only ski slopes are almost fifty miles from the Strip (see p.119). Three chair lifts lead to ten different slopes, graded from novice to advanced; lift passes cost $28 per day, and equipment rental is available.

Mount Charleston and Boulder City are both shown on the Out of the City map, pp110–11.

SKYDIVING

Skydive Las Vegas

1401 Airport Rd, Boulder City ©293-1860.

By reservation.

Leap from an airplane 12,500 feet over the Nevada desert, strapped to an instructor, then free-fall and parachute for a total of well over five minutes, for $199.

RAFTING, SKIING, SKYDIVING

Tennis

The best tennis courts on the Strip are at the *Desert Inn*; like those at *Caesars Palace*, the *New Frontier*, and the *Riviera*, they're free to guests, but non-guests have to pay. Everyone pays to use the courts at *Bally's*, the *Flamingo Hilton*, the *Las Vegas Hilton*, the *MGM Grand*, and the *Monte Carlo*. The *Plaza* is the only downtown hotel with tennis courts, available to guests only. Except at those places where guests do not have to pay, court rates typically run $10–$15 per hour; most playing areas are lighted so you can hit well into the night. By the way, tennis champ Andre Agassi hails from Las Vegas, though you're unlikely to see him out on the city courts (to view Agassi memorabilia, however, you might try the *All-Star Cafe* in the Showcase Mall, p.34).

WATER SPORTS

Las Vegas Bay Marina

Lake Shore Rd, Henderson. ☎565-9111.
Hours vary.

Among water craft available for rental at Las Vegas Bay Marina, at 25 miles out the closest point on Lake Mead to the city, are jetskis at $50 per hour or $150 for four hours, and speedboats at $50 per hour or $300 per day. Similar facilities are offered by Lake Mead Marina near Boulder City (☎293-3484), and Callville Bay (☎565-8958) and Echo Bay (☎394-4000), on the north shore of the lake.

For details of Las Vegas's only water park, Wet'n'Wild, located on the Strip, see p.72.

WATER SPORTS

SPECTATOR SPORTS

BASEBALL

The **Las Vegas Stars**, a class AAA team affiliated to the San Diego Padres, have in recent years repeatedly triumphed in the Pacific Coast League. They play around seventy home games between April and Labor Day each year at Cashman Field, 850 Las Vegas Blvd N (✆386-7200). Admission prices start at $4.

BOXING

In the last twenty years, Las Vegas has taken over from New York as the world capital of **boxing**. A heavyweight title fight brings so many high-rollers into town that the major casinos will pay almost any purse to the boxers concerned (upwards of $20 million per in some cases), and they're still doing so despite fiascos like the infamous ear-biting bout between Mike Tyson and Evander Holyfield.

The three principal players have long been *Caesars Palace*, which for big fights erects an arena in its back lot capable of holding up to 30,000 people; the *MGM Grand*, with its 15,000-seat Garden; and the *Mirage*. *Mandalay Bay* has ventured into hosting championship boxing as well, and some fights also take place at the University's Thomas & Mack Center, 4505 S Maryland Pkwy (✆895-3761). Ticket prices depend completely on demand; the cheapest seats for a welterweight fight can be as little as $50, but for Mike Tyson they're more likely to range between $500 and $2500.

It was just after a Mike Tyson fight at the *MGM Grand* that rap star Tupac Shakur was shot, on September 7, 1996. He died four days later.

In addition, the *Orleans*, 4500 W Tropicana Ave (✆365-7570), stages regular Friday-night boxing in its Mardi Gras ballroom, featuring three men's bouts and one women's, with tickets priced at $15 to $40.

COLLEGE SPORTS

The University of Nevada, Las Vegas, plays its home **bas-ketball** games at the Thomas & Mack Center, 4505 S Maryland Pkwy (✆895-3761), from November to May, and home **football** games at Sam Boyd Silver Bowl Stadium, Boulder Hwy (✆895-3900), between September and December.

ICE HOCKEY

From October through April, the **Las Vegas Thunder** (✆798-7825) plays around forty International Hockey League home games at the Thomas & Mack Center, 4505 S Maryland Pkwy (✆0895-3761). Ticket prices range upwards from $10.

Gay Las Vegas

While Las Vegas has long been a gay-friendly city, and looks to become even more so under liberal-minded mayor Oscar Goodman, elected in 1999, its tourist industry makes little provision for gays and lesbians. There are no specifically gay hotels, and none of the casinos goes very far toward attracting gay visitors.

As far as specifically gay **nightlife** is concerned, it's largely a question of joining in with the local scene. There's a scattering of gay bars and clubs throughout the city, but the main concentration these days is around the intersection **of Paradise Road** and **Naples Drive**, a mile east of the Strip and just south of the *Hard Rock Casino*. In addition, of course, most gay and lesbian travelers are likely to find something to suit their tastes amid the bustle, glamour, and kitsch of the Strip, and there's certainly plenty to enjoy in the shows and spectaculars reviewed in Chapter Nine, Entertainment.

INFORMATION

For up-to-date information on events and happenings in Las Vegas's gay community, be sure to get hold of the two free monthly **newspapers**, the *Las Vegas Bugle* and *Q-Tribe*.

Both are available at the gay and lesbian **bookstore** Get
Booked, 4640 Paradise Rd (daily 10am–midnight; ℭ737-
7780), one block north of Tropicana Avenue, and also at
the lively *Mariposa Café*, across the street at 4643 Paradise
Rd (daily 3pm–3am; ℭ650-9009).

The **Gay and Lesbian Center of Las Vegas**, 912 E
Sahara Ave (Mon–Fri 10am–7.30pm; ℭ733-9800) is a
drop-in center that provides information on community
resources, social clubs, and health-related issues.

Although Nevada state law does not recognize gay or lesbian weddings, Alternative Lifestyle Commitments (ℭ1-
888/638-4673) arranges same-sex ceremonies.

**The best single source of information on Las Vegas's
gay scene is the Web site *www.gayvegas.com*.**

GAY BARS AND CLUBS

Angles / Club Lace
Map 2, G4. 4633 Paradise Rd ℭ791-0100.
Daily 24hr.
Two distinct bars – *Angles* is predominantly for men, *Club Lace*
is more mixed but has some women-only nights – devoted
more to drinking and cruising than dancing. Between 10.30pm
and 2am on several nights of the week, $5 buys all the beer you
can drink.

Back Door Lounge
Map 4, I7. 1415 E Charleston Blvd ℭ385-2018.
Daily 24hr.
Neighborhood bar, on the fringes of downtown, that's popular
with older gay men. Free barbecue on Saturday nights and hol-
idays, and nightly early-evening happy hours.

Backstreet Bar & Grill

Map 1, D5. 5012 S Arville St ℂ876-1844.

Daily 24hr.

Very friendly country bar, a mile west of the Strip between
Flamingo and Tropicana, which hosts square dancing on
Tuesday evenings, line dancing on Thursdays (beginners welcome), country dancing on Fridays and Saturdays, and an
almighty "beer bust" on Sunday afternoons.

The Buffalo

Map 2, G4. 4640 Paradise Rd ℂ733-8355.

Daily 24hr.

Lively Levi's-and-leathers club in the heart of the main gay district that's the base for the Satyricons Motorcycle Club. Beer
busts (especially on Friday evenings and Sunday afternoons) are
a bigger deal than music or dancing.

**During an ever-popular "beer bust," you can, for a
(usually low) set price, drink all the beer you like.**

The Eagle

Map 1, E5. 3430 E Tropicana Ave ℂ458-8662.

Daily 24hr.

Dark, male-dominated Levi's-and-leathers bar, roughly four
miles east of the Strip, that's famous for hosting late-night beer
busts several times a week and an underwear night every
Wednesday. Not a desperately beautiful joint, it attracts a mainly older crowd.

Flex

Map 1, C4. 4371 W Charleston Blvd ℂ385-3539.

Daily 24hr. Cover varies.

Flamboyant gay club, several miles west of the Strip toward
Red Rocks, with an emphasis on music and dancing, and

occasional strip shows. Beer flows freely all week, and the whole place goes Latin on Sunday nights.

Freezone
Map 2, G4. 610 E Naples Drive ℂ794-2300.
Daily 24hr.
Busy gay-district bar, popular with women and men alike, which also serves good food.

Gipsy
Map 2, G4. 4605 Paradise Rd ℂ731-9677.
Daily except Mon 10pm–5am. Cover charge varies; usually $5.
High-profile dance club, whose success has spurred the emergence of the predominantly gay business district. Apart from the free cruise nights on Wednesdays, there's normally some form of live entertainment to justify the $5 cover charge, and there are beer busts most nights too. The elaborate lost-city-decor attracts young ingenues and local celebs.

Goodtimes
Map 1, E5. 1775 E Tropicana Ave ℂ736-9494.
Daily 24hr.
Welcoming neighborhood bar, in the same mini-mall as the irresistible Liberace Museum (see p.104), with daily happy hours from both 5am to 7am and 5pm to 7pm. Other than on the hectic Monday nights, it's a quiet, friendly place to hang out.

Tropical Island
Map 1, E5. 3430 E Tropicana Ave ℂ456-5525.
Daily 6pm–4am.
Neighborhood bar, with pool tables and darts, that's become the rendezvous of choice for local lesbians.

GAY BARS AND CLUBS

251

Getting married

Well over a hundred thousand **marriages** are performed in Las Vegas each year. Having a Vegas wedding has become a byword for tongue-in-cheek chic, and there are indeed drive-thru chapels where bride and groom do no more than roll down their car windows before being serenaded on their way by Elvis himself.

What's more surprising, however, is that most marriages in the city seem to be deeply **formal affairs**. Both the casinos and a horde of independent wedding chapels compete to offer elaborate and expensive ceremonies with all the traditional trimmings, from white gowns and black limousines, to garters and boutonniers. The happy couples are more likely to have saved and planned long in advance than to have succumbed to a spur-of-the-moment impulse.

You don't have to be a local resident or take a blood test to get wed in Las Vegas. Assuming you're both at least eighteen years old and carrying picture ID, and neither of you is already married, simply turn up at the Clark County Marriage License Bureau, downtown at 200 S Third St (Mon–Thurs 8am–midnight, and continuously from 8am on Fri to midnight on Sun; ℃455 4416), and buy a marriage license for $35 cash.

To get a divorce in Las Vegas, you have to have been a Nevada resident for at least six weeks.

With no waiting period required, the cheapest option is then to walk one block to the office of the Commissioner of Civil Marriages, 309 S Third St (Mon–Fri 8am–5pm), and pay another $35 cash to have a civil wedding performed.

Wedding chapels claim to charge as little as $50 for their most basic ceremonies, but at that sort of rate even the minister is regarded as an "extra" costing an additional $40. Reckon on paying at least $100 for the bare minimum, which is liable to be as romantic a process as checking in at a hotel, and to take about as long. The full deluxe service ranges up to around $500. **Photography** in particular can be expensive; many chapels won't let you bring a still camera, let alone make a video. When you pay for the services of their own photographers, you're not usually buying the right to keep the negatives, and may have to pay exorbitant rates for each individual print.

To arrange a gay or lesbian wedding – albeit not recognized under Nevada law – contact Alternative Lifestyle Commitments, ✆1-888/638-4673.

The Las Vegas Convention and Visitors Bureau (see p.11) can provide full listings of wedding chapels, as well as details of operators such as **Las Vegas Weddings and Rooms** (✆1-800/488-6283) that offer all-inclusive wedding packages. The busiest days in the calendar are New Year's Eve, which gives American couples the right to file a joint tax return for the entire preceding year, and Valentine's Day.

WEDDING CHAPELS

Candlelight Wedding Chapel

Map 3, E6. 2855 Las Vegas Blvd S ✆735-4179 or 1-800/962-1818, *candlelightchapel.com*.

Daily 8am–midnight.

Busy little chapel across from *Circus Circus*, where you get a garter with the $169 wedding package, or two white T-shirts with the $499 option.

Graceland Wedding Chapel

Map 4, E6. 619 Las Vegas Blvd S ✆474-6655 or 1-800/824-5732.

Mon–Thurs & Sun 9am–9pm, Fri & Sat 9am–midnight.

This comparatively tasteful white-painted church, complete with stained-glass windows, offers conventional ceremonies for $100–250, while an extra $120 buys the services of the King himself. Elvis prefers not to conduct actual weddings – although he will renew vows – but he makes a great best man, and sings six songs.

Little Chapel of the Flowers

Map 3, G3. 1717 Las Vegas Blvd S ✆735-4331 or 1-800/843-2410, *littlechapel.com*.

Daily 8am–10pm.

Rather traditional, not to say twee, establishment with two antique-furnished chapels off the same lobby. Weddings range between $200 and $1400.

Elvis married Priscilla at the *Aladdin* on May 1, 1967, nine months to the day before the birth of Lisa Marie, and eight years before Michael Jackson met Lisa Marie at a Jackson Five gig in Vegas. Those two, however, wed years later in the Dominican Republic.

Novelty weddings

When it comes to getting hitched in style, the sky is literally the limit in Las Vegas. Most wedding chapels can persuade Elvis to arrive in a pink Cadillac and sing *Love Me Tender*, but there are plenty of options guaranteed to make you the star of the show. Plighting your troth at *Excalibur* (©597-7777) is a great excuse to cavort in medieval costume, while at A.J. Hackett Bungy, at *Circus Circus* (©385-4321), you can take your vows perched on a tiny platform immediately before plummeting on an eighteen-story bungee jump. A Little White Chapel in the Sky (©382-5943) arranges marriages in a hot-air balloon from $500, while Las Vegas Helicopters (©736-0013) can provide a ministry to perform your ceremony either hovering over the Strip or on the rim of the Grand Canyon.

Little Church of the West

Map 2, C9. 4617 Las Vegas Blvd S ©739-7971 or 1-800/821-2452. Daily 8am–midnight.

Having originally formed part of the *Last Frontier* casino, the Little Church of the West is on the National Register of Historic Places, and has moved progressively down the Strip to its current site south of *Mandalay Bay*. It's among the more peaceful and quiet places to exchange your Vegas vows – if that's really what you want.

A Little White Chapel

Map 1, D4. 1301 Las Vegas Blvd S ©382-5943 or 1-800/545-8111. Daily 24 hrs.

Las Vegas's best-known location for celebrity weddings, where Bruce Willis and Demi Moore married each other, as did Jack and Vera Duckworth of British soap *Coronation Street*, while Michael Jordan and Joan Collins married other people. Having pioneered the "24-hr Drive-Up Wedding Window," it has since refined the concept by roofing over the driveway as the "Tunnel of Love," and painting naked cherubs on its blue-sky ceiling. Staffed by fifteen ministers, it can provide tasteful black baseball caps embroidered for "Bride" and "Groom," and is even planning to add an on-site massage parlor.

Casino chapels

Almost all of the major casinos have their own wedding chapels, which tend to eschew the kitschier elements of the independent chapels and offer ceremonies starting at around $400. Among the most popular are:

Bellagio ℂ791-7111

Excalibur ℂ597-7777

The Flamingo ℂ733-3232

New York–New York ℂ740-6625

Treasure Island ℂ894-7700

The Tropicana ℂ798-3778

Directory

AIRLINES Major airlines using McCarran International Airport include Air Canada ℡1-800/776-3000; America West ℡1-800/2-FLY AWA; American Airlines ℡1-800/433-7300; Canadian Airlines ℡1-800/426-7000; Continental ℡1-800/525-0280; Delta ℡1-800/221-1212; Hawaiian Airlines ℡1-800/367-5320; Northwest ℡1-800/225-2525; Southwest ℡1-800/435-9792; TWA ℡1-800/221-2000; United ℡1-800/241-6522.

AREA CODE The telephone area code for all Las Vegas numbers is ℡702.

BANKS AND EXCHANGE There's not a single bank on the Strip, but there can be no easier city in which to get cash or change money: the casinos gladly convert almost any currency, day and night, and their walls are festooned with every conceivable ATM machine.

CONVENTIONS During large conventions, which can attract up to 100,000 visitors, room rates in Las Vegas can rise enormously – partly due to the demand, but also because conventioneers tend not to gamble as much as tourists. The biggest annual events are the Consumer Electronic Show, in the second week of January; the Men's Apparel Guild (or MAGIC) in early March; and Comdex computer show in mid-November.

DISABLED TRAVELERS While all the major casinos offer designated rooms for the physically challenged – plus, of course, accessible gaming facilities – the buildings themselves are on such a vast scale that visiting Las Vegas can be an exhausting experience. The Convention and Visitors Authority runs an advice line at ☏892-7525; to arrange for a free disabled parking permit, call ☏229-6431.

EMERGENCIES For police or medical assistance, call ☏911.

FESTIVALS Las Vegas has far fewer annual festivals than most American cities. Apart from New Year's Eve and the World Series of Poker (held at the *Horseshoe* in April and May; see p.84), almost all the highlights of the calendar are sports-related, ranging from rodeo events like Helldorado in mid-June and the National Finals in December, to the Las Vegas Invitational golf tournament in October.

FILM PROCESSING You're likely to find film processing charges fairly outrageous at the specialty shops in town; most casinos do have places to develop film as well, but check on those prices first, too.

HOSPITALS 24-hour emergency rooms operate at the University Medical Center, 1800 W Charleston Blvd (☏383-2661), and Sunrise Hospital, 3186 Maryland Parkway (☏731-8080).

KIDS A list of the Top Ten attractions on the Strip for kids appears on p.23. Several casinos will look after your children while you gamble or simply explore; these include the *MGM Grand*, whose Youth Center costs $7 per hour for guests, or $9 for outsiders, and the various members of the Stations chain. Typically, you can leave your kids for a maximum of 3hr 30min in any 24-hour period. For a babysitter, call Around The Clock Child Care (☏365-1040 or 1-800/798-6768).

LAUNDROMATS Laundry facilities are available in all hotels.

LIBRARY 1401 E Flamingo Rd (Mon–Thurs 9am–9pm, Fri & Sat 9am–5pm, Sun 1–5pm).

MEDICAL HELP There's a 24-hour medical center on the eighth floor of the *Imperial Palace*, 3535 Las Vegas Blvd S.

PHARMACIES The closest to the Strip are Sav-On, 1360 E Flamingo Rd (24-hr; ✆731-5373), and White Cross, north of the *Stratosphere* at 1700 Las Vegas Blvd S (daily 7am–1am; ✆382-1733), which has a delivery service.

PHOTOGRAPHY The only casino in Las Vegas that allows visitors to take photographs of the action on its slot machines and gaming tables is the *Four Queens*, downtown.

POLICE Las Vegas police can be contacted on ✆795-3111.

POST OFFICE While you should be able to mail postcards, letters, and packages from your hotel, the nearest post office to the Strip is behind the *Stardust* at 3100 Industrial Rd (Mon–Fri 8.30am–5pm).

TAX Nevada's sales tax is 7.25 percent. Room tax in Las Vegas is currently set at nine percent on the Strip, and ten percent downtown; part is set aside to fund Strip monorail services and the Fremont Street Experience respectively.

TIME Las Vegas is on Pacific Standard Time, which is three hours behind Eastern Standard Time and seven hours behind Greenwich Mean Time, but moves its clocks forward by one hour to operate daylight saving between the first Sunday in April and the last Sunday in October.

TIPPING When in doubt, tip. The usual rate in restaurants or taxis is fifteen to twenty percent. In your hotel, for assistance with luggage, tip $1 per bag; for valet parking, $2; for maid service, $1 per day at the end of your stay; and for concrete help from a concierge, such as making a reservation, $5. You're supposed to tip dealers at the gaming tables a chip or two each time you win (you can also place bets on behalf of the dealer, if you choose). Bar staff, or cocktail waitresses bringing free drinks, normally expect $1 per drink.

CONTEXTS

A history of Las Vegas

Las Vegas has a shorter history than any other city in the world. The only city founded in the twentieth century to boast over a million inhabitants, it's also perhaps the only one that has consistently prioritized the need to attract visitors over the quality of life of its own residents.

Almost from the start, Las Vegas has been stuck with the consequences of throwing in its lot with **casino gambling**. Only recently has it begun to acquire industry on any scale; Boeing, which almost relocated to the city from Seattle in 1946, was one of many corporations to steer clear because of the taint of gambling. Similarly, the desire – and ability – of casino owners to keep city government as weak as possible has allowed Las Vegas to become a hideous sprawl, with an infrastructure that is at best haphazard and at worst downright inadequate.

Despite it all, however, Las Vegas has grown within a single human lifetime to become an astonishing and in many ways irresistible city. Some twists in the tale have been thanks to its being utterly in tune with its times, others can be put down to pure luck, but it's been an extraordinary journey, and you can only but wonder what the second century will bring.

A valley without a city

Little trace remains of the earliest human inhabitants of the Las Vegas Valley. Until around 1150 AD, the region lay on the extreme western periphery of the domains of the **Anasazi** Indians. The ruins of their dramatic "cliff dwellings" are scattered throughout the Colorado Plateau to the east, but the only significant relics of the Anasazi in Nevada are preserved in the Lost City Museum near Overton, sixty miles northeast of Las Vegas (see p.125). In more recent times, the valley was roamed by the nomadic

Paiute, whose descendants still occupy a small reservation northwest of the city.

What's now southern Nevada was claimed for Spain in 1598, as part of the Spanish colony of New Mexico, but no outsiders are known to have passed this way before 1829, by which time it belonged to the newly independent nation of Mexico. These first explorers were members of an expedition led by Antonio Armejo, seeking to extend the **Old Spanish Trail** from Santa Fe all the way to California. Encountering an unexpected oasis of grasslands fed by underground springs, they named it **Las Vegas** – "The Meadows."

Significant traffic along the Old Spanish Trail only began to appear in the late 1840s. In 1847, **Mormon** refugees established Salt Lake City beyond the western frontier of the United States, and proclaimed it the capital of the promised land of **Deseret**, which supposedly included much of Nevada and California. That same year, however, the US acquired New Mexico as part of the spoils of war with Mexico. The Mormons were granted the smaller Territory of Utah, while Nevada was at first part of the Territory of New Mexico and went on to achieve statehood in its own right in 1864.

Nonetheless, the Las Vegas Valley soon became a crucial staging post on the route between Utah and California, now known as the **Mormon Trail**. In 1855, Mormon leader Brigham Young decided to establish a colony there. Centered on a small adobe fort, the colony was known as **Bringhurst**, because there was already a town of Las Vegas, New Mexico. It lasted only three years before disintegrating into factionalism.

With the discovery of silver in southern Nevada in 1859, Las Vegas, however, survived as a supply center serving miners and prospectors. The former Mormon fort became the center of the **Las Vegas Ranch**, which was run by

Octavio Gass between 1865 and 1882, and then by Helen Stewart. Even in 1900, however, the census for the whole valley took up only half a sheet of paper; you can see it in the Nevada State Museum (see p.107), listing just seven families and a total of eighteen people.

The founding of Las Vegas

In 1903, Helen Stewart sold the Las Vegas Ranch to Montana senator **William Clark**, the proprietor of the San Pedro, Los Angeles and Salt Lake Railroad, for $55,000. Not only did the valley stand roughly halfway between Salt Lake City and Los Angeles, it was also the only point within hundreds of miles to offer a dependable water supply. Newly constructed railroad tracks were approaching Las Vegas from both directions, and they finally met near what's now Jean, 23 miles southwest, on January 30, 1905.

By then, freebooters had set up a speculative townsite west of the tracks near modern Las Vegas, but the official birth of **"Clark's Las Vegas Townsite"** came a few months later, on May 15. At the corner of Fremont and Main streets downtown, forty blocks, each divided into 32 lots, were auctioned off to buyers brought in by special trains from Los Angeles and Salt Lake City. Soon the nascent businesses and residences of a small western town occupied the space. The sale of liquor was confined to **Block 16**, bounded by First, Second, Ogden, and Stewart streets, which quickly gained a reputation for its raucous saloons and gambling dens.

Las Vegas was very much a railroad town in its early years, with its initial boost coming from the construction of locomotive repair shops in 1909. That same year, the southern portion of Lincoln County, in which it originally stood, was made **Clark County** in its own right, and, ironically enough, Nevada became the first state in the US to **outlaw gambling**.

THE FOUNDING OF LAS VEGAS

A boost from the Feds

When Nevada relegalized gambling in 1931, the *Las Vegas Review-Journal* commented that "People should not get overly excited over the effects of the new gambling bill – conditions will be little different than they are at the present time." The measure was a response to the recent experience of Prohibition, when "speakeasies" serving bootleg liquor had proved a major source of political corruption across the nation. Rather than go through the same problems with the then-burgeoning illegal casinos, Nevada's legislators decided to keep them above board, and gain a little tax revenue in the process. What they hadn't anticipated, however, was that every other state in the country decided to tackle the situation differently and crack down on gambling instead.

Reno was the first city to benefit from Nevada's new renown as a haven for gamblers. Las Vegas might never have amounted to anything more than a way station where railroad passengers could lay over and drink, had Congress not decided to dam nearby Boulder Canyon. The aim was to harness the Colorado River to provide cheap electricity and water for the entire southwest, but from the very start, the project amounted to a massive federal subsidy for the infant city.

The government deliberately housed the dam workers in purpose-built **Boulder City** – "a wholesome American community," in which gambling remains banned to this day – rather than the "boisterous frontier town" of Las Vegas. Not only did that fail to deter them from frittering away their pay-packets on Fremont Street, but the workers were immediately joined by a vast influx of **tourists**. In 1932 alone, the first year of the dam's construction, over a hundred thousand visitors came to admire the new "World Wonder."

Las Vegas had made its first attempts to encourage tourism during the 1920s, with the opening of a dude ranch and even a golf course. Its first out-of-town casino, the *Meadows*, opened in 1931 on Boulder Highway – not that it lasted long – while its first luxury hotel, the *Apache*, followed a year later. Las Vegas played host to its first **convention** in 1935, when the arrival of five thousand Shriners from California briefly doubled the local population.

By the time the dam builders left town in 1937, Las Vegas had grown used to the tourist dollar (and also to its first taste of air-conditioning, thanks to dam-powered "swamp coolers"). While it vigorously promoted such events as its "Helldorado" rodeo, and an annual regatta on Lake Mead (then known as Boulder Lake), its continuing appeal depended on two mighty pillars: legalized gambling and easy **divorce**. Then as now, any American citizen had only to spend six weeks in Nevada to take advantage of the state's liberal divorce laws. Glamorous movie depictions of desert-ranch sojourns, and real-life cases like the separation of Clark Gable and Ria Longham in March 1939, publicized Las Vegas across the nation.

The emergence of the Strip

While Las Vegas's destiny as a resort destination was already becoming clear in 1940, its population was still a mere eight thousand. Like Phoenix and Albuquerque, however, it prospered mightily during World War II. Far from possible enemy attack, the desert southwest made an ideal location for defense installations. Las Vegas itself swiftly acquired a large air force base, while what's now Henderson started out in 1941 as Basic Town Site, built to house the ten thousand employees of the huge Basic magnesium plant.

Inevitably, gambling also boomed during the war. Thus far, the casino industry had been almost exclusively concentrated between First and Third streets along Fremont Street downtown, well away from residential neighborhoods. However, as the illegal casinos of California were forced out of business, a new breed of entrepreneur began to show up in Las Vegas.

Although Guy McAfee, a former chief of LA's vice squad, opened the *Pair-O-Dice* in 1938, the first fully fledged resort to appear on the Strip was *El Rancho*, in 1941. Its location just outside the city line (on what's now an empty lot opposite the *Sahara*) enabled its owner, California hotelier Thomas Hull, to benefit from lower taxes and cheaper real estate prices. The original *Rancho* only had fifty rooms, but its lawns, palm trees, swimming pool, and central windmill tower came as a revelation. One impressed guest, William Moore, followed suit by opening the *Last Frontier* a mile south in 1942, and the career of the Strip as a "casino suburb" was launched.

As described on p.48, mobster **Benjamin "Bugsy" Siegel** was the powerhouse behind the early Strip's definitive occupant, the seven-million-dollar *Flamingo*. Shortly after its premature opening night in December 1946, heavy losses forced him to shut up shop. The *Flamingo* was back on its feet by March 1947, but Siegel's erstwhile partners were dissatisfied enough to have him murdered in LA in June. If anything, such murky goings-on merely added to the allure of Las Vegas for visitors who were drawn to the city precisely because, and not in spite of, its "Sin City" image.

> **Detailed histories of individual casinos appear through the Guide section of this book.**

The heyday of the Mob

With downtown Las Vegas becoming increasingly out-stripped, in 1950 Las Vegas's city authorities made a last great effort to annex the Strip. The attempt was thwarted when a consortium of casino owners and Clark County officials declared the Strip area to be the unincorporated township of **Paradise City** instead. That unholy alliance lay behind the Strip's developing status as the barely concealed corporate playground and cash cow for the criminal underworld of the entire United States.

The flow of new resorts in the 1950s seemed all but unstoppable. The luxurious *Desert Inn*, which opened in 1950, was the cream of the crop, featuring a chef imported from the *Ritz* in Paris and with a guest list that included the Duke and Duchess of Windsor and John F Kennedy. Next came the *Sands* in 1952, the *Riviera* in 1955 (which finally proved it was possible to build high-rise hotels in the desert), the *Dunes* later that year, and the *Hacienda* in 1957. However, sinister figures lurked in the shadows. To complete the *Desert Inn*, nominal owner Wilbur Clark had been obliged to sell a 75 percent stake to a Detroit syndicate led by Moe Dalitz, while when East Coast gangster Frank Costello was shot in New York in 1957, the monthly profit figures from the new *Tropicana* were found in his pocket.

Until the late 1940s, Nevada state authorities played no part in the licensing of casinos. In 1950, the **Kefauver Committee on Organized Crime**, set up by the US Senate, held hearings in Las Vegas to gather evidence of links between casinos and the Mafia, and established that licenses had been granted to known criminals. In belated response, Nevada established its Gaming Control Board in 1955, with the aim of vetting potential casino owners. In 1960, the board went further by issuing the legendary Black Book, of underworld figures who were barred from even entering any casino in the state.

Meanwhile, Las Vegas was establishing itself as the **entertainment** center of the world. Frank Sinatra debuted at the *Desert Inn* in 1951, while Liberace received $50,000 to open the *Riviera* in 1955. The *New Frontier* played host to

The bomb

In 1950 the Atomic Energy Commission decided that a remote area of Nellis Air Force Base, sixty miles northwest of Las Vegas, would be ideal for testing atomic bombs, and designated it the **Nevada Test Site**. Publicly, the citizens of Las Vegas were assured that they were in no danger, as they'd be shielded by the Spring Mountains, though more sanguine assessments, behind closed doors in the White House, felt the potential price, of perhaps a few thousand victims of radiation poisoning, was worth paying.

Las Vegas embraced the bomb, turning it into another show for tourists. The first explosion, at Frenchmans Flat on January 26, 1951, was close enough to shatter windows in the city, though it took seven minutes for the shock wave to arrive. While the mushroom cloud was visible from the city, sightseers began to drive out to get a better look; soon, traffic on test days out to the best viewpoints on Mount Charleston would be bumper to bumper.

Blasts continued above ground until 1958 (indeed tests were conducted underground until 1992), with unfailing popularity. Schedules would be released months in advance, so tourists could time their vacations to join in the fun. The *Sands* ran a "Miss Atomic Bomb" contest in May 1957. The Atomic Energy Commission even encouraged the Boy Scouts to have an atomic energy merit badge.

Las Vegas was spared the worst of the fallout; prevailing winds blew east instead, to St George, Utah, where in 1954 *The Conqueror*, a John Wayne movie, was being filmed. Radiation is thought to have contributed to the cancer-related deaths of three-fourths of the cast, including Wayne.

Ronald Reagan with the Adorabelles in 1954; Sammy Davis Jr in 1955, when his family became the first black

audience members on the Strip; and the young Elvis
Presley, who bombed abysmally, in 1956. As the stars gravi-
tated toward the Vegas honeypot, nightclubs across America
went out of business.

The opening of the city's Convention Center in 1959, on
Paradise Road, was yet another factor that boosted the Strip
at the expense of downtown; conventioneers stayed almost
exclusively in the nearby Strip hotels. At first, almost all
came from the western states, but with the advent of jet
planes in 1960 they began to arrive from all over the country, and not for the last time the airport had to expand.
California's ever-growing car culture made road links
increasingly important too; work on the I-15 freeway started in the late 1950s, although it was not to be completed
until into the 1970s.

Howard Hughes and the new Las Vegas

At the start of the 1960s, Las Vegas was the epitome of
cool. Even the glamorous young John F Kennedy, as both
senator and President-elect, beat a path to the *Sands* to be
brushed by the magic of the legendary **Rat Pack** – Frank
Sinatra, Dean Martin, Sammy Davis Jr, Peter Lawford, and
Joey Bishop.

As President, on the other hand, Kennedy stopped taking Sinatra's calls. His brother Robert, the new US
Attorney General, went further, castigating Las Vegas as
"the bank of America's organized crime." RFK had long
loathed Jimmy Hoffa, the president of the International
Brotherhood of Teamsters, whose pension fund was the
principal investor in several Strip casinos. Both Las Vegas
and the Teamsters were forced to clean up their act,
thought not before the Teamsters achieved their last and
greatest gasp, financing the construction in 1966 of *Caesars
Palace*, the first of the great themed casinos. (*Godfather*
author Mario Puzo, incidentally, described visiting a Hell-

themed casino in Reno as early as 1939, but *Caesars* was something very new for Las Vegas.)

What really signaled the beginning of the end for Mob rule in Vegas was the arrival of reclusive airline tycoon **Howard Hughes** at the *Desert Inn* in late 1966, having just sold TWA for $546 million. When the owners tired of his stingy – specifically, non-gambling – ways, he simply bought the hotel. Hughes went on to buy the *Sands*, the *Silver Slipper*, and the *New Frontier*, together with vast tracts of real estate throughout the city, but more important still was his sheer example. Personally he's a candidate for the weirdest human being in history, but financially he was regarded as utterly beyond reproach, and individual entrepreneurs and Wall Street corporations alike soon followed in his wake.

Kirk Kerkorian – like Hughes, a former aviator, who started out in the 1940s ferrying passengers such as Bugsy Siegel between LA and Las Vegas – went on to open the world's largest hotel in Las Vegas on three separate occasions. The first was the *International* in 1969, which witnessed the second coming of Elvis Presley as a karate-kicking lounge lizard, and became the *Las Vegas Hilton* within a year; the second was the original *MGM Grand* in 1973, now as *Bally's* also owned by Hilton; and the third was the current *MGM Grand*.

The defining figure of modern Las Vegas, **Steve Wynn**, made his debut on the scene in the early 1970s. He somehow parlayed ownership of a small piece of the parking lot at *Caesars Palace* – acquired by Howard Hughes as part of a bid to buy *Caesars*, then sold to Wynn for no obvious reason – into gaining control of downtown's *Golden Nugget* in 1973. His success in re-inventing the *Nugget* as a glittering glamour joint, coupled with a stain-free image, swiftly turned him into a major player.

Hard times

Throughout the 1970s, Las Vegas continued to struggle free from the Mob. Almost every veteran casino went through its own catharsis, as endless federal swoops and stings uncovered "skimming" operations in one after another. Just as the worst seemed finally to be over, however, the city took its biggest blow yet, with the opening of legal casinos in **Atlantic City**, in 1978.

In its early years, the growth of gambling on the East Coast hit Las Vegas very hard, with tourists and investors alike flocking to New Jersey rather than Nevada. Following the notorious fires at the *MGM Grand* in 1980, which killed 84 people and injured hundreds more, and the *Las Vegas Hilton* in 1981, which cost eight lives, things reached the stage where the last direct flight service between New York and Las Vegas was discontinued in 1983.

And yet Las Vegas survived, just as it has continued to survive the explosion of gambling to cover almost all the United States. Atlantic City has found itself on the ropes instead, and is now seen as having simply prepared novice gamblers for the sophisticated pleasures of Las Vegas. Donald Trump's much-vaunted *Taj Mahal* in Atlantic City was originally regarded as the trump card that defeated Steve Wynn, who had opened *Golden Nugget Atlantic City* in 1980. Wynn, however, can now be seen to have won the battle, by switching his attention back to Las Vegas before he lost his shirt.

The modern city and the development boom

When Steve Wynn opened the *Mirage* in November 1989, backed by junk-bond mega-dollars raised in conjunction with finance whiz-kid Michael Milken, he appeared to be taking a breathtaking risk. The first top-flight casino to be built for sixteen years, it required a daily profit of one million dollars from its gaming tables just to stay open, much less be in the black. Las Vegas, however, has been on a roll ever since.

The long-established Circus Circus crew swiftly opened *Excalibur*, then leapfrogged to *Luxor* and *Mandalay Bay*. Wynn himself went from *Treasure Island* by way of the *Monte Carlo* to the sumptuous *Bellagio*, Kerkorian constructed his latest *MGM Grand*, and a succession of miniature cities has sprung up along the Strip – New York, Venice, and Paris, for a start. Even downtown got into the act, throwing a roof over its head and calling itself the **Fremont Street Experience**.

The 1990s also saw Las Vegas succeed in adding world-class dining and shopping to its bedrock appeal of casino gambling. The one false step along the way was the widely publicized assertion in mid-decade that the city was now a family destination. Everyone knows it's a place to get away from the kids and behave irresponsibly, not to bring them along, and the casinos these days deny they ever suggested anything else.

This book goes to press at the end of 1999, at a time when Las Vegas's self-confidence as the world's pre-eminent adult resort seems unshakable. New mayor Oscar Goodman, previously a self-publicizing attorney notorious for defending diehard mobsters, has come to office promising an inclusive coalition to improve the lives of all the valley's diverse citizens. City boosters point out that only fifteen percent of Americans have so far seen Vegas, and they're expecting the rest to turn up any day now.

Books

The following is a small selection of books that proved enjoyable or useful during the writing of this guide. Las Vegas changes so fast that although exposés of the city's early rise to fame abound, there's currently no up-to-date history that covers the boom of the 1990s.

All publishers listed below are in the US, unless otherwise specified.

Architecture

Francis Anderton and John Chase, *Las Vegas* (Ellipsis, UK). Beautifully written, highly intelligent little pocket book that describes and illustrates every major building in the Las Vegas of 1996.

Alan Hess, *Viva Las Vegas* (Chronicle). A comprehensive, lovingly illustrated survey of Las Vegas's architectural history, which consistently throws fascinating sidelights on the development of the city.

Robert Venturi, Denise Scott Brown, Steve Izenour, *Learning From Las Vegas* (The MIT Press). Seminal architectural treatise that was in 1972 the first work to hail the Strip as something new and intriguing, and introduced the great debate between "ducks" and "decorated sheds" to the aesthetics of Las Vegas.

Biography and history

Susan Berman, *Lady Las Vegas* (TV Books). The book of the excellent TV series is a messy disappointment; Berman has some good family anecdotes from the days when her father ran the *Flamingo*, but as a history of the city it's vague and timid.

Shawn Levy, *Rat Pack Confidential* (Doubleday, US; Fourth Estate, UK). Enjoyable hymn to the "last great showbiz party," when Las Vegas prostrated itself at the feet of Frank Sinatra and the boys.

Eugene P Moehring, *Resort City In The Sunbelt; Las Vegas 1930–70* (University of Nevada Press). A dry but very detailed history that aims to show how much Las Vegas has in common with other western cities, as well as what makes it unique.

Nicholas Pileggi, *Casino* (Pocket Star Books, US; Corgi, UK). The mind-boggling true-life story of Frank "Lefty" Rosenthal and the "skimming" of the *Stardust* by organized crime during the 1970s, which became the basis of Martin Scorsese's movie.

Ed Reid and Ovid Demaris, *The Green Felt Jungle* (Pocket Books, o/p). This classic journalistic expose from 1963 of Las Vegas's seamy underbelly did nothing whatsoever to dent the city's growth; murders, the Mob, prostitution, it's all here.

Hal K Rothman (ed), *Reopening The American West* (University of Arizona Press). An essay collection that's worth buying for Mike Davis's eye-opening account of the environmental issues facing Las Vegas.

Jack Sheehan (ed), *The Players: The Men Who Made Las Vegas* (University of Nevada Press). Very readable warts'n'all biographies of the major figures in Las Vegas's casino history.

John L Smith, *No Limit* (Huntington Press). An entertaining chronicle of the genesis of Bob Stupak's folly, the *Stratosphere*.

John L Smith, *Running Scared: The Life and Treacherous Times of Las Vegas Casino King Steve Wynn* (Barricade Books). In which it turns out, despite Smith's best efforts, that there's not much more to Steve Wynn than meets the eye.

David Spanier, *Welcome To The Pleasuredome* (University of Nevada Press). This comprehensive overview of Las Vegas in all its glory, absurdity, and venality dates from 1992; many of the characters are still around, but a new edition would be nice.

BIOGRAPHY AND HISTORY

Gambling

Thomas A Bass, *The Newtonian Casino* (Penguin, UK); titled *The Eudaemonic Pie* in the US (Penguin US, o/p). Every gambler's dream: the true saga of how a group of computer graduates at the end of the 1970s constructed a shoe-size computer to predict the revolutions of the roulette wheel. So did they beat the casinos? Read on . . .

Edward Thorp, *Beat The Dealer* (Vintage Books). The card-counter's bible; mathematical proof that it is possible to win at blackjack if you're equipped with the perfect brain. The casinos soon learned not to fear those who attempted to follow this first of many fiendishly complicated systems.

Barney Vinson, *Las Vegas Behind The Tables parts 1 and 2* (Gollehon Press). A casino insider gives the low-down on the gambling business and all that goes with it; fascinating reading, even if it makes you want to give up for good.

Literature

Stephen King, *The Stand* (New American Library, US; Hodder & Stoughton, UK). Plague-ridden horror yarn, in which Satan himself takes up residence in the *MGM Grand*.

Andres Martinez, *24/7: Living It Up and Doubling Down in the New Las Vegas* (Villard). Journalists story of taking his book advance and putting it on the line at Vegas's gambling tables – thus creating the plot for this nonfiction tale.

Robert B Parker, *Chance* (Berkley Books). Fictional detective Spenser keeps his head above the murky waters of Las Vegas as he delves into some very dirty business indeed.

Mario Puzo *Fools Die* (Signet). No, it's not *The Godfather*, and not especially well written either, but this tale of high-stakes gambling, casino cons, Mafioso, and the like manages to be diverting enough.

Hunter S Thompson, *Fear and Loathing in Las Vegas* (Random House, US; Paladin, UK). Classic account of the drug-propelled "gonzo" journalist's lost weekend in early 1970s Las Vegas. What's really striking is how much further over the top the place has gone since then.

Mike Tronnes (ed), *Literary Las Vegas* (Henry Holt, US; Mainstream Publishing, UK). Superb collection of book extracts and magazine articles, which provides the full flavor of the changing city over the last fifty years.

Top twelve Las Vegas movies

Las Vegas has become, with its glittering new signs and casinos, an increasingly popular setting for **films**; below are a dozen that use the city to best – or most ludicrous – advantage. Not included are films such as *Rain Man* (1988) and *Swingers* (1996), in which a few key scenes take place amid all the neon glory.

Bugsy (1991)

Casino (1995)

Diamonds Are Forever (1960)

Fear and Loathing in Las Vegas (1997)

Honeymoon In Vegas (1993)

Indecent Proposal (1993)

The Las Vegas Story (1952)

Leaving Las Vegas (1995)

Mars Attacks (1996)

Oceans 11 (1960)

Showgirls (1995)

Viva Las Vegas (1964)

INDEX

Stay in touch with us!

ROUGHNEWS is Rough Guides' free newsletter.
In four issues a year we give you news, travel issues, music reviews, readers' letters and the latest dispatches from authors on the road.

I would like to receive ROUGHNEWS: please put me on your free mailing list.

NAME . . . .

ADDRESS . . . .

Please clip or photocopy and send to: Rough Guides, 62-70 Shorts Gardens, London WC2H 9AB, England

or Rough Guides, 375 Hudson Street, New York, NY 10014, USA.

ROUGH GUIDES: Travel

ROUGH GUIDES: Mini Guides, Travel Specials and Phrasebooks

MINI GUIDES

Antigua
Bangkok
Barbados
Big Island of Hawaii
Boston
Brussels
Budapest
Dublin
Edinburgh
Florence
Honolulu
Lisbon
London Restaurants
Madrid
Maui
Melbourne
New Orleans
St Lucia

Seattle
Sydney
Tokyo
Toronto

TRAVEL SPECIALS

First-Time Asia
First-Time Europe
More Women Travel

PHRASEBOOKS

Czech
Dutch
Egyptian Arabic
European
French

German
Greek
Hindi & Urdu
Hungarian
Indonesian
Italian
Japanese
Mandarin
  Chinese
Mexican
  Spanish
Polish
Portuguese
Russian
Spanish
Swahili
Thai
Turkish
Vietnamese

AVAILABLE AT ALL GOOD BOOKSHOPS

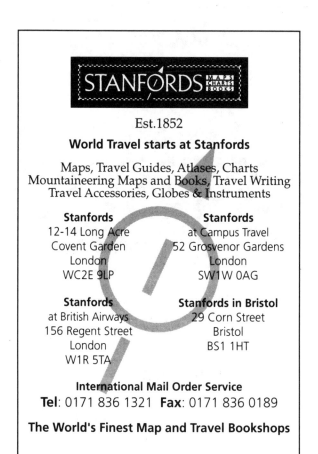

the perfect
getaway vehicle

for top quality, low cost, fully inclusive car rental in over 4,000 locations worldwide. to hire your perfect getaway vehicle call

reservations on:
0990 300 428
and quote ref RG

holiday
autos

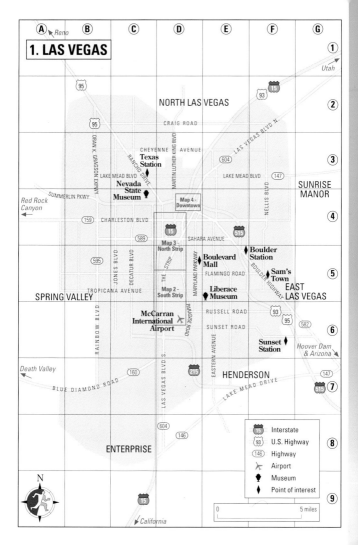

1. LAS VEGAS

Reno

Utah

NORTH LAS VEGAS

CRAIG ROAD

CHEYENNE AVENUE

Texas Station

LAKE MEAD BLVD

Nevada State Museum

Map 4 - Downtown

SUNRISE MANOR

LAKE MEAD BLVD

Red Rock Canyon

SUMMERLIN PKWY

ORAN K. GRAGSON EXPWY

RANCHO DRIVE

MARTIN LUTHER KING BLVD

LAS VEGAS BLVD N.

NELLIS BLVD

CHARLESTON BLVD

SAHARA AVENUE

Map 3 - North Strip

Boulevard Mall

Boulder Station

Sam's Town

FLAMINGO ROAD

DECATUR BLVD

JONES BLVD

THE STRIP

MARYLAND PARKWAY

BOULDER HIGHWAY

SPRING VALLEY

TROPICANA AVENUE

Map 2 - South Strip

Liberace Museum

EAST LAS VEGAS

RAINBOW BLVD

McCarran International Airport

RUSSELL ROAD

SUNSET ROAD

PARADISE ROAD

EASTERN AVENUE

Sunset Station

Hoover Dam & Arizona

Death Valley

BLUE DIAMOND ROAD

LAS VEGAS BLVD S.

HENDERSON

LAKE MEAD DRIVE

ENTERPRISE

N

California

Interstate	
U.S. Highway	
Highway	
Airport	
Museum	
Point of interest	

0   5 miles

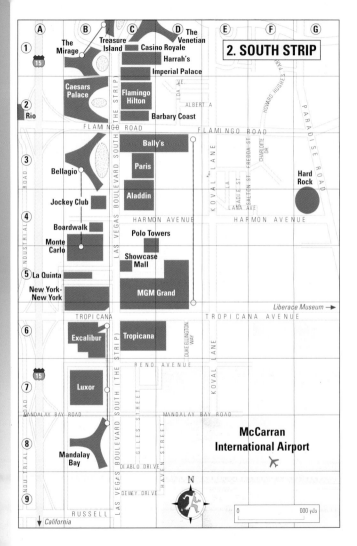

2. SOUTH STRIP

(A) (B) (C) (D) (E) (F) (G)

① The Mirage
Treasure Island
Casino Royale
The Venetian
Harrah's
Imperial Palace

② Rio
Caesars Palace
Flamingo Hilton
Barbary Coast
THE STRIP
FLAMINGO ROAD
FLAMINGO ROAD
HOWARD HUGHES PKWY
PARADISE ROAD

③ Bellagio
Bally's
Paris
Aladdin
Jockey Club
Hard Rock
KOVAL LANE
LANE
LADIE ST
DALTON ST
FREDDA ST
CHARLOTTE DR

④ Boardwalk
Monte Carlo
Polo Towers
Showcase Mall
HARMON AVENUE
HARMON AVENUE

⑤ La Quinta
New York-New York
MGM Grand
Liberace Museum →

⑥ Excalibur
Tropicana
TROPICANA
TROPICANA AVENUE
DUKE ELLINGTON WAY
RENO AVENUE
KOVAL LANE

⑦ Luxor
GILES STREET
MANDALAY BAY ROAD

⑧ Mandalay Bay
MANDALAY BAY ROAD
DIABLO DRIVE
HAVEN STREET
McCarran International Airport

⑨ RUSSELL
DEWEY DRIVE
LAS VEGAS BOULEVARD SOUTH (THE STRIP)
↓ California
N
0   000 yds

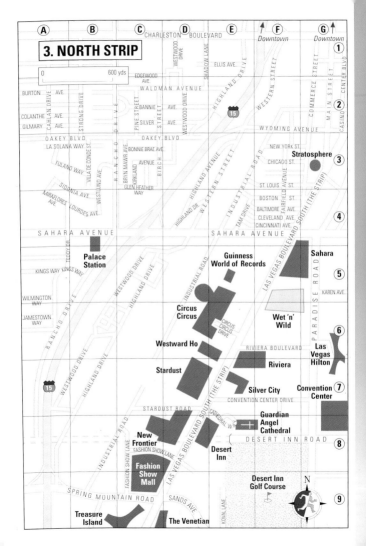

3. NORTH STRIP

CHARLESTON BOULEVARD

| A | B | C | D | E | F | G |

0   600 yds

Downtown   Downtown

Places / Streets:

ELLIS AVE.

WESTWOOD DRIVE

SHADOW LANE

HIGHLAND DRIVE

WESTERN STREET

COMMERCE STREET

MAIN STREET

CASINO CENTER BLVD.

BURTON   AVE.

EDGEWOOD AVE.

WALDMAN AVENUE

CAHLAN DRIVE

STRONG DRIVE

PINE STREET

BANNIE   AVE.

RANCHO DRIVE

WESTWOOD DRIVE

COLANTHE   AVE.

SILVER   AVE.

STREET

GILMARY   AVE.

OAKEY BLVD.   OAKEY BLVD.

WYOMING AVENUE

LA SOLANA WAY

BONNIE BRAE AVE.

NEW YORK ST.

Stratosphere

FULANO WAY

VILLA DE CONDE ST.

BRYN MAWR AVE.

AVENUE

BIRCH

CHICAGO ST.

HIGHLAND AVENUE

FAIRFIELD AVENUE

SIDONIA AVE.

WESTLING AVE.

KIRKLAND

ST. LOUIS ST.

LAS VEGAS BOULEVARD SOUTH (THE STRIP)

MIRAFLORES AVE.

LOURDES AVE.

GLEN HEATHER WAY

HIGHLAND DR.

WESTERN STREET

BOSTON ST.

BALTIMORE   AVE.

TAM DRIVE

INDUSTRIAL ROAD

CLEVELAND AVE.

CINCINNATI AVE.

SAHARA   AVENUE   SAHARA AVENUE

TEDDY DR.

Palace Station

Guinness World of Records

Sahara

KINGS WAY   KINGS WAY

WESTWOOD DRIVE

HIGHLAND DRIVE

INDUSTRIAL ROAD

PARADISE ROAD

KAREN AVE.

WILMINGTON WAY

Circus Circus

Wet 'n' Wild

JAMESTOWN WAY

RANCHO DRIVE

CIRCUS CIRCUS DRIVE

Westward Ho

RIVIERA BOULEVARD

Las Vegas Hilton

WESTWOOD DRIVE

HIGHLAND DRIVE

Stardust

Riviera

Convention Center

STARDUST ROAD

Silver City

CONVENTION CENTER DRIVE

CATHEDRAL WAY

Guardian Angel Cathedral

INDUSTRIAL ROAD

New Frontier

FASHION SHOW LANE

DESERT INN ROAD

FASHION SHOW LANE

Fashion Show Mall

Desert Inn

SPRING MOUNTAIN ROAD

SANDS AVE.

Desert Inn Golf Course

KOVAL LANE

N

Treasure Island

The Venetian

| 1 | 2 | 3 | 4 | 5 | 6 | 7 | 8 | 9 |

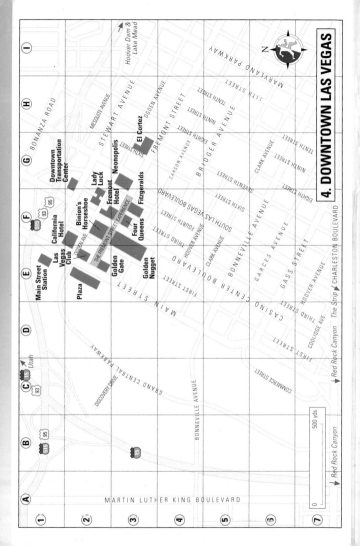

4. DOWNTOWN LAS VEGAS

Hoover Dam & Lake Mead

MARYLAND PARKWAY

BONANZA ROAD

MESQUITE AVENUE

STEWART AVENUE

OGDEN AVENUE

FREMONT STREET

CARSON AVENUE

BRIDGER AVENUE

CLARK AVENUE

Downtown Transportation Center

El Cortez

Neonopolis

Lady Luck

Fremont Hotel

Fitzgeralds

Binion's Horseshoe

Four Queens

California Hotel

THE FREMONT STREET EXPERIENCE

Main Street Station

Las Vegas Club

Plaza

Golden Gate

Golden Nugget

SOUTH LAS VEGAS BOULEVARD

FOURTH STREET

THIRD STREET

SECOND STREET

FIRST STREET

HOOVER AVENUE

CASINO CENTER BOULEVARD

BONNEVILLE AVENUE

GARCES AVENUE

CLARK AVENUE

GASS STREET

HOOVER AVENUE

CHARLESTON BOULEVARD

Red Rock Canyon   The Strip

Utah

GRAND CENTRAL PARKWAY

DISCOVERY DRIVE

MAIN STREET

BONNEVILLE AVENUE

COOLIDGE AVE

COMMERCE STREET

Red Rock Canyon

MARTIN LUTHER KING BOULEVARD

500 yds

N